The Legends of the Jews Volume 4

Louis Ginzberg

Contents

I. JOSHUA 7

II. THE JUDGES 18

III. SAMUEL AND SAUL 41

IV. DAVID 55

V. SOLOMON 83

VI. JUDAH AND ISRAEL 118

VII. ELIJAH 127

VIII. ELISHA AND JONAH 154

IX. THE LATER KINGS OF JUDAH 164

X. THE EXILE 185

XI. THE RETURN OF THE CAPTIVITY 219

XII. ESTHER 232

THE LEGENDS OF THE JEWS VOLUME 4

by

Louis Ginzberg

THE LEGENDS OF THE JEWS VOLUME IV
BIBLE TIMES AND CHARACTERS
FROM JOSHUA TO ESTHER

I. JOSHUA

THE SERVANT OF MOSES

THE early history of the first Jewish conqueror in some respects is like the early history of the first Jewish legislator. Moses was rescued from a watery grave, and raised at the court of Egypt. Joshua, in infancy, was swallowed by a whale, and, wonderful to relate, did not perish. At a distant point of the sea-coast the monster spewed him forth unharmed. He was found by compassionate passers-by, and grew up ignorant of his descent. The government appointed him to the office of hangman. As luck would have it, he had to execute his own father. By the law of the land the wife of the dead man fell to the share of his executioner, and Joshua was on the point of adding to parricide another crime equally heinous. He was saved by a miraculous sign. When he approached his mother, milk flowed from her breasts. His suspicions were aroused, and through the inquiries he set a foot regarding his origin, the truth was made manifest.

Later Joshua, who was so ignorant that he was called a fool, became the minister of Moses, and God rewarded his faithful service by making him the successor to Moses. He was designated as such to Moses when, at the bidding of his master, he was carrying on war with the Amalekites. In this campaign God's care of Joshua was plainly seen. Joshua had condemned a portion of the Amalekites to death by lot, and the heavenly sword picked them out for extermination. Yet there was as great a difference between Moses and Joshua as between the sun and the moon. God did not withdraw His help from Joshua, but He was by no means so close to him as to Moses. This appeared immediately after Moses had passed away. At the moment when the Israelitish leader was setting out on his journey to the great beyond, he summoned his successor and bade him put questions upon all points about which he felt uncertain. Conscious of his own industry and devotion, Joshua replied that he had no questions to ask, seeing that he had carefully studied the teachings of Moses. Straightway he forgot three hundred Halakot, and doubts assailed him concerning seven hundred others. The people threatened Joshua's life, because he was not able to resolve their difficulties in the law. It was vain to turn to God, for the Torah once revealed was subject to human, not to heavenly, authority. Directly after Moses' death, God commanded Joshua to go to war, so that the people might forget its grievance against him. But it is false to think that the great conqueror was nothing more than a military hero. When God appeared to him, to give him instructions concerning the war, He found him with the Book of Deuteronomy in his hand, whereupon God called to him: "Be strong and of good courage; the book of the law shall not depart out of thy mouth."

ENTERING THE PROMISED LAND

The first step in preparation for war was the selection of spies. To guard against a repetition of what had happened to Moses, Joshua chose as his messengers Caleb and Phinehas, on whom he could place dependence in all circumstances. They were accompanied on their mission by two demons, the husbands of the she-devils Lilith and Mahlah. When Joshua was planning his campaign, these devils offered their services to him; they proposed that they be sent out to reconnoitre the land. Joshua refused the offer, but formed their appearance so frightfully that the residents of Jericho were struck with fear of them. In Jericho the spies put up with Rahab. She had been leading an immoral life for forty years, but at the approach of Israel, she paid homage to the true God, lived the life of a pious convert, and, as the wife of Joshua, became the ancestress of eight prophets and of the prophetess Huldah. She had opportunity in her own house of beholding the wonders of God.

When the king's bailiffs came to make their investigations, and Rahab wanted to conceal the Israelitish spies, Phinehas calmed her with the words: "I am a priest, and priests are like angels, visible when they wish to be seen, invisible when they do not wish to be seen."

After the return of the spies, Joshua decided to pass over the Jordan. The crossing of the river was the occasion for wonders, the purpose of which was to clothe him with authority in the eyes of the people. Scarcely had the priests, who at this solemn moment took the place of the Levites as bearers of the Ark, set foot in the Jordan, when the waters of the river were piled up to a height of three hundred miles. All the peoples of the earth were witnesses of the wonder. In the bed of the Jordan Joshua assembled the people around the Ark. A Divine miracle caused the narrow space between its staves to contain the whole concourse. Joshua then proclaimed the conditions under which God would give Palestine to the Israelites, and he added, if these conditions were not accepted, the waters of the Jordan would descend straight upon them. Then they marched through the river. When the people arrived on the further shore, the holy Ark, which had all the while been standing in the bed of the river, set forward of itself, and, dragging the priests after it, overtook the people.

The day continued eventful. Unassailed, the Israelites marched seventy miles to Mount Gerizim and Mount Ebal, and there performed the ceremony bidden by Moses in Deuteronomy: six of the tribes ascended Mount Gerizim, and six Mount Ebal. The priests and the Levites grouped themselves about the holy Ark in the vale between the two peaks. With their faces turned toward Gerizim, the Levites uttered the words: "Happy the man that maketh no idol, an abomination unto the Lord," and all the people answered Amen. After reciting twelve blessings similar to this in form, the Levites turned to Mount Ebal, and recited twelve curses, counterparts of the blessings, to each of which the people responded again with Amen. Thereupon an altar was erected on Mount Ebal with the stones, each weighing forty seim, which the Israelites had taken from the bed of the river while passing through the Jordan. The altar was plastered with lime, and the Torah written upon it in seventy languages, so that the heathen nations might have the opportunity of learning the law. At the end it was said explicitly that the heathen outside of Palestine, if they would but abandon the worship of idols, would be received kindly by the Jews.

All this happened on one day, on the same day on which the Jordan was crossed, and the assembly was held on Gerizim and Ebal, the day on which the people arrived at Gilgal, where they left the stones of which the altar had been built. At Gilgal Joshua performed the rite of circumcision on those born in the desert, who had remained uncircumcised on account of the rough climate and for other reasons. And here it was that the manna gave out. It had ceased to fall at the death of Moses, but the supply that had been stored up had lasted some time longer. As soon as the people were under the necessity of providing for their daily wants, they grew negligent in the study of the Torah. Therefore the angel admonished Joshua to loose his shoes from off his feet, for he was to mourn over the decline of the study of the Torah, and bare feet are a sign of mourning. The angel reproached Joshua in particular with having allowed the preparations for war to interfere with the study of the Torah and with the ritual service. Neglect of the latter might be a venial sin, but neglect of the former is worthy of condign punishment. At the same time the angel assured Joshua that he had come to aid him, and he entreated Joshua not to draw back from him, like Moses, who had refused the good offices of the angel. He who spoke to Joshua was none other than the archangel Michael.

CONQUEST OF THE LAND

Joshua's first victory was the wonderful capture of Jericho. The whole of the city was declared anathema, because it had been conquered on the Sabbath day. Joshua reasoned that as the Sabbath is holy, so also that which conquered on the Sabbath should be holy. The brilliant victory was followed by the luckless defeat at Ai. In this engagement perished Jair, the son of Manasseh, whose loss was as great as if the majority of the Sanhedrin had been destroyed. Presently Joshua discovered that the cause of the defeat was the sinfulness of Israel, brought upon it by Achan, who had laid hands on some of the spoils of Jericho. Achan was a hardened transgressor and criminal from of old. During the life of Moses he had several times appropriated to his own use things that had been declared anathema, and he had committed other crimes worthy of the death penalty. Before the Israelites crossed the Jordan, God had not visited Achan's sins upon the people as a whole, because at that time it did not form a national unit yet. But when Achan abstracted an idol and all its appurtenances from Jericho, the misfortune of Ai followed at once.

Joshua inquired of God, why trouble had befallen Israel, but God refused to reply. He was no tale-bearer; the evil-doer who had caused the disaster would have to be singled out by lot. Joshua first of all summoned the high priest from the assembly of the people. It appeared that, while the other jewels in his breastplate gleamed bright, the stone representing the tribe of Judah was dim. By lot Achan was set apart from the members of his tribe. Achan, however, refused to submit to the decision by lot. He said to Joshua: "Among all living men thou and Phinehas are the most pious. Yet, if lots were cast concerning you two, one or other of you would be declared guilty. Thy teacher Moses has been dead scarcely one month, and thou has already begun to go astray, for thou hast forgotten that a man's guilt can be proved only through two witnesses."

Endued with the holy spirit, Joshua divined that the land was to be assigned to the tribes and families of Israel by lot, and he realized that nothing ought to be done to bring this method of deciding into disrepute. He, therefore, tried to persuade Achan to make a clean breast of his transgression. Meantime, the Judeans, the tribesmen of Achan, rallied about him, and throwing themselves upon the other tribes, they wrought fearful havoc and bloodshed. This determined Achan to confess his sins. The confession cost him his life, but it saved him from losing his share in the world to come.

In spite of the reverses at Ai, the terror inspired by the Israelites grew among the Canaanitish peoples. The Gibeonites planned to circumvent the invaders, and form an alliance with them. Now, before Joshua set out on his campaign, he had issued three proclamations: the nation that would leave Canaan might depart unhindered; the nation that would conclude peace with the Israelites, should do it at once; and the nation that would choose war, should make its preparations. If the Gibeonites had sued for the friendship of the Jews when the proclamation came to their ears, there would have been no need for subterfuges later. But the Canaanites had to see with their own eyes what manner of enemy awaited them, and all the nations prepared for war. The result was that the thirty-one kings of Palestine perished, as well as the satraps of many foreign kings, who were proud to own possessions in the Holy Land. Only the Girgashites departed out of Palestine, and as a reward for their docility God gave them Africa as an inheritance.

The Gibeonites deserved no better fate than all the rest, for the covenant made with them rested upon a misapprehension, yet Joshua kept his promise to them, in order to sanctify the name of God, by showing the world how sacred an oath is to the Israelites. In the course of events it became obvious that the Gibeonites were by no means worthy of being received into the Jewish communion, and David, following Joshua's example, excluded them forever, a sentence that will remain in force even in the Messianic time.

THE SUN OBEYS JOSHUA

The task of protecting the Gibeonites involved in the offensive and defensive alliance made with them, Joshua fulfilled scrupulously. He had hesitated for a moment whether to aid the Gibeonites in their distress, but the words of God sufficed to recall him to his duty. God said to him: "If thou dost not bring near them that are far off, thou wilt remove them that are near by." God granted Joshua peculiar favor in his conflict with the assailants of the Gibeonites. The hot hailstones which, at Moses' intercession, had remained suspended in the air when they were about to fall upon the Egyptians, were now cast down upon the Canaanites. Then happened the great wonder of the sun's standing still, of the great wonders since the creation of the world.

The battle took place on a Friday. Joshua knew it would pain the people deeply to be compelled to desecrate the holy Sabbath day. Besides, he noticed that the heathen were using sorcery to make the heavenly hosts intercede for them in the fight against the Israelites. He, therefore, pronounced the Name of the Lord, and the sun, moon and stars stood still. The sun at first refused to obey Joshua's behest, seeing that he was older than man by two days. Joshua replied that there was no reason why a free-born youth should refrain from enjoining silence upon an old slave whom he owns, and had not God given heaven and earth to our father Abraham? Nay, more than this, had not the sun himself bowed down like a slave before Joseph? "But," said the sun, "who will praise God if I am silent?" Whereupon Joshua: "Be thou silent, and I will intone a song of praise." And he sang thus:

1. Thou hast done mighty things, O Lord, Thou has performed great deeds. Who is like unto Thee? My lips shall sing unto Thy name.

2. My goodness and my fortress, my refuge, I will sing a new song unto Thee, with thanksgiving I will sing unto Thee, Thou art the strength of my salvation.

3. All the kings of the earth shall praise Thee, the princes of the world shall sing unto Thee, the children of Israel shall rejoice in Thy salvation, they shall sing and praise Thy power.

4. In Thee, O God, did we trust; we said, Thou art our God, for Thou wast our shelter and our strong tower against our enemies.

5. To Thee we cried, and we were not ashamed; in Thee we trusted, and we were delivered; when we cried unto Thee, Thou didst hear our voice, Thou didst deliver our souls from the sword.

6. Thou hast shown unto us Thy mercy, Thou didst give unto us Thy salvation, Thou didst rejoice our hearts with Thy strength.

7. Thou wentest forth for our salvation; with the strength of Thy arm Thou didst redeem Thy people; Thou did console us from the heavens of Thy holiness, Thou didst save us from tens of thousands.

8. Sun and moon stood still in heaven, and Thou didst stand in Thy wrath against our oppressors, and Thou didst execute Thy judgements upon them.

9. All the princes of the earth stood up, the kings of the nations had gathered themselves together, they were not moved at Thy presence, they desired Thy battles.

10. Thou didst rise against them in Thine anger, and Thou didst bring down Thy wrath upon them, Thou didst destroy them in Thy fury, and Thou didst ruin them in Thy rage.

11. Nations raged from fear of Thee, kingdoms tottered because of Thy wrath, Thou didst wound kings in the day of Thine anger.

12. Thou didst pour out Thy fury upon them, Thy wrathful anger took hold of them, Thou didst turn their iniquity upon them, and Thou didst cut them off in their wickedness.

13. They spread a trap, they fell therein, in the net they hid their foot was caught.

14. Thine hand found all Thine enemies, who said, through their sword they possessed the land, through their arm thy dwelt in the city.

15. Thou didst fill their faces with shame, Thou didst bring their horns down

to the ground.

16. Thou didst terrify them in Thy wrath, and thou didst destroy them from before Thee.

17. The earth quaked and trembled from the noise of Thy thunder against them; Thou didst not withhold their souls from earth, and Thou didst bring down their lives to the grave.

18. Thou didst pursue them in Thy storm, Thou didst consume them in the whirlwind, Thou didst turn their rain into hail, they fell in floods, so that they could not rise.

19. Their carcasses were like rubbish cast out in the middle of the streets.

20. They were consumed, and they perished before Thee, Thou hast delivered Thy people in Thy might.

21. Therefore our hearts rejoice in Thee, our souls exult in Thy salvation.

22. Our tongues shall relate Thy might, we will sing and praise Thy wondrous works.

23. For Thou didst save us from our enemies, Thou didst deliver us from those who rose up against us, Thou didst destroy them from before us, and depress them beneath our feet.

24. Thus shall all Thine enemies perish, O Lord, and the wicked shall be like chaff driven by the wind, and Thy beloved shall be like trees planted by the waters.

WAR WITH THE ARMENIANS

Joshua's victorious course did not end with the conquest of the land. His war with the Armenians, after Palestine was subdued, marked the climax of his heroic deeds. Among the thirty-one kings whom Joshua had slain, there was one whose son, Shobach by name, was king of Armenia. With the purpose of waging war with Joshua, he united the forty-five kings of Persia and Media, and they were joined by the renowned hero Japheth. The allied kings in a letter informed Joshua of their design against him as follow: "The noble, distinguished council of the kings of Persia and Media to Joshua, peace! Thou wolf of the desert, we well know what thou didst to our kinsmen. Thou didst destroy our palaces; without pity thou didst slay young and old; our fathers thou didst mow down with the sword; and their cities thou didst turn into desert. Know, then, that in the space of thirty days, we shall come to thee, we, the forty-five kings, each having sixty thousand warriors under him, all them armed with bows and arrows, girt about with swords, all of us skilled in the ways of war, and with us the hero Japheth. Prepare now for the combat, and say not afterward that we took thee at unawares."

The messenger bearing the letter arrived on the day before the Feast of Weeks. Although Joshua was greatly wrought up by the contents of the letter, he kept his counsel until after the feast, in order not to disturb the rejoicing of the people. Then, at the conclusion of the feast, he told the people of the message that had reached him, so terrifying that even he, the veteran warrior, trembled at the heralded approach of the enemy. Nevertheless Joshua determined to accept the challenge. From the first words his reply was framed to show the heathen how little their fear possessed him whose trust was set in God. The introduction to his epistle reads as follows: "In the Name of the Lord, the God of Israel, who saps the strength of the iniquitous warrior, and slays the rebellious sinner. He breaks up the assemblies of marauding transgressors, and He gathers together in council the pious and the just scattered abroad, He the God of all gods, the Lord of all lords, the God of Abraham, Isaac, and Jacob. God is the Lord of war! From me, Joshua, the servant of God, and from the holy and chosen congregation to the impious nations, who pay worship to images, and prostrate themselves before idols: No peace unto you, saith my God! Know that ye acted foolishly to awaken the slumbering lion, to rouse up the lion's whelp, to excite his wrath. I am ready to pay you your recompense. Be ye prepared to meet me, for within a week I shall be with you to slay your warriors to a man."

Joshua goes on to recite all the wonders God had done for Israel, who need fear no power on earth; and he ends his missive with the words: "If the hero Japheth is with you, we have in the midst of us the Hero of heroes, the Highest above all the high."

The heathen were not a little alarmed at the tone of Joshua's letter. Their terror grew when the messenger told of the exemplary discipline maintained in the Isrealitish army, of the gigantic stature of Joshua, who stood five ells high, of his royal apparel, of his crown graven with the Name of God. At the end of seven days

Joshua appeared with twelve thousand troops. When the mother of King Shobach, who was a powerful witch, espied the host, she exercised her magic art, and enclosed the Isrealitish army in seven walls. Joshua thereupon sent forth a carrier pigeon to communicate his plight to Nabiah, the king of the trans-Jordanic tribes. He urged him to hasten to his help and bring the priest Phinehas and the sacred trumpets with him. Nabiah did not tarry. Before the relief detachment arrived, his mother reported to Shobach that she beheld a star arise out of the East against which her machinations were vain. Shobach threw his mother from the wall, and he himself was soon afterward killed by Nabiah. Meantime Phinehas arrived, and, at the sound of his trumpets, the wall toppled down. A pitched battle ensued, and the heathen were annihilated.

ALLOTMENT OF THE LAND

At the end of seven years of warfare, Joshua could at last venture to parcel out the conquered land among the tribes. This was the way he did it. The high priest Eleazar, attended by Joshua and all the people, and arrayed in the Urim and Thummim, stood before two urns. One of the urns contained the names of the tribes, the other the names of the districts into which the land was divided. The holy spirit caused him to exclaims "Zebulon." When he put his hand into the first urn, lo, he drew forth the word Zebulon, and from the other came the word Accho, meaning the district of Accho. Thus it happened with each tribe in succession. In order that the boundaries might remain fixed, Joshua had had the Hazubah planted between the districts. The rootstock of this plant once established in a spot, it can be extirpated only with the greatest difficulty. The plough may draw deep furrows over it, yet it puts forth new shoots, and grows up again amid the grain, still marking the old division lines.

In connection with the allotment of the land Joshua issued ten ordinances intended, in a measure, to restrict the rights in private property: Pasturage in the woods was to be free to the public at large. Any one was permitted to gather up bits of wood in the field. The same permission to gather up all grasses, wherever they might grow, unless they were in a field that had been sown with fenugreek, which needs grass for protection. For grafting purposes twigs could be cut from any plant except the olive-trees. Water springs belonged to the whole town. It was lawful for any one to catch fish in the Sea of Tiberias, provided navigation was not impeded. The area adjacent to the outer side of a fence about a field might be used by any passer-by to ease nature. From the close of the harvest until the seventeenth day of Marheshwan fields could be crossed. A traveler who lost his way among vineyards could not be held responsible for the damage done in the effort to recover the right path. A dead body found in a field was to be buried on the spot where it was found.

The allotment of the land to the tribes and subdividing each district among the tribesmen took as much time as the conquest of the land.

When the two tribes and a half from the land beyond Jordan returned home after an absence of fourteen years, they were not a little astonished to hear that the boys who had been too young to go to the wars with them had in the meantime shown themselves worthy of the fathers. They had been successful in repulsing the Ishmaelitish tribes who had taken advantage of the absence of the men capable of bearing arms to assault their wives and children.

After a leadership of twenty – eight years, marked with success, in war and in peace, Joshua departed this life. His followers laid the knives he had used in circumcising the Israelites into his grave, and over it they erected a pillar as a memorial of the great wonder of the sun's standing still over Ajalon. However, the mourning for Joshua was not so great as might justly have been expected. The cultivation of the recently conquered land so occupied the attention of the tribes that they came nigh forgetting the man to whom chiefly they owed their possession of it. As a punishment for their ingratitude, God, soon after Joshua's death, brought also the life of the high priest Eleazar and of the other elders to a close, and the mount on which Joshua's body was interred began to tremble, and threatened to engulf the Jews.

II. THE JUDGES

THE FIRST JUDGE

After the death of Joshua the Israelites inquired to God whether they were to go up against the Canaanites in war. They were given the answer: "If ye are pure of heart, go forth unto the combat; but if your hearts are sullied with sin, then refrain." They inquired furthermore how to test the heart of the people. God ordered them to cast lots and set apart those designated by lot, for they would be the sinful among them. Again, when the people besought God to give it a guide and leader, an angel answered: "Cast lots in the tribe of Caleb." The lot designated Kenaz, and he was made prince over Israel.

His first act was to determine by lot who were the sinners in Israel, and what their inward thought. He declared before the people: "If I and my house be set apart by lot, deal with us as we deserve, burn us with fire." The people assenting, lots were cast, and 345 of the tribe of Judah were singled out, 560 of Reuben, 775 of Simon, 150 of Levi, 665 of Issachar, 545 of Zebulon, 380 of Gad, and 665 of Asher, 480 of Manasseh, 448 of Ephraim, and 267 of Benhamin. So 6110 persons were confined in prison, until God should let it be know what was to be done with them. The united prayers of Kenaz, Eleazar the high priest, and the elders of the congregation, were answered thus: "Ask these men now to confess their iniquity, and they shall be burnt with fire." Kenaz thereupon exhorted them: "Ye know that Achan, the son of Zabdi, committed the trespass of taking the anathema, but the lot fell upon him, and he confessed his sin. Do ye likewise confess your sins, that ye may come to life with those whom God will revive on the day of the resurrection."

One of the sinful, a man by the name of Elah, said in reply thereto: "If thou desirest to bring forth the truth, address thyself to each of the tribes separately." Kenaz began with his own, the tribe of Judah. The wicked of Judah confessed to the sin of worshipping the golden calf, like unto their forefathers in the desert. The Reubenites had burnt sacrifices to idols. The Levites said: "We desired to prove whether the Tabernacle is holy." Those of the tribe of Issachar replied: "We consulted idols to know what will become of us." The sinners of Zebulon: "We desired to eat the flesh of our sons and daughters, to know whether the Lord loves them." The Danites admitted, they had taught their children out of the books of the Amorites, which they had hidden then under Mount Abarim, where Kenaz actually found them. The Naphtalites confessed to the same transgression, only they had concealed the books in the tent of Elah, and there they were found by Kenaz. The Gadites acknowledged having led an immoral life, and the sinners of Asher, that they had found, and had hidden under Mount Shechem, the seven golden idols called by the Amorites the holy nymphs the same seven idols which had been made in a miraculous way after the deluge by the seven sinners, Canaan, Put, Shelah, Nimrod, Elath, Diul, and Shuah. They were of precious stones from Havilah, which radiated light, making night bright as day. Besides, they possessed a rare virtue: if a blind Amorite kissed one of the idols, and at the same time touched its eyes, his sight was restored. After the sinners of Asher, those of Manasseh made their confession they had desecrated the Sabbath. The Ephraimites owned to having sacrificed their children to Moloch. Finally, the Benjamites said: "We desired to prove whether the law emanated from God or from Moses."

At the command of God these sinners and all their possessions were burnt with fire at the brook of Pishon. Only the Amorite books and the idols of precious stones remained unscathed. Neither fire nor water could do them harm. Kenaz decided to consecrate the idols to God, but a revelation came to him, saying: "If God were to accept what has been declared anathema, why should not man?" He was assured that God would destroy the things over which human hands had no power. Kenaz, acting under Divine instruction, bore them to the summit of a mountain, where an altar was erected. The books and the idols were placed upon it, and the people offered many sacrifices and celebrated the whole day as a festival. During the night following, Kenaz saw dew rise from the ice in Paradise and descend upon the books. The letters of their writing were obliterated by it, and then an angel came and annihilated what was left. During the same night an angel carried off the seven gems, and threw them to the bottom of the sea. Meanwhile a second angel brought twelve other gems, engraving the names of the twelve sons of Jacob upon them, one name upon each. No two of these gems were alike: the first, to bear the name of Reuben, was like sardius; the second, for Simon, like topaz; the third, Levi, like emerald; the fourth, Judah, like carbuncle; the fifth, Issachar, like sapphire; the sixth, Zebulon, like jasper; the seventh, Dan, like ligure; the eighth, Naphtali, like amethyst; the ninth, Gad, like agate; the tenth, Asher, like chrysolite; the eleventh, Joseph, like beryl; and the twelfth, Benjamin, like onyx.

Now God commanded Kenaz to deposit twelve stones in the holy Ark, and there they were to remain until such time as Solomon should build the Temple, and attach them to the Cherubim. Furthermore, this Divine communication was made to Kenaz: "And it shall come to pass, when the sin of the children of men shall have been completed by defiling My Temple, the Temple they themselves shall build, that I will take these stones, together with the tables of the law, and put them in the place whence they were removed of old, and there they shall remain until the end of all time, when I will visit the inhabitants of the earth. Then I will take them up, and they shall be an everlasting light to those who love me and keep my commandments."

When Kenaz bore the stones to the sanctuary, they illumined the earth like unto the sun at midday.

CAMPAIGNS OF KENAZ

After these preparations Kenaz took the field against the enemy, with three hundred thousand men. The first day he slew eight thousand of the foe, and the second day five thousand. But not all the people were devoted to Kenaz. Some murmured against him, and calumniating him, said: "Kenaz stays at home, while we expose ourselves on the field." The servants of Kenaz reported these words to him. He ordered the thirty-seven men who had railed against him to be incarcerated, and he swore to kill them, if God would but grant him assistance for the sake of His people.

Thereupon he assembled three hundred men of his attendants, supplied them with horses, and bade them be prepared to make a sudden attack during the night, but to tell none of the plans he harbored in his mind. The scouts sent ahead to reconnoitre reported that the Amorites were too powerful for him to risk an engagement. Kenaz, however, refused to be turned away from his intention. At midnight he and his three hundred trusty attendants advanced upon the Amorite camp. Close upon it, he commanded his men to halt, but to resume their march and follow him when they should hear the notes of the trumpet. If the trumpet was not sounded, they were to return home.

Alone Kenaz ventured into the very camp of the enemy. Praying to God fervently, he asked that a sign be given him: "Let this be the sign of the salvation Thou wilt accomplish for me this day: I shall draw my sword from its sheath, and brandish it so that it glitters in the camp of the Amorites. If the enemy recognize it as the sword of Kenaz, then I shall know Thou wilt deliver them into my hand; if not, I shall understand Thou hast not granted my prayer, but dost purpose to deliver me into the hand of the enemy for my sins."

He heard the Amorites say: "Let us proceed to give battle to the Israelites, for our sacred gods, the nymphs, are in their hands, and will cause their defeat." When he heard these words, the spirit of God came over Kenaz. He arose and swung his sword above his head. Scarce had the Amorites seen it gleam in the air when they exclaimed: "Verily, this is the sword of Kenaz, who has come to inflict wounds and pain. But we know that our gods, who are held by the Israelites, will deliver them into our hands. Up, then, to battle!" Knowing that God had heard his petition, Kenaz threw himself upon the Amorites, and mowed down forty-five thousand of them, and as many perished at the hands of their own brethren, for God had sent the angel Gabriel to his aid, and he had struck the Amorites blind, so that they fell upon one another. On account of the vigorous blows dealt by Kenaz on all sides, his sword stuck to his hand. A fleeing Amorite, whom he stopped, to ask him how to loose it, advised him to slay a Hebrew, and let his warm blood flow over his hand. Kenaz accepted his advice, but only in part: instead of a Hebrew, he slew the Amorite himself, and his blood freed his hand from the sword.

When Kenaz came back to his men, he found them sunk in profound sleep, which had overtaken them that they might not see the wonders done for their leader. They were not a little astonished, on awakening, to behold the whole plain strewn with the dead bodies of the Amorites. Then Kenaz said to them: "Are the ways of God like unto the ways of man? Through me the Lord hath sent deliverance to this people. Arise now and go back to your tents." The people recognized that a great miracle had happened, and they said: "Now we know that God hath wrought salvation for His people; He hath no need of numbers, but only of holiness."

On his return from the campaign, Kenaz was received with great rejoicing. The whole people now gave thanks to God for having put him over them as their leader. They desired to know how he had won the great victory. Kenaz only answered: "Ask those who were with me about my deeds." His men were thus forced to confess that they knew nothing, only, on awakening, they had seen the plain full of dead bodies, without being able to account for their being there. Then Kenaz turned to the thirty-seven men imprisoned, before he left for the war, for having cast aspersions upon him. "Well," he said, "what charge have you to make against me?" Seeing that death was inevitable, they confessed they were of the sort of sinners whom Kenaz and the people had executed, and God had now surrendered them to him on account of their misdeeds. They, too, were burnt with fire.

Kenaz reigned for a period of fifty-seven years. When he felt his end draw nigh, he summoned the two prophets, Phinehas and Jabez, together with the priest Phinehas, the son of Eleazar. To these he spake: "I know the heart of this people, it will turn from following after the Lord. Therefore do I testify against it." Phinehas, the son of Eleazar, replied: "As Moses and Joshua testified, so do I testify against it; for Moses and Joshua prophesied concerning the vineyard, the beautiful planting of the Lord, which knew not who had planted it, and did not recognize Him who cultivated it, so that the vineyard was destroyed, and brought forth no fruit. These are the words my father commanded me to say unto this people."

Kenaz broke out into loud wailing, and with him the elders and the people, and they wept until eventide, saying: "Is it for the iniquity of the sheep that the shepherd must perish? May the Lord have compassion upon His inheritance that it may not work in vain."

The spirit of God descended upon Kenaz, and he beheld a vision. He prophesied that this world would continue to exist only seven thousand years, to be followed then by the Kingdom of Heaven. These words spoken, the prophetical spirit departed from him, and he straightway forgot what he had uttered during his vision. Before he passed away, he spoke once more, saying: "If such be the rest which the righteous obtain after their death, it were better for them to die than live in this corrupt world and see its iniquities."

As Kenaz left no male heirs, Zebul was appointed his successor. Mindful of the great service Kenaz had performed for the nation, Zebul acted a father's part toward the three unmarried daughters of his predecessor. At his instance, the people assigned a rich marriage portion to each of them; they were given great domains as their property. The oldest of the three, Ethema by name, he married to Elizaphan; the second, Pheila, to Odihel; and the youngest, Zilpah, to Doel.

Zebul, the judge, instituted a treasury at Shiloh. He bade the people bring contributions, whether of gold or of silver. They were only to take heed not to carry anything thither that had originally belonged to an idol. His efforts were crowned with success. The free-will offerings to the temple treasure amounted to twenty talents of gold and two hundred and fifty talents of silver.

Zebul's reign lasted twenty-five years. Before his death he admonished the people solemnly to be God-fearing and observant of the law.

OTHNIEL

Othniel was a judge of a very different type. His contemporaries said, that before the sun of Joshua went down, the sun of Othniel, his successor in the leadership of the people , appeared on the horizon. The new leader's real name was Judah; Othniel was one of his epithets, as Jabez was another.

Among the judges, Othniel represents the class of scholars. His acumen was so great that he was able, by dint of dialect reasoning, to restore the seventeen hundred traditions which Moses had taught the people, and which had been forgotten in the time of mourning for Moses. Nor was his zeal for the promotion of the study of the Torah inferior to his learning. The descendants of Jethro left Jericho, the district assigned to them, and journeyed to Arad, only that thy might sit at the feed to Othniel. His wife, the daughter of his half-brother Caleb, was not so well pleased with him. She complained to her father that her husband's house was bare of all earthly goods, and his only possession was knowledge of the Torah.

The first event to be noted in Othniel's forty years' reign is his victory over

Adoni-bezek. This chief did not occupy a prominent position among the Canaanitish rulers. He was not even accounted a king, nevertheless he had conquered seventy foreign kings. The next event was the capture of Luz by the Israelites. The only way to gain entrance into Luz was by a cave, and the road to the cave lay through a hollow almond tree. If the secret approach to the city had not been betrayed by one of its residents, it would have been impossible for the Israelites to reach it. God rewarded the informer who put the Israelites in the way of capturing Luz. The city he founded was left unmolested both by Sennacherib and Nebuchadnezzar, and not event the Angel of Death has power over its inhabitants. They never die, unless, weary of life, they leave the city.

The same good fortune did not mark Othniel's reign throughout. For eight years Israel suffered oppression at the hands of Cushan, the evil-doer who in former days had threatened to destroy the patriarch Jacob, as he was now endeavoring to destroy the descendants of Jacob, for Cushan is only another name for Laban.

Othniel, however, was held so little answerable for the causes that had brought on the punishment of the people, that God granted him eternal life; he is one of the few who reached Paradise alive.

BOAZ AND RUTH

The story of Ruth came to pass a hundred years after Othniel's reign. Conditions in Palestine were of such a nature that if a judge said to a man, "Remove the mote from thine eye," his reply was, "Do thou remove the beam from thine own." To chastise the Israelites God sent down them one of the ten seasons of famine which He had ordained, as disciplinary measures for mankind, from the creation of the world until the advent of Messiah. Elimelech and his sons, who belonged to the aristocracy of the land, attempted neither to improve the sinful generation whose transgressions had called forth the famine, nor alleviated the distress that prevailed about them. They left Palestine, and thus withdrew themselves from the needy who had counted upon their help. They turned their faced to Moab. There, on account of their wealth and high descent, they were made officers in the army. Mahlon and Chilion, the sons of Elimelech, rose to still higher distinction, they married the daughters of the Moabite king Eglon. But this did not happen until after the death of Elimelech, who was opposed to intermarriage with the heathen. Neither the wealth nor the family connections of the two men helped them before God. First they sank into poverty, and, as they continued in their sinful ways, God took their life.

Naomi, their mother, resolved to return to her home. Her two daughters-in-law were very dear to her on account of the love they had borne her sons, a love strong even in death, for they refused to marry again. Yet she would not take them with her to Palestine, because she foresaw contemptuous treatment in store for them as Moabitish women. Orpah was easily persuaded to remain behind. She accompanied her mother-in-law a distance of four miles, and then she took leave of her, shedding only four tears as she bade her farewell. Subsequent events showed that she had not been worthy of entering into the Jewish communion, for scarcely had she separated from Naomi when she abandoned herself to an immoral life. But with God nothing goes unrewarded. For the four miles which Orpah travelled with Naomi, she was recompensed by bringing forth four giants, Goliath and his three brothers.

Ruth's bearing and history were far different. She was determined to become a Jewess, and her decision could not be shaken by what Naomi, in compliance with the Jewish injunction, told her of the difficulties of the Jewish law. Naomi warned her that the Israelites had been enjoined to keep Sabbaths and feast days, and that the daughters of Israel were not in the habit of frequenting the theatres and circuses of the heathen. Ruth only affirmed her readiness to follow Jewish customs. And when Naomi said: "We have one Torah, one law, one command; the Eternal our God is one, there is none beside Him," Ruth answered: "Thy people shall be my people, thy God my God." So the two women journeyed together to Bethlehem. They arrived there on the very day on which the wife of Boaz was buried, and the concourse assembled for the funeral saw Naomi as she returned to her home.

Ruth supported herself and her mother-in-law sparsely with the ears of grain which she gathered in the fields. Association with so pious a woman as Naomi had already exercised great influence upon her life and ways. Boaz was astonished to notice that if the reapers let more than two ears fall, in spite of her need she did not pick them up, for the gleaning assigned to the poor by law does not refer to quantities of more than two ears inadvertently dropped at one time. Boaz also admired her grace, her decorous conduct, her modest demeanor. When he learned who she was, he commended her for her attachment to Judaism. To his praise she returned: "Thy ancestors found no delight even in Timna, the daughter of a royal house. As for me, I am a member of a low people, abominated by thy God, and excluded from the assembly of Israel." For the moment Boaz failed to recollect the Halakah bearing on the Moabites and Ammonites. A voice from heaven reminded him that only their males were affected by the command of exclusion. This he told to Ruth, and he also told her of a vision he had had concerning her descendants. For the sake of the good she had done to her mother-in-law, kings and prophets would spring from her womb.

Boaz showed kindness not only to Ruth and Naomi, but also to their dead. He took upon himself the decent burial of the remains of Elimelech and his two sons. All this begot in Naomi the thought that Boaz harbored the intention of marrying Ruth. She sought to coax the secret, if such there was, from Ruth. When she found that nothing could be elicited from her daughter-in-law, she made Ruth her partner in a plan to force Boaz into a decisive step. Ruth adhered to Naomi's directions in every particular, except that she did not wash and anoint herself and put on fine raiment, until after she had reached her destination. She feared to attract the attention of the lustful, if she walked along the road decked out in unusual finery.

The moral conditions in those days were very reprehensible. Though Boaz was high-born and a man of substance, yet he slept on the threshing-floor, so that his presence might act as a check upon profligacy. In the midst of his sleep, Boaz was startled to find some one next to him. At first he thought it was a demon. Ruth calmed his disquietude with these words: "Thou art the head of the court, thy ancestors were princes, thou art thyself an honorable man, and a kinsman of my dead husband. As for me, who am in the flower of my years, since I left the home of my parents where homage is rendered unto idols, I have been constantly menaced by the dissolute young men around. So I have come hither that thou, who art the redeemer, mayest spread out thy skirt over me." Boaz gave her the assurance that if his older brother Tob failed her, he would assume the duties of a redeemer. The next day he came before the tribunal of the Sanhedrin to have the matter adjusted. Tob soon made his appearance, for an angel led him to the place where he was wanted, that Boaz and Ruth might not have long to wait. Tob, who was not learned in the

Torah, did not know that the prohibition against the Moabites had reference only to males. Therefore, he declined to marry Ruth. So she was taken to wife by the octogenarian Boaz. Ruth herself was forty years old at the time of her second marriage, and it was against all expectations that her union with Boaz should be blessed with offspring, a son Obed the pious. Ruth lived to see the glory of Solomon, but Boaz died on the day after the wedding.

DEBORAH

Not long after Ruth, another ideal woman arose in Israel, the prophetess Deborah.

When Ehud died, there was none to take his place as judge, and the people fell off from God and His law. God, therefore, sent an angel to them with the following message: "Out of all the nations on earth, I chose a people for Myself, and I thought, so long as the world stands, My glory will rest upon them. I sent Moses unto them, My servant, to teach them goodness and righteousness. But they strayed from My ways. And now I will arouse their enemies against them, to rule over them, and they will cry out: 'Because we forsook the ways of our fathers, hath this come over us.' Then I will send a woman unto them, and she will shine for them as a light for forty years."

The enemy whom God raised up against Israel was Jabin, the king of Hazor, who oppressed him sorely. But worse than the king himself was his general Sisera, one of the greatest heroes know to history. When he was thirty years old, he had conquered the whole world. At the sound of his voice the strongest of walls fell in a heap, and the wild animals in the woods were chained to the spot by fear. The proportions of his body were vast beyond description. If he took a bath in the river, and dived beneath the surface, enough fish were caught in his beard to feed a multitude, and it required no less than nine hundred horses to draw the chariot in which he rode.

To rid Israel of this tyrant, God appointed Deborah and her husband Barak. Barak was an ignoramus, like most of his contemporaries. It was a time singularly deficient to scholars. In order to do something meritorious in connection with the Divine service, he carried candles, at his wife's instance, to the sanctuary, where-from he was called Lipidoth, "Flames." Deborah was in the habit of making the wicks on the candles very thick, so that they might burn a long time. Therefore God distinguished her. He said: "Thou takest pains to shed light in My house, and I will let thy light, thy flame, shine abroad in the whole land." Thus it happened that Deborah became a prophetess and a judge. She dispensed judgement in the open air, for it was not becoming that men should visit a woman in her house.

Prophetess though she was, she was yet subject to the frailties of her sex. Her self-consciousness was inordinate. She sent for Barak to come to her instead of going to him, and in her song she spoke more of herself than was seemly. The result was that the prophetical spirit departed from her for a time while she was composing her song.

The salvation of Israel was effected only after the people, assembled on the Mount of Judah, had confessed their sins publicly before God and besought His help. A seven days' fast was proclaimed for men and women, for young and old. Then God resolved to help the Israelites, not for their sakes, but for the sake of keeping the oath he had sworn to their forefathers, never to abandon their seed. Therefore He sent Deborah unto them.

The task allotted to Deborah and Barak, to lead the attack upon Sisera, was by no means slight. It is comparable with nothing less than Joshua's undertaking to conquer Canaan. Joshua had triumphed over only thirty-one of the sixty-two kings of Palestine, leaving at large as many as he had subdued. Under the leadership of Sisera these thirty-one unconquered kings opposed Israel. No less than forty thousand armies, each counting a hundred thousand warriors, were arrayed against Deborah and Barak. God aided Israel with water and fire. The river Kishon and all the fiery hosts of heaven except the star Meros fought against Sisera. The Kishon had long before been pledged to play its part in Sisera's overthrow. When the Egyptians were drowned in the Red Sea, God commanded the Angel of the Sea to cast their corpses on the land, that the Israelites might convince themselves of the destruction of their foes, and those of little faith might not say afterward that the Egyptians like the Israelites had reached dry land. The Angel of the Sea complained of the impropriety of withdrawing a gift. God mollified him with the promise of future compensation. The Kishon was offered as security that he would received half as many bodies again as he was now giving up. When Sisera's troops sought relief from the scorching fire of the heavenly bodies in the coolness of the waters of the Kishon, God commanded the river to redeem its pledge. And so the heathen were swept down into the Sea by the waves of the river Kishon, whereat the fishes in the Sea exclaimed: "And the truth of the Lord endureth forever."

Sisera's lot was no better than the lot of the men. He fled from the battle on horseback after witnessing the annihilation of his vast army. When Jael saw him approach, she went to meet him arrayed in rich garments and jewels. She was unusually beautiful, and her voice was the most seductive ever a woman possessed. These are the words she addressed to him: "Enter and refresh thyself with food, and sleep until evening, and then I will send my attendants with thee to accompany thee, for I know thou wilt not forget me, and thy recompense will not fail." When Sisera, on stepping into her tent, saw the bed strewn with roses which Jael had prepared for him, he resolved to take her home to his mother as his wife, as soon as his safety should be assured.

He asked her for milk to drink, saying: "My soul burns with the flame which I saw in the stars contending for Israel." Jael went forth to milk her goat, meantime supplicating God to grant her His help: "I pray to Thee, O Lord, to strengthen Thy maid-servant against the enemy. By this token shall I know that Thou wilt aid me if, when I enter the house, Sisera will awaken and ask for water to drink." Scarcely had Jael crossed the threshold when Sisera awakened and begged for water to quench his burning thirst. Jael gave him wine mixed with water, which caused him to drop into a sound sleep again. The woman then took a wooden spike in her left hand, approached the sleeping warrior, and said: "This shall be the sign that Thou wilt deliver him into my hand if I draw him from the bed down on the ground without awaking him." She tugged at Sisera, and in very truth he did not awaken even when he dropped from the bed to the floor. Then Jael prayed: "O God, strengthen the arm of Thy maid-servant this day, for Thy sake, for the sake of Thy people, and for the sake of those that hope in Thee." With a hammer she drove the spike into the temple of Sisera, who cried out as he was expiring: "O that I should lose my life by the hand of a woman!" Jael's mocking retort was: "Descend to hell and join thy fathers, and tell them that thou didst fall by the hand of a woman."

Barak took charge of the body of the dead warrior, and he sent it to Sisera's mother, Themac, with the message: "Here is thy son, whom thou didst expect to see returning laden with booty." He had in mind the vision of Themac and her women-in-waiting. When Sisera went forth to battle, their conjuring tricks had shown him to them as he lay on the bed of a Jewish woman. This they had interpreted to mean that he would return with Jewish captives. "One damsel, two damsels for ever man." they had said. Great, therefore, was the disappointment of Sisera's mother. No less than a hundred cries did she utter over him.

Deborah and Barak thereupon intoned a song of praise, thanking God for the deliverance of Israel out of the power of Sisera, and reviewing the history of the people since the time of Abraham.

After laboring for the weal of her nation for forty years, Deborah departed this life. Her last words to the weeping people were an exhortation not to depend upon the dead. They can do nothing for the living. So long as a man is alive, his prayers are efficacious for himself and for others. They avail naught once he is dead.

The whole nation kept a seventy days' period of mourning in honor of Deborah, and the land was at peace for seven years.

GIDEON

Elated by the victory over Sisera, Israel sang a hymn of praise, the song of Deborah, and God, to reward them for their pious sentiments, pardoned the transgression of the people. But they soon slipped back into the old ways, and the old troubles harassed them. Their backsliding was due to the witchcraft of a Midianite priest named Aud. He made the sun shine at midnight, and so convinced the Israelites that the idols of Midian were mightier than God, and God chastised them by delivering them into the hands of the Midianties. They worshipped their own images reflected in the water, and they were stricken with dire poverty. They could not bring so much as a meal offering, the offering of the poor. On the eve of one Passover, Gideon uttered the complaint: "Where are all the wondrous works which God did for our fathers in this night, when he slew the first-born of the Egyptians, and Israel went forth from slavery with joyous hearts?" God appeared unto him, and said: "Thou who art courageous enough to champion Israel, thou art worthy that Israel should be saved for thy sake."

An angel appeared, and Gideon begged him for a sign, that he would achieve the deliverance of Israel. He excused his petition with the precedent of Moses, the first prophet, who likewise has asked for a sign. The angel bade him pour water on the rock, and then gave him the choice of how he would have the water transformed. Gideon desired to see one-half changed into blood, and one-half into fire. Thus it happened. The blood and the fire mingled with each other, yet the blood did not quench the fire, nor did the fire dry out the blood. Encouraged by this and other signs, Gideon undertook to carry on the war against the Midianites with a band of three hundred God-fearing men, and he was successful. Of the enemy one hundred and twenty thousand corpses covered the field, and all the rest fled precipitately.

Gideon enjoyed the privilege of bringing salvation to Israel because he was a good son. His old father feared to thresh his grain on account of the Midianites, and Gideon once went out to him in the field and said: "Father, thou art too old to do this work; go thou home, and I shall finish thy task for thee. If the Midianites should surprise me out here, I can run away, which thou canst not do, on account of thy age."

The day on which Gideon gained his great victory was during the Passover, and the cake of barley bread that turned the camp of the enemy upside down, of which the Midianite dreamed, was a sign that God would espouse the cause of His people to reward them for bringing a cake of barley bread as an 'Omer offering.

After God had favored Israel with great help through him, Gideon had an ephod made. In the high priest's breastplate, Joseph was represented among the twelve tribes by Ephraim alone, not by Manasseh, too. To wipe out this slight upon his own tribe, Gideon made an ephod bearing the name of Manasseh. He consecrated it to God, but after his death homage was paid to it as an idol. In those days the Israelites were so addicted to the worship of Beelzebub that they constantly carried small images of this god with them in their pockets, and every now and then they were in the habit of bringing the image forth and kissing it fervently. Of such idolaters were the vain and light fellows who helped Abimelech, the son of Gideon by his concubine from Shechem, to assassinate the other sons of his father. But God is just. As Abimelech murdered his brothers upon a stone, so Abimelech himself met his death through a millstone. It was proper, then, that Jotham, in his parable, should compare Abimelech to a thorn-bush, while he characterized his predecessors, Othniel, Deborah, and Gideon, as an olive-tree, or a fig-tree, or a vine. This Jotham, the youngest of the sons of Gideon, was more than a teller of parables. He knew then that long afterward the Samaritans would claim sanctity for Mount Gerizim, on account of the blessing pronounced from it upon the tribe. For this reason he chose Gerizim from which to hurl his curse upon Shechem and it inhabitants.

The successor to Abimelech equalled, if he did not surpass, him in wickedness. Jair erected an altar unto Baal, and on penalty of death he forced the people to prostrate themselves before it. Only seven men remained firm in the true faith, and refused to the last to commit idolatry. Their names were Deuel, Abit Yisreel, Jekuthiel, Shalom, Ashur, Jehonadab, and Shemiel. They said to Jair: "We are mindful of the lessons given us by our teachers and our mother Deborah. 'Take ye heed,' they said, 'that your heart lead you not astray to the right or to the left. Day and night ye shall devote yourselves to the study of the Torah.' Why, then, dost thou seek to corrupt the people of the Lord, saying, 'Baal is God, let us worship him'? If he really is what thou sayest, then let him speak like a god, and we will pay him worship." For the blasphemy they had uttered against Baal, Jair commanded that the seven men be burnt. When his servants were about to carry out his order, God sent the angel Nathaniel, the lord over the fire, and he extinguished the fire though not before the servants of Jair were consumed by it. Not only did the seven men escape the danger of suffering death by fire, but the angel enabled them to flee unnoticed, by striking all the people present with blindness. Then the angel approached Jair, and said to him: "Hear the words of the Lord ere thou diest. I appointed thee as prince over my people, and thou didst break My covenant, seduce My people, and seek to burn My servants with fire, but they were animated and freed by the living, the heavenly fire. As for thee, thou wilt die, and die by fire, a fire in which thou wilt abide forever."

Thereupon the angel burnt him with a thousand men, whom he had taken in the act of paying homage to Baal.

JEPHTHAH

The first judge of any importance after Gideon was Jephthah. He, too, fell short of being the ideal Jewish ruler. His father had married a woman of another tribe, an unusual occurrence in a time when a woman who left her tribe was held in contempt. Jephthah, the offspring of this union, had to bear the consequences of his mother's irregular conduct. So many annoyances were put upon him that he was forced to leave his home and settle in a heathen district.

At first Jephthah refused to accept the rulership which the people offered him in an assembly at Mizpah, for he had not forgotten the wrongs to which he had been subjected. In the end, however, he yielded, and placed himself at the head of the people in the war against Getal, the king of the Ammonites. At his departure, he vowed before God to sacrifice to Him whatsoever came forth out of the doors of his house to meet him when he returned a victor from the war.

God was angry and said: "So Jephthah has vowed to offer unto me the first thing that shall meet him! If a dog were the first to meet him, would a dog be sacrificed to me? Now shall the vow of Jephthah be visited on his first-born, on his own offspring, yea, his prayer shall be visited on his only daughter. But I assuredly shall deliver my people, not for Jephthah's sake, but for the sake of the prayers of Israel."

The first to meet him after his successful campaign was his daughter Sheilah. Overwhelmed by anguish, the father cried out: "Rightly was the name Sheilah, the one who is demanded, given to thee, that thou shouldst be offered up as a sacrifice. Who shall set my heart in the balance and my soul as the weight, that I may stand and see whether that which happened to me is joy or sorrow? But because I opened my mouth to the Lord, and uttered a vow, I cannot take it back." Then Sheilah spoke, saying: "Why dost thou grieve for my death, since the people was delivered? Dost thou not remember what happened in the day of our forefathers, when the father offered his son as a burnt offering, and the son did not refuse, but consented gladly, and the offerer and the offered were both full of joy? Therefore, do as thou hast spoken. But before I die I will ask a favor of thee. Grant me that I may go with my companions upon the mountains, sojourn among the hills, and tread upon the rocks to shed my tears and deposit there the grief for my lost youth. The trees of the field shall weep for me, and the beasts of the field mourn for me. I do not grieve for my death, nor because I have to yield up my life, but because when my father vowed his heedless vow, he did not have me in mind. I fear, therefore, that I may not be an acceptable sacrifice, and that my death shall be for nothing." Sheilah and her companions went forth and told her case to the sages of the people, but none of them could give her any help. Then she went up to Mount Telag, where the Lord appeared to her at night, saying unto her: "I have closed the mouth of the sages of my people in this generation, that they cannot answer the daughter of Jephthah a word; that my vow be fulfilled and nothing of what I have thought remain undone. I know her to be wiser than her father, and all the wise men, and now her soul shall be accepted at her request, and her death shall be very precious before My face all the time." Sheilah began to bewail her fate in these words: "Hearken, ye mountains, to my lamentations, and ye hills, to the tears of my eyes, and ye rocks, testify to the weeping of my soul. My words will go up to heaven, and my tears will be written in the firmament. I have not been granted the joy of wedding, nor was the wreath of my betrothal completed. I have not been decked with ornaments, nor have I been scented with myrrh and with aromatic perfumes. I have not been anointed with the oil that was prepared for me. Alas, O mother, it was in vain thou didst give birth to me, the grave was destined to be my bridal chamber. The oil thou didst prepare for me will be spilled, and the white garments my mother sewed for me, the moth will eat them; the bridal wreath my nurse wound for me will wither, and my garments in blue and purple, the worms will destroy them, and my companions will all their days lament over me. And now, ye trees, incline your branches and weep over my youth; ye beasts of the forest, come and trample upon my virginity, for my years are cut off, and the days of my life grow old in darkness."

Her lamentations were of as little avail as her arguments with her father. In vain she sought to prove to him from the Torah that the law speaks only of animal sacrifices, never of human sacrifices. In vain she cited the example of Jacob, who had vowed to give God a tenth of all the possessions he owned, and yet did not attempt later to sacrifice one of his sons. Jephthah was inexorable. All he would yield was a respite during which his daughter might visit various scholars, who were to decide whether he was bound by his vow. According to the Torah his vow was entirely invalid. He was not even obliged to pay his daughter's value in money. But the scholars of his time had forgotten this Halakah, and they decided that he must keep his vow. The forgetfulness of the scholars was of God, ordained as a punishment upon Jephthah for having slaughtered thousands of Ephraim.

One man there was living at the time who, if he had been questioned about the case, would have been able to give a decision. This was the high priest Phinehas. But he said proudly: "What! I, a high priest, the son of a high priest, should humiliate myself and go to an ignoramus!" Jephthah on the other hand said: "What! I, the chief of the tribes of Israel, the first prince of the land, should humiliate myself and go to one of the rank and file!" So only the rivalry between Jephthah and Phinehas caused the loss of a young life. Their punishment did not miss them. Jephthah dies a horrible death. Limb by limb his body was dismembered. As for the high priest, the holy spirit departed from him, and he had to give up his priestly dignity.

As it had been Jephthah's task to ward off the Ammonites, so his successor Abdon was occupied with protecting Israel against the Moabites. The king of Moab sent messengers to Abdon, and they spoke thus: "Thou well knowest that Israel took possession of cities that belonged to me. Return them." Abdon's reply was: "Know ye not how the Ammonites fared? The measure of Moab's sins, it seems, out against the enemy, slew forty-five thousand of their number, and routed the rest.

SAMSON

The last judge but one, Samson, was not the most important of the judges, but he was the greatest hero of the period and, except Goliath, the greatest hero of all times. He was the son of Manoah of the tribe of Dan, and his wife Zelalponit of the tribe of Judah, and he was born to them at a time when they had given up all hope of having children. Samson's birth is a striking illustration of the shortsightedness of human beings. The judge Ibzan had not invited Manoah and Zelalponit to any of the one hundred and twenty feasts in honor of the marriage of his sixty children, which were celebrated at his house and at the house of their parents-in-law, because he thought that "the sterile she-mule" would never be in a position to repay his courtesy. It turned out that Samson's parents were blessed with an extraordinary son, while Ibzan saw his sixty children die during his lifetime.

Samson's strength was superhuman, and the dimensions of his body were gigantic he measured sixty ells between the shoulders. Yet he had one imperfection, he was maimed in both feet. The first evidence of his gigantic strength he gave when he uprooted two great mountains, and rubbed them against each other. Such feats he was able to perform as often as the spirit of God was poured out over him. Whenever this happened, it was indicated by his hair. In began to move and emit a bell-like sound, which could be heard far off. Besides, while the spirit rested upon him, he was able with one stride to cover a distance equal to that between Zorah and Eshtaol. It was Samson's supernatural strength that made Jacob think that he would be the Messiah. When God showed him Samson's latter end, then he realized that the new era would not be ushered in by the hero-judge.

Samson won his first victory over the Philistines by means of the jawbone of the ass on which Abraham had made his way to Mount Moriah. It had been preserved miraculously. After this victory a great wonder befell. Samson was at the point of perishing from thirst, when water began to flow from his own mouth as from a spring.

Besides physical prowess, Samson possessed also spiritual distinctions. He was unselfish to the last degree. He had been of exceeding great help to the Israelites, but he never asked the smallest service for himself. When Samson told Delilah that he was a "Nazarite unto God," she was certain that he had divulged the true secret of his strength. She knew his character too well to entertain the idea that he would couple the name of God with an untruth. There was a weak side to his character, too. He allowed sensual pleasures to dominate him. The consequences was that "he who went astray after his eyes, lost his eyes." Even this severe punishment produced no change of heart. He continued to lead his old life of profligacy in prison, and he was encouraged thereto by the Philistines, who set aside all considerations of family purity in the hope of descendants who should be the equals of Samson in giant strength and stature.

As throughout life Samson had given proofs of superhuman power, so in the moment of death. He entreated God to realize in him the blessing of Jacob, and endow him with Divine strength. He expired with these words upon his lips: "O Master of the world! Vouchsafe unto me in this life a recompense for the loss of one of my eyes. For the loss of the other I will wait to be rewarded in the world to come." Even after his death Samson was a shield unto the Israelites. Fear of him had so cowed the Philistines that for twenty years they did not dare attack the Israelites.

THE CRIME OF THE BENJAMITES

A part of the money which Delilah received from the Philistine lords as the price of Samson's secret, she gave to her son Micah, and he used it to make an idol for himself. This sin was the more unpardonable as Micah owed his life to a miracle performed by Moses. During the times of the Egyptian oppression, if the prescribed number of bricks was not furnished by the Israelites, their children were used as building material. Such would have been Micah's fate, if he had not been saved in a miraculous way. Moses wrote down the Name of God, and put the words on Micah's body. The dead boy came to life, and Moses drew him out of the wall of which he made a part. Micah did not show himself worthy of the wonder done for him. Even before the Israelites left Egypt, he made his idol, and it was he who fashioned the golden calf. At the time of Othniel the judge, he took up his abode at a distance of not more than three miles from the sanctuary at Shiloh, and won over the grandson of Moses to officiate as priest before his idol.

The sanctuary which Micah erected harbored various idols. He had three images of boys, and three of calves, one lion, an eagle, a dragon, and a dove. When a man came who wanted a wife, he was directed to appeal to the dove. If riches were his desire, he worshipped the eagle. For daughters both, to the calves; to the lion for strength, and to the dragon for long life. Sacrifices and incense alike were offered to these idols, and both had to be purchased with cash money from Micah, even didrachms for a sacrifice, and one for incense.

The rapid degeneration in the family of Moses may be accounted for by the fact that Moses had married the daughter of a priest who ministered to idols. Yet, the grandson of Moses was not an idolater of ordinary calibre. His sinful conduct was not without a semblance of morality. From his grandfather he had heard the rule that a man should do "Abodah Zarah" for hire rather than be dependent upon his fellow-creatures. The meaning of "Abodah Zarah" here naturally is "strange," in the sense of "unusual" work, but he took the term in its ordinary acceptation of "service of strange gods." So far from being a whole-souled idolater, he adopted methods calculated to harm the cause of idol worship. Whenever any one came leading an animal with the intention of sacrificing it, he would say: "What good can the idol do thee? It can neither see nor hear nor speak." But as he was concerned about his won livelihood, and did not want to offend the idolaters too grossly, he would continue: "If thou bringest a dish of flour and a few eggs, it will suffice." This offering he would himself eat.

Under David he filled the position of treasurer. David appointed him because he thought that a man who was willing to become priest to an idol only in order to earn his bread, must be worthy of confidence. However sincere his repentance may have been, he relapsed into his former life when he was removed from his office by Solomon, who filled all position with new incumbents at his accession to the throne. Finally he abandoned his idolatrous ways wholly, and became so pure a man that the was favored by God with the gift of prophecy. This happened on the day on which the man of God out of Judah came to Jeroboam, for the grandson of Moses is none other than the old prophet at Beth-el who invited the man of God out of Judah to come to his house.

The mischief done by Micah spread further and further. Especially the Benjamites distinguished themselves for their zeal in paying homage to his idols. God therefore resolved to visit the sins of Israel and Benjamin upon them. The opportunity did not delay to come. It was not long before the Benjamites committed the outrage of Gibeah. Before the house of Bethac, a venerable old man, they imitated the disgraceful conduct of the Sodomites before the house of Lot. When the other tribes exacted amends from the Benjamites, and were denied satisfaction, bloody combats ensued. At first the Benjamites prevailed, in spit of the fact that the Urim and Thummim questioned by Phinehas had encouraged the Israelites to take up the conflict, with the words: "Up to war, I shall deliver them into your hands." After the tribes had again and again suffered defeat, they recognized the intention of God, to betray them as a punishment for their sins. They therefore ordained a day of fasting and convocation before the holy Ark, and Phinehas the son of Eleazar entreated God in their behalf: "What means this, that Thou leadest us astray? Is the deed of the Benjamites right in Thine eyes? Then why didst Thou not command us to desist from the combat? But if what our brethren have done is evil in Thy sight, then why dost Thou cause us to fall before them in battle? O God of our fathers, hearken unto my voice. Make it known this day unto Thy servant whether the war waged with Benjamin is pleasing in Thine eyes, or whether thou desirest to punish Thy people for its sins. Then the sinners among us will amend their ways. I am mindful of what happened in the days of my youth, at the time of Moses. In the zeal of my soul I slew two for the sin of Zimri, and when his well-wishers sought to kill me, Thou didst send an angel, who cut off twenty-four thousand of them and delivered me. But now eleven of Thy tribes have gone forth to do Thy bidding, to avenge and slay, and, lo, they have themselves been slain, so that they are made to believe that Thy revelations are lying and deceitful. O Lord, God of our forefathers, naught is hidden before Thee. Make it manifest why this misfortune has overtaken us."

God replied to Phinehas at great length, setting forth why eleven tribes had suffered so heavily. The Lord had wanted to punished them for having permitted Micah and his mother Delilah to pursue their evil ways undisturbed, though they were zealous beyond measure in avenging the wrong done to the woman at Gibeah. As soon as all those had perished who were guilty of having aided and abetted Micah in his idolatrous practices, whether directly or indirectly, God was willing to help them in their conflicts with the Benjamites.

So it came. In the battle fought soon after, seventy-five thousand Benjamites fell slain. Only six hundred of the tribe survived. Fearing to remain in Palestine, the small band emigrated to Italy and Germany.

At the same time the punishment promised them by God overtook the two chief sinners. Micah lost his life by fire, and his mother rotted alive; worms crawled from her body.

In spite of the great mischief caused by Micah, he had one good quality, and God permitted it to plead for him when the angel stood up against him as his accusers. He was extremely hospitable. His house always stood wide open to the wanderer, and to his hospitality he owed it that he was granted a share in the future world. In hell Micah is the first in the sixth division, which is under the guidance of the angel Hadriel, and he is the only one in the division who is spared hell tortures. Micah's sons was Jeroboam, whose golden calves were sinful far beyond anything his father had done.

In those days God spake to Phinehas: "Thou art one hundred and twenty years old, thou hast reached the natural term of man's life. Go now, betake thyself to the mountain Danaben, and remain there many years. I will command the eagles to sustain thee with food, so that thou returnest not to men until the time when thou lockest fast the clouds and openest them again. Then I will carry thee to the place where those are who were before thee, and there thou wilt tarry until I visit the world, and bring thee thither to taste of death."

III. SAMUEL AND SAUL

ELKANAH AND HANNAH

THE period of the Judges is linked to the period of the Kingdom by the prophet Samuel, who anointed both Saul and David as kings. Not only was Samuel himself a prophet, but his forebears also has been prophets, and both his parents, Elkanah and Hannah, were endowed with the gift of prophecy. Aside from this gift, Elkanah possessed extraordinary virtue. He was a second Abraham, the only pious man of his generation, who saved the world from destruction when God, made wroth by the idolatry of Micah, was on the point of annihilating it utterly. His chief merit was that he stimulated the people by his example to go on pilgrimages to Shiloh, the spiritual centre of the nation. Accompanied by his whole household, including kinsmen, he was in the habit of making the three prescribed pilgrimages annually, and though he was a man of only moderate means, his retinue was equipped with great magnificence. In all the towns through which it passed, the procession caused commotion. The lookers-on invariably inquired into the reason of the rare spectacle, and Elkanah told them: "We are going to the house of the Lord at Shiloh, for thence come forth the law. Why should you not join us?" Such gentle, persuasive words did not fail of taking effect. In the first year five households undertook the pilgrimage, the next year ten, and so on until the whole town followed his example. Elkanah chose a new route every year. Thus he touched at many towns, and their inhabitants were led to do a pious deed.

In spite of his God-fearing ways, Elkanah's domestic life was not perfectly happy. He had been married ten years, and his union with Hannah had not been blessed with offspring. The love he bore his wife compensated him for his childlessness, but Hannah herself insisted upon his taking a second wife. Peninnah embraced every opportunity of vexing Hannah. In the morning her derisive greeting to Hannah would be: "Dost thou not mean to rise and wash thy children, and send them to school?" Such jeers were to keep Hannah mindful of her childlessness. Perhaps Peninnah's intentions were laudable: she may have wanted to bring Hannah to the point of praying to God for children. However it may have been forced from her, Hannah's petition for a son was fervent and devout. She entreats God: "Lord of the world! Hast Thou created aught in vain? Our eyes Thou hast destined for sight, our ears for hearing, our mouth for speech, our nose to smell therewith, our hands for work. Didst Thou not create these breasts above my heart to give suck to a babe? O grant me a son, that he may draw nourishment therefrom. Lord, Thou reignest over all beings, the mortal and the heavenly beings. The heavenly beings neither eat nor drink, they do not propagate themselves, nor do they die, but they live forever. Mortal man eats, drinks, propagates his kind and dies. If, now, I am of the heavenly beings, let me live forever. But if I belong to mortal mankind, let me do my part in establishing the race."

Eli the high priest, who at first misinterpreted Hannah's long prayer, dismissed her with the blessing: "May the son to be born unto thee acquire great knowledge in the law." Hannah left the sanctuary, and at once her grief-furrowed countenance changes. She felt beyond a doubt that the blessing of Eli would be fulfilled.

THE YOUTH OF SAMUEL

Hannah's prayer was heard. At the end of six months and a few days, Samuel was born to her, in the nineteenth year of her married life, and the one hundred and thirtieth of her age. Samuel was of a frail constitution, and required tender care and nurture. For this reason he and his mother could not accompany Elkanah on his pilgrimages. Hannah withheld her boy from the sanctuary for some years. Before Samuel's birth a voice from heaven had proclaimed that in a short time a great man would be born, whose name would be Samuel. All men children of that time were accordingly named Samuel. As they grew up, the mothers were in the habit of getting together and telling of their children's doings, in order to determine which of them satisfied the expectations the prophecy had aroused. When the true Samuel was born, and by his wonderful deed excelled all his companions, it became plain to whom the word of God applied. His preeminence now being undisputed, Hannah was willing to part with him.

The following incident is an illustration of Samuel's unusual qualities manifested even in infancy. He was two years old when his mother brought him to Shiloh to leave him there permanently. An occasion at once presented itself for the display of his learning and acumen, which were so great as to arouse the astonishment of the high priest Eli himself. On entering the sanctuary Samuel noticed that they were seeking a priest to kill the sacrificial animal. Samuel instructed the attendants that a non-priest was permitted to kill the sacrifice. The high priest Eli appeared at the moment when, by Samuel's directions, the sacrifice was being killed by a non-priest. Angered by the child's boldness, he was about to have him executed, regardless of Hannah's prayer for his life. "Let him die," he said, "I shall pray for another in his place." Hannah replied: "I lent him to the Lord. Whatever betide, he belongs neither to thee nor to me, but to God." Only then, after Samuel's life was secure, Hannah offered up her prayer of thanksgiving. Beside the expression of her gratitude, it contains also many prophecies regarding Samuel's future achievements, and it recited the history of Israel from the beginning until the advent of Messiah. Her prayer incidentally brought relief to the Sons of Korah. Since the earth had swallowed them, they had been constantly sinking lower and lower. When Hannah uttered the words, "God bringeth down to Sheol, and bringeth up," they came to a standstill in their downward course.

Hannah was spared to witness, not only the greatness of her son, but also the undoing of her rival. Every time Hannah bore a child, Peninnah lost two of hers, until eight of her ten children had died, and she would have had to surrender all, had not Hannah interceded for her with prayer.

ELI AND HIS SONS

Shortly before Samuel entered upon his novitiate in the sanctuary, Eli succeeded to the three highest offices in the land: he was made high priest, president of the Sanhedrin, and ruler over the political affairs of Israel. Eli was a pious man, and devoted to the study of the Torah, wherefore he attained to a good old age and to high honors. In his office as high priest he was successor to no less a personage than Phinehas, who had lost his high-priestly dignity on account of his haughty bearing toward Jephthah. With Eli the line of Ithamar rose to power instead of the line of Eleazar. However, the iniquitous deed of his two sons brought dire misfortune upon Eli and upon his family, though the Scriptural account of their conduct may not be taken literally. The sons of Eli transgressed only in that they sometimes kept the women waiting who came to the sanctuary to bring the purification offerings, and so they retarded their return to their families. This was bad enough for priest of God. Their misdeeds recoiled upon their father, who was not strict enough in rebuking them. Eli's punishment was that he aged prematurely, and, besides, he had to give up his various offices.

During his lifetime, his youngest son Phinehas, the worthier of the two, officiated as high priest. The only reproach to which Phinehas laid himself open was that he made no attempt to mend his brother's ways.

The worst of God's decree against Eli he learned from Elkanah, the man of God who came unto Eli, and who announced that the high-priestly dignity would be wrested from his house, and once more conferred upon the family of Eleazar, and, furthermore, his descendant would all die in their prime. The latter doom can be averted by good deeds, devotion in prayer, and zealous study of the Torah. These means were often employed successfully. But against the loss of the high priest's office there is no specific. The house of Eli forfeited it irrevocably. Abiathar, the great-grandson of Eli's son Phinehas, the last of the high priest of the line of Ithamar, had to submit to the fate of seeing David transfer his dignity to Zadok, in whose family it remained forever.

The sons of Eli brought misfortune also upon the whole of Israel. To their sins and the ease with which the people condoned them was attributed the unhappy issue of the war with the Philistines. The holy Ark, the receptacle for the broken table of the law, which accompanied the people to the camp, did not have the expected effect of compelling victory for the Israelites. What Eli feared happened. He enjoined upon his sons not to appear before him if they should survive the capture of the Ark. But they did not survive it; they died upon the battlefield on which their nation had suffered bitter defeat. The Philistines, to be sure, had to pay dearly for their victory, especially those who had spoken contemptuous words when the holy Ark had appeared in the Israelitish camp: "The God of the Israelites had ten plagues, and those he expended upon the Egyptians. He no longer has it in His power to do harm." But God said: "Do ye but wait to see. I shall bring plague down upon you like of which hath never been." This new plague consisted in mice crawling forth out of the earth, and jerking the entrails out of the bodies of the Philistines while they eased nature. If the Philistines sought to protect themselves by using brass vessels, the vessels burst at the touch of the mice, and, as before, the Philistines were at their mercy. After some months of suffering, when they realized that their god Dagon was the victim instead of the victor, they resolved to send the Ark back to the Israelites. Many of the Philistines, however, were not yet convinced of God's power. The experiment with the milch kine on which there had come no yoke was to establish the matter for them. The result was conclusive. Scarcely had the cows begun to draw the cart containing the Ark when they raised their voices in song:

Arise thou, O Acacia! Soar aloft in the fulness of thy splendor,
Thou who art adorned with gold embroidery,
Thou who art reverenced within the Holiest of the palace,
Thou who art covered by the two Cherubim!

When the holy Ark was thus brought into the Israelitish domain, there was exceeding great rejoicing. Yet the people were lacking in due reverence. They unloaded the holy vessel while doing their usual work. God punished them severely. The seventy members of the Sanhedrin perished, and with them fifty thousand of the people. The punishment was meet for another reason. At first sight of the Ark some of the people had exclaimed: "Who vexed these that thou didst feel offended, and what had mollified thee now?"

THE ACTIVITIES OF SAMUEL

In the midst of the defeats and other calamities that overwhelmed the Israelites, Samuel's authority grew, and the respect for him increased, until he was acknowledged the helper of his people. His first efforts were directed toward counteracting the spiritual decay in Israel. When he assembled the people at Mizpah for prayer, he sought to distinguish between the faithful and the idolatrous, in order to mete out punishment to the disloyal. He had all the people drink water, whose effect was to prevent idolaters from opening their lips. The majority of the people repented of their sins, and Samuel turned to God in their behalf: "Lord of the world! Thou requirest naught of man but that he should repent of his sins. Israel is penitent, do Thou pardon him." The prayer was granted, and when, after his sacrifice, Samuel led an attack upon the Philistines, victory was not withheld from the Israelites. God terrified the enemy first by an earthquake, and then by thunder and lightning. Many were scattered and wandered about aimlessly; many were precipitated into the rents torn in the earth, the rest had their faces scorched, and in their terror and pain their weapons dropped from their hands.

In peace as in war Samuel was the type of a disinterested, incorruptible judge, who even refused compensation for the time, trouble, and pecuniary sacrifices entailed upon him by his office. His sons fell far short of resembling their father in these respects. Instead of continuing Samuel's plan of journeying from place to place to dispense judgment, they had the people come to them, and they surrounded themselves with a crew of officials who preyed upon the people for their maintenance. In a sense, therefore, the curse with which Eli threatened Samuel in his youth was accomplished: both he and Samuel had sons unworthy of their fathers. Samuel at least had the satisfaction of seeing his sons mend their ways. One of them is the prophet Joel, whose prophecy forms a book of the Bible.

Though, according to this account, the sons of Samuel were by no means so iniquitous as might be inferred from the severe expressions of the Scripture, still the demand for a king made by the leaders of the people was not unwarranted. All they desired was a king in the place of a judge. What enkindled the wrath of God and caused Samuel vexation, was the way in which the common people formulated the demand. "We want a king," they said, "that we may be like the other nations."

THE REIGN OF SAUL

There were several reasons for the choice of Saul as king. He had distinguished himself as a military hero in the unfortunate engagement of the Philistines with Israel under the leadership of the sons of Eli. Goliath captured the tables of the law. When Saul heard of this in Shiloh, he marched sixty miles to the camp, wrested the tables from the giant, and returned to Shiloh on the same day, bringing Eli the report of the Israelitish misfortune. Besides, Saul possessed unusual beauty, which explains why the maidens whom he asked about the seer in their city sought to engage him in a lengthy conversation. At the same time he was exceedingly modest. When he and his servant failed to find the asses they were looking for, he said, "My father will take thought of us," putting his servants on a level with himself, and when he was anointed king, he refused to accept the royal dignity until the Urim and Thummin were consulted. His chief virtue, however, was his innocence. He was as free from sin as "a one year old child." No wonder, then, he was held worthy of the prophetic gift. The prophecies he uttered concerned themselves with the war of Gog and Magog, the meting out of reward and punishment at the last judgment. Finally, his choice as king was due also to the merits of his ancestors, especially his grandfather Abiel, a man interested in the public welfare, who would have the streets lighted so that people might go to the houses of study after dark.

Saul's first act as king was his successful attack upon Nahash, king of the Ammonites, who had ordered the Gileadites to remove the injunction from the Torah barring the Ammonites from the congregation of Israel. In his next undertaking, the campaign against the Philistines, he displayed his piety. His son Jonathan had fallen under the severe ban pronounced by Saul against all who tasted food on a certain day, and Saul did not hesitate to deliver him up to death. Jonathan's trespass was made know by the stones in the breastplate of the high priest. All the stones were bright, only the one bearing the name Benjamin had lost its brilliancy. By lot it was determined that its dimmed lustre was due to the Benjamite Jonathan. Saul desisted from his purpose of executing Jonathan only when it appeared that he had transgressed his father's command by mistake. A burnt offering and his weight in gold paid to the sanctuary were considered an atonement for him. In the same war Saul had occasion to show his zeal for the scrupulous observance of the sacrificial ordinances. He reproached his warriors with eating the meat of the sacrifices before the blood was sprinkled on the altar, and he made it his task to see to it that the slaughtering knife was kept in the prescribed condition. As recompense, an angel brought him a sword, there being none beside Saul in the whole army to bear one.

Saul manifested a different spirit in the next campaign, the war with the Amalekites, whom, at the bidding of God, he was to exterminate. When the message of God's displeasure was conveyed to Saul by the prophet Samuel, he said: "If the Torah ordains that a heifer of the herd shall be beheaded in the valley as an atonement for the death of a single man, how great must be the atonement required for the slaughter of so many men? And granted they are sinners, what wrong have their cattle done to deserve annihilation? And granted that the adults are worthy of their fate, what have the children done?" Then a voice proclaimed from heaven, "Be not overjust." Later on, when Saul commissioned Doeg to cut down the priests at Nob, the same voice was heard to say, "Be not overwicked." It was this very Doeg, destined to play so baleful a part in his life, who induced Saul to spare Agag, the king of Amalekites. His argument was the law prohibits the slaying of an animal and its young on the same day. How much less permissible is it to destroy at one time old and young, men and children. As Saul had undertaken the war of extermination against Amalek only because forced into it, he was easily persuaded to let the people keep a part of the cattle alive. As far as he himself was concerned, he could have had no personal interest in the booty, for he was so affluent that he took a census of the army by giving a sheep to every one of his soldiers, distributing not less than two hundred thousand sheep.

Compared with David's sins, Saul's were not sufficiently grievous to account for the withdrawal of the royal dignity from him and his family. The real reason was Saul's too great mildness, a drawback in a ruler. Moreover, his family was of such immaculate nobility that his descendants might have become too haughty. When Saul disregarded the Divine command about the Amalekites, Samuel announced to him that his office would be bestowed upon another. The name of his successor was not mentioned on that occasion, but Samuel gave him a sign by which to recognize the future king: he who would cut off the corner of Saul's mantle, would reign in his stead. Later on, when David met Saul in the cave and cut off a piece of the king's skirt, Saul knew him for a certainty to be his destined successor.

So Saul lost his crown on account of Agag, and yet did not accomplish his purpose of saving the life of the Amalekite king, for Samuel inflicted a most cruel death upon Agag, and that not in accordance with Jewish, but with heathen, forms of justice. No witnesses of Agag's crime could be summoned before the court, nor could it be proved that Agag, as the law requires, had been warned when about to commit the crime. Though due punishment was meted out to Agag, in a sense it came too late. Had he been killed by Saul in the course of the battle, the Jews would have been spared the persecution devised by Haman, for, in the short span of time that elapsed between war and his execution, Agag became the ancestor of Haman.

The Amalekite war was the last of Saul's notable achievements. Shortly afterward he was seized by the evil spirit, and the rest of his days were passed mainly in persecuting David and his followers. Saul would have died immediately after the Amalekite war, if Samuel had not interceded for him. The prophet prayed to God that the life of the disobedient king be spared, at least so long as his own years had not come to their destined close: "Thou regardest me equal to Moses and Aaron. As Moses and Aaron did not have their handiwork destroyed before their eyes during their life, so may my handiwork not cease during my life." God said: "What shall I do? Samuel will not let me put an end to Saul's days, and if I let Samuel die in his prime, people will speak ill of him. Meanwhile David's time is approaching, and one reign may not overlap the time assigned to another by his hairbreadth." God determined to let Samuel age suddenly, and when he died at fifty-two, the people were under the impression the days of an old man had come to an end. So long as he lived, Saul was secure. Scarcely was he dead, when the Philistines began to menace the Israelites and their king. Soon it appeared how well justified had been the mourning services for the departed prophet in all the Israelitish towns. It was not remarkable that the mourning for Samuel should have been universal. During his active administration as judge, he had been in the habit of journeying through every part of the country, and so he was known personally to all the people. This practice of his testifies not only to the zeal with which he devoted himself to his office, but also to his wealth, for the expenses entailed by these journeys were defrayed from his own purse. Only one person in all the land took no part in the demonstrations of grief. During the very week of mourning Nabal held feasts. "What!" God exclaimed, "all weep and lament over the death of the pious, and this reprobate engages in revelry!" Punishment was not withheld. Three days after the week of mourning for Samuel Nabal dies.

There was none that felt the death of Samuel more keenly than Saul. Left alone and isolated, he did not shrink from extreme measures to enter into communication with the departed prophet. With his two adjutants, Abner and Amasa, he betook himself to Abner's mother, the witch of En-dor. The king did not reveal his identity, but the witch had no difficulty in recognizing her visitor. In necromancy the peculiar rule holds good that, unless it is summoned by a king, a spirit raised from the dead appears head downward and feet in the air. Accordingly, when the figure of Samuel stood upright before them, the witch knew that the king was with her. Though the witch saw Samuel, she could not hear what he said, while Saul heard his words, but could not see his person another peculiar phenomenon in necromancy: the conjuror sees the spirit, and he for whom the spirit had been raised only hears it. Any other person present neither sees nor hears it.

The witch's excitement grew when she perceived a number of spirits arise by the side of Samuel. The dead prophet, when he was summoned back to earth, thought that the judgement day had arrived. He requested Moses to accompany him and testify to his always having executed the ordinances of the Torah as Moses had established them. With these two great leaders a number of the pious arose, all believing that the day of judgment was at hand. Samuel was apparelled in the "upper garment" his mother had made for him when she surrendered him to the sanctuary. This he had worn throughout his life, and in it he was buried. At the resurrection all the dead wear their grave clothes, and so it came about that Samuel stood before Saul in his well-known "upper garment."

Only fragments of the conversation between Samuel and Saul have been preserved in the Scriptures. Samuel reproached Saul with having disturbed him. "Was it not enough," he said, "for thee to enkindle the wrath of thy Creator by calling up the spirits of the dead, must thou need change me into an idol? For is it not said that like unto the worshippers so shall the worshipped be punished?" Samuel then consented to tell the king God's decree, that he had resolved to rend the kingdom out of his hand, and invest David with the royal dignity. Whereupon Saul: "These are not the words thou spakest to me before." "When we dwelt together," rejoined Samuel, "I was in the world of lies. Now I abide in the world of truth, and thou heardest lying words from me, for I feared thy wrath and thy revenge. Now I abide in the world of truth, and thou hearest words of truth from me. As to the thing the Lord hath done unto thee, thou hast deserved it, for thou didst not obey the voice of the Lord, nor execute his fierce wrath upon Amalek." Saul asked: "Can I still save myself by flight?" "Yes," replied Samuel, "if thou fleest, thou art safe. But if thou acceptest God's judgment, by to-morrow thou wilt be united with me in Paradise."

When Abner and Amasa questioned Saul about his interview with Samuel, he replied: "Samuel told me I should go into battle to-morrow, and come forth victorious. More than that, my sons will be given exalted positions in return for their military prowess." The next day his three sons went with him to the war, and all were stricken down. God summoned the angels and said to them: "Behold the being I have created in my world. A father as a rule refrains from taking his sons even to a banquet, lest he expose them to the evil eye. Saul goes to war knowing that he will lose his life, yet he takes his sons with him, and cheerfully accepts the punishment I ordain."

So perished the first Jewish king, as a hero and a saint. His latter days were occupied with regrets on account of the execution of the priest of Nob, and his remorse secured pardon for him. Indeed, in all respects his piety was so great that not even David was his equal: David had many wives and concubines; Saul had but on wife. David remained behind, fearing to lose his life in battle with his son Absalom; Saul went into the combat knowing he should not return alive. Mild and generous, Saul led the life of a saint in his own house, observing even the priestly laws of purity. Therefore God reproached David with having pronounced a curse upon Saul in his prayer. Also, David in his old age was punished for having cut off the corner of Saul's mantle, for no amount of clothing would keep him warm. Finally, when a great famine fell upon the land during the reign of David, God told him it had been inflicted upon him because Saul's remains had not been buried with the honor due to him, and at that moment a heavenly voice resounded calling Saul "the elect of God."

THE COURT OF SAUL

The most important figure at the court of Saul was his cousin Abner, the son of the witch of En-dor. He was a giant of extraordinary size. A wall measuring six ells in thickness could be moved more easily than one of Abner's feet. David once chanced to get between the feet of Abner as he lay asleep, and he was almost crushed to death, when fortunately Abner moved them, and David made his escape. Conscious of his vast strength he once cried out: "If only I could seize the earth at some point, I should be able to shake it." Even in the hour of death, wounded mortally by Joab, he grasped his murderer like a worsted ball. He was about to kill him, but the people crowded round them, and said to Abner: "If thou killest Joab, we shall be orphaned, and our wives and children will be prey to the Philistines." Abner replied: "What can I do? He was about to extinguish my light." The people consoled him: "Commit thy cause to the true Judge." Abner thereupon loosed his hold upon Joab, who remained unharmed, while Abner fell dead instantly. God had decided against him. The reason was that Joab was in a measure justified in seeking to avenge the death of his brother Asahel. Asahel, the supernaturally swift runner, so swift that he ran through a field without snapping the ears of wheat, had been the attacking party. He had sough to take Abner's life, and Abner contended, that in killing Asahel he had but acted in self-defense. Before inflicting the fatal wound, Joab held a formal court of justice over Abner. He asked: "Why didst thou no render Asahel harmless by wounding him rather than kill him?" Abner replied that he could not have done it. "What," said Joab, incredulous, "if thou wast able to strike him under the fifth rib, dost thou mean to say thou couldst not have made him innocuous by a wound, and saved him alive?"

Although Abner was a saint, even a "lion in the law," he perpetrated many a deed that made his violent death appear just. It was in his favor that he had refused to obey Saul's command to do away with the priests of Nob. Yet a man of his stamp should not have rested content with passive resistance. He should have interposed actively, and kept Saul from executing his blood design. And granted that Abner could not have influenced the king's mind in this matter, at all events he is censurable for having frustrated a reconciliation between Saul and David. When David, holding in his hand the corner of the king's mantle which he had cut off, sought to convince Saul of his innocence, it was Abner who turned the king against the suppliant fugitive. "Concern not thyself about it," he said to Saul. "David found the rag on a thornbush in which thou didst catch the skirt of thy mantle as thou didst pass it." On the other hand, no blame attaches to Abner for having espoused the cause of Saul's son against David for two years and a half. He knew that God had designated David for the royal office, but, according to an old tradition, God had promised two kings to the tribe of Benjamin, and Abner considered it his duty to transmit his father's honor to the son of Saul the Benjamite.

Another figure of importance during Saul's reign, but a man of radically different character, was Doeg. Doeg, the friend of Saul from the days of his youth, died when he was thirty-four years old, yet at that early age he had been president of the Sanhedrin and the greatest scholar of his time. He was called Edomi, which means, not Edomite, but "he who causes the blush of shame," because by his keen mind and his learning he put to shame all who entered into argument with him. But his scholarship lay only on his lips, his heart was not concerned in it, and his one aim was to elicit admiration. Small wonder, then, that his end was disastrous. At the time of his death he had sunk so low that he forfeited all share in the life to come. Wounded vanity caused his hostility to David, who had got the better of him in a learned discussion. From that moment he bent all his energies to the task of ruining David. He tried to poison Saul's mind against David, by praising the latter inordinately, and so arousing Saul's jealousy. Again, he would harp on David's Moabite descent, and maintain that on account of it he could not be admitted into the congregation of Israel. Samuel and other prominent men had to bring to bear all the weight of their authority to shield David against the consequences of Doeg's sophistry.

Doeg's most grievous transgression, however, was his informing against the priests of Nob, whom he accused of high treason and executed as traitors. For all his iniquitous deeds he pressed the law into his service, and derived justification of his conduct from it. Abimelech, the high priest at Nob, admitted that he had consulted the Urim and Thummim for David. This served Doeg as the basis for the charge of treason, and he stated it as an unalterable Halakah that the Urim and Thummim may be consulted only for a king. In vain Abner and Amasa and all the other members of the Sanhedrin demonstrated that the Urim and Thummim may be consulted for any on whose undertaking concerns the general welfare. Doeg would not yield, and as no one could be found to execute the judgement, he himself officiated as hangman. When the motive of revenge actuated him, he held cheap alike the life and honor of his fellow-man. He succeeded in convincing Saul that David's marriage with the king's daughter Michal had lost its validity from the moment David was declared a rebel. As such, he said, David was as good as dead, since a rebel was outlawed. Hence his wife was no longer bound to him. Doeg's punishment accorded with his misdeeds. He who had made impious use of his knowledge of the law, completely forgot the law, and even his disciples rose up against him, and drove him from the house of study. In the end he died a leper.

Dreadful as this death was, it was not accounted an atonement for his sins. One angel burned his soul, and another scattered his ashes in all the house of study and prayer. The son of Doeg was Saul's armor-bearer, who was killed by David for daring to slay the king even though he longed for death.

Along with Abner and Doeg, Jonathan distinguished himself in the reign of his father. His military capacity was joined to deep scholarship. To the latter he owed his position as Ab Bet Din. Nevertheless he was one of the most modest men known in history. Abinadab was another one of Saul's sons who was worthy of his father, wherefore he was sometimes called Ishvi. As for Saul's grandson Mephibosheth. He, too, was reputed a great man. David himself did not scorn to sit at his feet, and he revered Mephibosheth as his teacher. The wrong done him by David in granting one-half his possessions to Ziba, the slave of Mephibosheth, did not go unavenged. When David ordered the division of the estate of Mephibosheth, a voice from heaven prophesied: "Jeroboam and Rehoboam shall divide the kingdom between themselves."

IV. DAVID

DAVID'S BIRTH AND DESCENT

DAVID, the "elect of God," was descended from a family which itself belonged to the elect of Israel. Those ancestors of his who are enumerated in the Bible by name are all of them men of distinguished excellence. Besides, David was a descendant of Miriam, the sister of Moses, and so the strain of royal aristocracy was reinforced by the priestly aristocracy. Nor was David the first of his family to occupy the throne of a ruler. His great-grandfather Boaz was one and the same person with Ibzan, the judge of Bethlehem. Othniel, too, the first judge in Israel after the death of Joshua, and Caleb, the brother of Othniel, were connected with David's family. As examples of piety and virtue, David had his grandfather and more particularly his father before him. His grandfather's whole life was a continuous service of God, whence his name Obed, "the servant," and his father Jesse was one of the greatest scholars of his time, and one of the four who died wholly untainted by sin. If God had not ordained death for all the descendants of our first parents after their fall, Jesse would have continued to live forever. As it was, he died at the age of four hundred, and then a violent death, by the hand of the Moabite king, in whose care David, trusting in the ties of kinship between the Moabites and the seed of Ruth, left his family when he was fleeing before Saul. Jesse's piety will not go unrewarded. In the Messianic time he will be one of the eight princes to rule over the world.

In spite of his piety, Jesse was not always proof against temptation. One of his slaves caught his fancy, and he would have entered into illicit relations with her, had his wife, Nazbat, the daughter of Adiel, not frustrated the plan. She disguised herself as the slave, and Jesse, deceived by the ruse, met his own wife. The child borne by Nazbat was given out as the son of the freed slave, so that the father might not discover the deception practiced upon him. This child was David.

In a measure David was indebted for his life to Adam. At first only three hours of existence had been allotted to him. When God caused all future generations to pass in review before Adam, he besought God to give David seventy of the thousand years destined for him. A deed of gift, signed by God and the angel Metatron, was drawn up. Seventy years were legally conveyed from Adam to David, and in accordance with Adam's wishes, beauty, dominion, and poetical gift went with them.

ANOINTED KING

Beauty and talent, Adam's gifts to David, did not shield their possessor against hardship. As the supposed son of a slave, he was banished from association with his brothers, and his days were passed in the desert tending his father's sheep. It was his shepherd life that prepared him for his later exalted position. With gentle consideration he led the flocks entrusted to him. The young lambs he guided to pastures of tender grass; the patches of less juicy herbs he reserved for the sheep; and the full-grown sturdy rams were given the tough weeds for food. Then God said: "David knows how to tend sheep, therefore he shall be the shepherd of my flock Israel."

In the solitude of the desert David had opportunities of displaying his extraordinary physical strength. One day he slew four lions and three bears, though he had no weapons. His most serious adventure was with the reem. David encountered the mammoth beast asleep, and taking it for a mountain, he began to ascend it. Suddenly the reem awoke, and David found himself high up in the air on its horns. He vowed, if he were rescued, to build a temple to God one hundred ells in height, as high as the horns of the reem. Thereupon God sent a lion. The king of beasts inspired even the reem with awe. The reem prostrated himself, and David could easily descend from his perch. At that moment a deer appeared. The lion pursued after him, and David was saved from the lion as well as the reem.

He continued to lead the life of a shepherd until, at the age of twenty-eight, he was anointed king by Samuel, who was taught by a special revelation that the despised youngest son of Jesse was to be king. Samuel's first charge had been to anoint one of the sons of Jesse, but he was not told which one. When he saw the oldest, Eliab, he thought him the king of God's choice. God had allowed him to be deceived, in order to punish Samuel for his excessive self-consciousness in calling himself the seer. It was thus proved to him that he could not foresee all things. However, Samuel's error was pardonable. God's first choice had rested upon Eliab. Only on account of his violent nature, his swiftness to anger against David, the position destined for him was transferred to his youngest brother. Eliab was in a sense compensated by seeing his daughter become the wife of Rehoboam. Thus he, too, enjoys the distinction of being among the ancestors of the Judaic kings, and Samuel's vision of Eliab as king was not wholly false.

The election of David was obvious from what happened with the holy oil with which he was anointed. When Samuel had tried to pour the oil on David's brothers, it had remained in the horn, but at David's approach it flowed of its own accord, and poured itself out over him. The drops on his garments changed into diamonds and pearls, and after the act of anointing him, the horn was as full as before.

The amazement was great that the son of a slave should be made king. Then the wife of Jesse revealed her secret, and declared herself the mother of David.

The anointing of David was for a time kept a secret, but its effect appeared in the gift of prophecy which manifested itself in David, and in his extraordinary spiritual development. His new accomplishments naturally earned envy for him. None was more bitterly jealous than Doeg, the greatest scholar of his time. When he heard that Saul was about to have David come to court as his attendant, Doeg began to praise David excessively, with the purpose of arousing the king's jealousy and making David hateful in his eyes. He succeeded, yet Saul did not relinquish his plan of having David at court. David had become known to Saul in his youth, and at that time the king had conceived great admiration for him. The occasion was one on which David had shown cleverness as well as love of justice. A rich woman had had to leave her home temporarily. She could not carry her fortune with her, nor did she wish to entrust it to any one. She adopted the device of hiding her gold in honey jars, and these she deposited with a neighbor. Accidentally he discovered what was in the jars, and he abstracted the gold. On her return the woman received her vessels, but the gold concealed in them was gone. She had no evidence to bring up against her faithless neighbor, and the court dismissed her complaint. She appealed to the king, but he was equally powerless to help. When the woman came out of the palace of the king, David was playing with his companions. Seeing her dejection, he demanded an audience of the king, that truth might prevail. The king authorized him to do as he saw fit. David ordered the honey jars to be broken, and two coins were found to adhere to the inner side of the vessels. The thief had overlooked them, and they proved his dishonesty.

ENCOUNTER WITH GOLIATH

David was not long permitted to enjoy the ease of life at court. The aggressive manner assumed by Goliath drove him to the front. It was a curious chance that designated David to be the slayer of Goliath, who was allied with him by the ties of blood. Goliath, it will be remembered, was the son of the Moabitess Orpah, the sister-in-law of David's ancestress Ruth, and her sister as well, both having been the daughters of the Moabite king Eglon. David and Goliath differed as widely as their grandams, for in contrast to Ruth, the pious, religious Jewess, Orpah had led a life of unspeakable infamy. Her son Goliath was jeered at as "the son of a hundred fathers and one mother." But God lets naught go unrewarded, even in the wicked. In return for the forty steps Orpah had accompanied her mother-in-law Naomi, Goliath the Philistine, her son, was permitted to display his strength and skill for forty days, and in return for the four tears Orpah had shed on parting from her mother-in-law, she was privileged to give birth to four giant sons.

Of the four, Goliath was the strongest and greatest. What the Scriptures tell about him is but a small fraction of what might have been told. The Scriptures refrain intentionally from expatiating upon the prowess of the miscreant. Nor do they tell how Goliath, impious as he was, dared challenge the God of Israel to combat with him, and how he tried by every means in his power to hinder the Israelites in their Divine worship. Morning and evening he would appear in the camp at the very time when the Israelites were preparing to say the Shema.

All the more cause, then, for David to hate Goliath and determine to annihilate him. His father encouraged him to oppose Goliath, for he considered it David's duty to protect Saul the Benjamite against the giant, as Judah, his ancestor, had in ancient days pledged himself for the safety of Benjamin, the ancestor of Saul. For Goliath was intent upon doing away with Saul. His grievance against him was that once, when, in a skirmish between the Philistines and the Israelites, Goliath had succeeded in capturing the holy tables of the law, Saul had wrested them from the giant. In consequence of his malady, Saul could not venture to cross swords with Goliath, and he accepted David's offer to enter into combat in his place. David put on Saul's armor, and when it appeared that the armor of the powerfully-built king fitted the erstwhile slender youth, Saul recognized that David had been predestined for the serious task he was about to undertake, but at the same time David's miraculous transformation did not fail to arouse his jealousy. David, for this reason, declined to array himself as a warrior for his contest with Goliath. He wanted to meet him as a simple shepherd. Five pebbles came to David of their own accord, and when he touched them, they all turned into one pebble. The five pebbles stood for God, the three Patriarchs, and Aaron. Hophni and Phinehas, the descendants of the last, had only a short time before been killed by Goliath.

Scarcely did David begin to move toward Goliath, when the giant became conscious of the magic power of the youth. The evil eye David cast on his opponent sufficed to afflict him with leprosy, and in the very same instant he was rooted to the ground, unable to move. Goliath was so confused by his impotence that he scarcely knew what he was saying, and he uttered the foolish threat that he would give David's flesh to the cattle of the field, as though cattle ate flesh. One can see, David said to himself, that he is crazy, and there can be no doubt he is doomed. Sure of victory, David retorted that he would cast the carcass of the Philistine to the fowls of the air. At the mention of fowls, Goliath raised his eyes skyward, to see whether there were any birds about. The upward motion of his head pushed his visor slightly away from his forehead, and in that instant the pebble aimed by David struck him on the exposed spot. An angel descended and cast him to the ground face downward, so that the mouth that had blasphemed God might be choked with earth. He fell in such wise that the image of Dagon which he wore on his breast touched the ground, and his head came to lie between the feet of David, who now had no difficulty in dispatching him.

Goliath was encased, from top to toe, in several suits of armor, and David did not know how to remove them and cut off the head of the giant. At this juncture Uriah the Hittite offered him his services, but under the condition that David secure him an Israelitish wife. David accepted the condition, and Uriah in turn showed him how the various suits of armor were fastened together at the heels of the giant's feet.

David's victory naturally added fuel to the fire of Saul's jealousy. Saul sent Abner, his general, to make inquiry whether David, who, he knew, was of the tribe of Judah, belonged to the clan of the Perez or to the clan of the Zerah. In the former case his suspicion that David was destined for kingship would be confirmed. Doeg, David's enemy from of old, observed that David, being the descendant of the Moabitess Ruth, did not even belong to the Jewish communion, and Saul need entertain no fears from that quarter. A lively discussion arose between Abner and Doeg, as to whether the law in Deuteronomy regarding Moabites affected women as well as men. Doeg, an expert dialectician, brilliantly refuted all of Abner's arguments in favor of the admission of Moabitish women. Samuel's authority had to be appealed to in order to establish for all times the correctness of Abner's view. Indeed, the dispute could be settled only by recourse to threats of violence. Ithra, the father of Amasa, in Arab fashion, for which reason he was sometimes called the Ishmaelite, threatened to hew down any one with his sword who refused to accept Samuel's interpretation of the law, that male Moabites and male Ammonites are forever excluded from the congregation of Israel, but not Moabite and Ammonite women.

PURSUED BY SAUL

As God stood by David in his duel with Goliath, so he stood by him in many other of his difficulties. Often when he thought all hope lost, the arm of God suddenly succored him, and in unexpected ways, not only bringing relief, but also conveying instruction on God's wise and just guidance of the world.

David once said to God: "The world is entirely beautiful and good, with the one exception of insanity. What use does the world derive from a lunatic, who runs hither and thither, tears his clothes, and is pursued by a mob of hooting children?" "Verily, a time will come," said God in reply, "when thou wilt supplicate me to afflict thee with madness." Now, it happened when David, on his flight before Saul, came to Achish, the king of the Philistines, who lived in Gath, that the brothers of Goliath formed the heathen king's body-guard, and they demanded that their brother's murderer be executed. Achish, though a heathen, was pious, for which reason he is called Abimelech in the Psalms, after the king of Gerar, who also was noted for piety. He therefore sought to pacify David's enemies. He called their attention to the fact that Goliath had been the one to challenge the Jews to combat, and it was meet, therefore, that he should be left to bear the consequences. The brothers rejoined, if that view prevailed, then Achish would have to give up his throne to David, for, according to the conditions of the combat, the victor was to have dominion over the vanquished as his servants. In his distress, David besought God to let him appear a madman in the eyes of Achish and his court. God granted his prayer. As the wife and daughter of the Philistine king were both bereft of reason, we can understand his exclamation: "Do I lack madmen, that ye have brought this fellow to play the madman in my presence?" Thus it was that David was rescued. Thereupon he composed the Psalm beginning with the words, "I will bless the Lord at all times," which includes even the time of lunacy.

On another occasion David expressed his doubt of God's wisdom in having formed such apparently useless creatures as spiders are. They do nothing but spin a web that has no value. He was to have striking proof that even a spider's web may serve an important purpose. On one occasion he had taken refuge in a cave, and Saul and his attendants, in pursuit of him, were about to enter and seek him there. But God sent a spider to weave its web across the opening, and Saul told his men to desist from fruitless search in the cave, for the spider's web was undeniable proof that no one had passed through its entrance.

Similarly, when David became indebted to one of them for his life, he was cured of his scorn for wasps. He had thought them good for nothing but to breed maggots. David once surprised Saul and his attendants while they were fast asleep in their camp, and he resolved to carry off, as proof of his magnanimity, the cruse that stood between the feet of the giant Abner, who like the rest was sleeping. Fortunately his knees were drawn up, so that David could carry out his intention unhindered. But as David was retiring with the cruse, Abner stretched out his feet, and pinned David down as with two solid pillars. His life would have been forfeit, if a wasp had not stung Abner, who mechanically, in his sleep, moved his feet, and released David.

There were still other miracles that happened to David in his flight. Once, when Saul and his men compassed David round about, an angel appeared and summoned him home, to repulse the raid of the Philistines upon the land. Saul gave up the pursuit of David, but only after a majority had so decided, for some had been of the opinion that the seizure of David was quite as important as the repulse of the Philistines. Again, in his battle with the Amalekites, David enjoyed direct intervention from above. Lightning in flashes and sheets illumined the dark night, so enabling him to carry on the struggle.

WARS

David's first thought after ascending the throne was to wrest Jerusalem, sacred since the days of Adam, Noah, and Abraham, from the grasp of the heathen. The plan was not easy of execution for various reasons. The Jebusites, the possessors of Jerusalem, were the posterity of those sons of Heth who had ceded the Cave of Machpelah to Abraham only on condition that their descendants should never be forcibly dispossessed of their capital city Jerusalem. In perpetuation of this agreement between Abraham and the sons of Heth, monuments of brass were erected, and when David approached Jerusalem with hostile intent, the Jebusites pointed to Abraham's promise engraven upon them and still plainly to be read. They maintained that before David could take the city, which they had surrounded with a high wall, he would have to destroy the monuments. Joab devised a plan of getting into Jerusalem. He set up a tall cypress tree near the wall, bent it downward, and standing on David's head, he grasped the very tip of the tree. When the tree rebounded, Joab sat high above the wall, and could jump down upon it. Once in the city, he destroyed the monuments, and possessed himself of Jerusalem. For David a miracle had happened; the wall had lowered itself before him so that he could walk into the city without difficulty. David, however, was not desirous of using forcible means. He therefore offered the Jebusites six hundred shekels, fifty shekels for each Israelitish tribe. The Jebusites accepted the money, and gave David a bill of sale.

Jerusalem having been acquired, David had to prepare for war with the Philistines, in which the king gave proof at once of his heroic courage and his unshakable trust in God. The latter quality he displayed signally in the battle that took place in the Valley of the Giants. God had commanded David not to attack the host of the Philistines until he heard "the sound of marching in the tops of the mulberry trees." God desired to pass judgment upon the tutelary angels of the heathen, before surrendering the heathen themselves to the pious, and the motion of the tops of the trees was to indicate that the battle could proceed. The enemy advanced until there were but four ells between them and the Israelites. The latter were about to throw themselves against the Philistines, but David restrained them, saying: "God forbade me to attack the Philistines before the tops of the trees begin to move. If we transgress God's command, we shall certainly die. If we delay, it is probable that we shall be killed by the Philistines, but, at least, we shall die as pious men that keep God's command. Above all, let us have confidence in God." Scarcely had he ended his speech when the tops of the trees rustled, and David made a successful assault upon the Philistines. Whereupon God said to the angels, who were constantly questioning him as to why he had taken the royal dignity from Saul and given it to David: "See the difference between Saul and David."

Of David's other campaigns, the most notable is his war with Shobach the Aramean, whom he conquered in spite of his gigantic size and strength. Shobach was very tall, as tall as a dove-cote, and one look at him sufficed to strike terror to the heart of the beholder. The Aramean general indulged in the belief that David would treat the Syrians gently on account of the monument, still in existence at that time, which Jacob and Laban had erected on the frontier between Palestine and Aram as a sign of their covenant that neither they nor their descendants should wage war with each other. But David destroyed the monument. Similarly, the Philistines had placed trust in a relic from Isaac, the bridle of a mule which the Patriarch had given to Abimelech, the king of the Philistines, as a pledge of the covenant between Israel and his people. David took it from them by force.

However, David was as just as he was bold. Disregard of the covenants made by the Patriarchs was far removed from his thoughts. Indeed, before departing for the wars with the Arameans and the Philistines, he had charged the Sanhedrin to investigate carefully the claims of the two nations. The claims of the Philistines were shown to be utterly unfounded. In no sense were they the descendants of those Philistines who had concluded a treaty with Isaac; they had immigrated from

Cyprus at a much later date. The Arameans, on the other hand, had forfeited their claims upon considerate treatment, because under the "Aramean" Balaam, and later again, in the time of Othniel, under their king Cushan-rishathaim, they had attacked and made war upon the Israelites.

AHITHOPHEL

Among David's courtiers and attendants, a prominent place is occupied by his counsellor Ahithophel, with whom the king was connected by family ties, Bath-sheba being his granddaughter. Ahithophel's wisdom was supernatural, for his counsels always coincided with the oracles rendered by the Urim and Thummim, and great as was his wisdom, it was equalled by his scholarship. Therefore David did not hesitate to submit himself to his instruction, even though Ahithophel was a very young man, at the time of his death not more than thirty-three years old. The one thing lacking in him was sincere piety, and this it was that proved his undoing in the end, for it induced him to take part in Absalom's rebellion against David. Thus he forfeited even his share in the world to come.

To this dire course of action he was misled by astrologic and other signs, which he interpreted as prophecies of his own kingship, when in reality they pointed to the royal destiny of his granddaughter Bath-sheba. Possessed by his erroneous belief, he cunningly urged Absalom to commit an unheard-of crime. Thus Absalom would profit nothing by his rebellion, for, though he accomplished his father's ruin, he would yet be held to account and condemned to death for his violation of family purity, and the way to the throne would be clear for Ahithophel, the great sage in Israel.

The relation between David and Ahithophel had been somewhat strained even before Absalom's rebellion. Ahithophel's feelings had been hurt by his being passed over at the time when David, shortly after ascending the throne, invested, on a single day, no less than ninety thousand functionaries with positions.

On that day a remarkable incident occurred. When the Ark was to be brought up from Geba to Jerusalem, the priests who attempted to take hold of it were raised up in the air and thrown violently to the ground. In his despair the king turned for advice to Ahithophel, who retorted mockingly: "Ask thy wise men whom thou hast but now installed in office." It was only when David uttered a curse on him who knows a remedy and withholds it from the sufferer, that Ahithophel advised that a sacrifice should be offered at every step taken by the priests. Although the measure proved efficacious, and no further disaster occurred in connection with the Ark, yet Ahithophel's words had been insincere. He knew the real reason of the misadventure, and concealed it from the king. Instead of following the law of having the Ark carried on the shoulders of priests, David had had it put on a wagon, and so incurred the wrath of God.

Ahithophel's hostility toward David showed itself also on the following occasion. When David was digging the foundations of the Temple, a shard was found at a depth of fifteen hundred cubits. David was about to lift it, when the shard exclaimed: "Thou canst not do it." "Why not?" asked David. "Because I rest upon the abyss." "Since when?" "Since the hour in which the voice of God was heard to utter the words from Sinai, 'I am the Lord thy God,' causing the earth to quake and sink into the abyss. I lie here to cover up the abyss." Nevertheless David lifted the shard, and the waters of the abyss rose and threatened to flood the earth. Ahithophel was standing by, and he thought to himself: "Now David will meet with his death, and I shall be king." Just then David said: "Whoever knows how to stem the tide of waters, and fails to do it, will one day throttle himself." Thereupon Ahithophel had the Name of God inscribed upon the shard, and the shard thrown into the abyss. The waters at once commenced to subside, but they sank to so great a depth that David feared the earth might lose her moisture, and he began to sing the fifteen "Songs of Ascents," to bring the waters up again.

Nevertheless David's curse was realized. Ahithophel ended his days by hanging himself. His last will contained the following three rules of conduct: 1. Refrain from doing aught against a favorite of fortune. 2. Take heed not to rise up against the royal house of David. 3. If the Feast of Pentecost falls on a sunny day, then sow wheat.

Posterity has been favored with the knowledge of but a small part of Ahithophel's wisdom, and that little through two widely different sources, through Socrates, who was his disciple, and through a fortune-book written by him.

JOAB

Joab, the warrior, was a contrast to Ahithophel in every essential. He was David's right hand. It was said, if Joab had not been there to conduct his wars, David would not have had leisure to devote himself to the study of the Torah. He was the model of a true Jewish hero, distinguished at the same time for his learning, piety, and goodness. His house stood wide open for all comers, and the campaigns which he undertook redounded invariably to the benefit of the people. They were indebted to him for luxuries even, and more than that, he took thought for the welfare of scholars, he himself being the president of the Sanhedrin.

It interested Joab to analyze the character of men and their opinions. When he heard King David's words: "Like as a father pitieth his children, so the Lord pitieth them that fear him," he expressed his astonishment that the comparison should be made with the love of a father for a child, and not with the love of a mother; mother love as a rule is considered the stronger and the more self-sacrificing. He made up his mind to keep his eyes open, and observe whether David's idea was borne out by facts. On one of his journeys he happened into the house of a poor old man who had twelve children, all of whom the father supported, however meagrely, with the toil of his own hands. Joab proposed that he sell him one of the twelve children; he would thus be relieved of the care of one, and the selling-price could be applied to the better support of the rest. The good father rejected the proposition brusquely. Then Joab approached the mother, offering her a hundred gold denarii for one of the children. At first she resisted the temptation, but finally she yielded. When the father returned in the evening, he cut the bread, as was his wont, into fourteen pieces, for himself, his wife, and his twelve children. In allotting the portions he missed a child, and insisted upon being told its fate. The mother confessed what had happened during his absence. He neither ate nor drank, and next morning he set out, firmly resolved to return the money to Joab and to slay him if he should refuse to surrender the child. After much parleying, and after the father had threatened him with death, Joab yielded the child to the old man, with the exclamation: "Yes, David was right when he compared God's love for men to a father's love for his child. This poor fellow who has twelve children to support was prepared to fight me to the death for one of them, which the mother, who calmly stayed at home, had sold to me for a price."

Among all the heroic achievements of Joab, the most remarkable is the taking of the Amalekite capital. For six months the flower of the Israelitish army, twelve thousand in number, under the leadership of Joab, had been besieging the capital city of the Amalekites without result. The soldiers made representations to their general, that it would be well for them to return home to their wives and children. Joab urged that this not only would earn for them contempt and derision, but also would invite new danger. The heathen would be encouraged to unite against the Israelites. He proposed that they hurl him into the city by means of a sling, and then wait forty days. If at the end of this period they saw blood flow from the gates of the fortress, it should be a sign to them that he was still alive.

His plan was executed. Joab took with him one thousand pieces of money and his sword. When he was cast from the sling, he fell into the courtyard of a widow, whose daughter caught him up. In a little while he regained consciousness. He pretended to be an Amalekite taken prisoner by the Israelites, and thrown into the city by his captors, who thus wished to inflict death. As he was provided with money, which he dispensed lavishly among his entertainers, he was received kindly, and was given the Amalekite garb. So apparelled, he ventured, after ten days, on a tour of inspection through the city, which he found to be of enormous size.

His first errand was to an armorer, to have him mend his sword, which had been broken by his fall. When the artisan scanned Joab's weapon, he started back—he had never seen a sword like it. He forged a new one, which snapped in two almost at once when Joab grasped it firmly. So it happened with a second sword, and with a third. Finally he succeeded in fashioning one that was acceptable. Joab asked the smith whom he would like him to slay with the sword, and the reply was, "Joab, the general of the Israelitish king." "I am he," said Joab, and when the smith in astonishment turned to look at him, Joab ran him through so skillfully that the victim had no realization of what was happening. Thereupon he hewed down five hundred Amalekite warriors whom he met on his way, and not one escaped to betray him. The rumor arose that Asmodeus, the king of demons, was raging among the inhabitants of the city, and slaying them in large numbers.

After another period of ten days, which he spent in retirement with his hosts,

Joab sallied forth a second time, and caused such bloodshed among the Amalekites that his gory weapon clave to his hand, and his right hand lost all power of independent motion, it could be made to move only in a piece with his arm. He hastened to his lodging place to apply hot water to his hand and free it from the sword. On his way thither the woman who had caught him up when he fell into the city called to him: "Thou eatest and drinkest with us, yet thou slayest our warriors." Seeing himself betrayed, he could not but kill the woman. Scarcely had his sword touched her, when it was separated from his hand, and his hand could move freely, for the dead woman had been with child, and the blood of the unborn babe loosed the sword.

After Joab had slain thousands, the Israelites without, at the very moment when they were beginning to mourn their general as dead, saw blood issue from the city, and joyfully they cried out with one accord: "Hear, O Israel, the Lord is our God, the Lord is One." Joab mounted a high tower, and in stentorian tones shouted: "The Lord will not forsake his people." Inspired with high and daring courage, the Israelites demanded permission to assault the city and capture it. As Joab turned to descend from the tower, he noticed that six verses of a Psalm were inscribed on his foot, the first verse running thus: "The Lord answers thee in the day of trouble, the name of the God of Jacob is thy defense." Later David added three verses and completed the Psalm. Thereupon the Israelites took the Amalekite capital, destroyed the heathen temples in the city, and slew all its inhabitants, except the king, whom, with his crown of pure gold on his head, they brought before David.

DAVID'S PIETY AND HIS SIN

Neither his great achievements in war nor his remarkable good fortune moved David from his pious ways, or in aught changed his mode of life. Even after he became king he sat at the feet of his teachers, Ira the Jairite and Mephibosheth. To the latter he always submitted his decisions on religious questions, to make sure that they were in accordance with law. Whatever leisure time his royal duties afforded him, he spent in study and prayer. He contented himself with "sixty breaths" of sleep. At midnight the strings of his harp, which were made of the gut of the ram sacrificed by Abraham on Mount Moriah, began to vibrate. The sound they emitted awakened David, and he would arise at once to devote himself to the study of the Torah.

Besides study, the composition of psalms naturally claimed a goodly portion of his time. Pride filled his heart when he had completed the Psalter, and he exclaimed: "O Lord of the world, is there another creature in the universe who like me proclaims thy praise?" A frog came up to the king, and said: "Be not so proud; I have composed more psalms than thou, and, besides, every psalm my mouth has uttered I have accompanied with three thousand parables." And, truly, if David indulged in conceit, it was only for a moment. As a rule he was the exemplar of modesty. The coins which were stamped by him bore a shepherd's crook and pouch on the obverse, and on the reverse the Tower of David. In other respects, too, his bearing was humble, as though he were still the shepherd and not the king.

His great piety invested his prayer with such efficacy that he could bring things in heaven down to earth. It is natural that so godly a king should have used the first respite granted by his wars to carry out his design of erecting a house of worship to God. But in the very night in which David conceived the plan of building the Temple, God said to Nathan the prophet: "Hasten to David. I know him to be a man with whom execution follows fast upon the heels of thought, and I should not like him to hire laborers for the Temple work, and then, disappointed, complain of me. I furthermore know him to be a man who obligates himself by vows to do good deeds, and I desire to spare him the embarrassment of having to apply to the Sanhedrin for absolution from his vow."

When David heard Nathan's message for him, he began to tremble, and he said: "Ah, verily, God hath found me unworthy to erect His sanctuary." But God replied with these words: "Nay, the blood shed by thee I consider as sacrificial blood, but I do not care to have thee build the Temple, because then it would be eternal and indestructible." "But that would be excellent," said David. Whereupon the reply was vouchsafed him: "I foresee that Israel will commit sins. I shall wreak My wrath upon the Temple, and Israel will be saved from annihilation. However, thy good intentions shall receive their due reward. The Temple, though it be built by Solomon, shall be called thine."

David's thinking and planning were wholly given to what is good and noble. He is one of the few pious men over whom the evil inclination had no power. By nature he was not disposed to commit such evil-doing as his relation to Bath-sheba involved. God Himself brought him to his crime, that He might say to other sinners: "Go to David and learn how to repent." Nor, indeed, may David be charged with gross murder and adultery. There were extenuating circumstances. In those days it was customary for warriors to give their wives bills of divorce, which were to have validity only if the soldier husbands did not return at the end of the campaign. Uriah having fallen in battle, Bath-sheba was a regularly divorced woman. As for the death of her husband, it cannot be laid entirely at David's door, for Uriah had incurred the death penalty by his refusal to take his ease in his own house, according to the king's bidding. Moreover, from the first, Bath-sheba had been destined by God for David, but by way of punishment for having lightly promised Uriah the Hittite an Israelitish woman to wife, in return for his aid in unfastening the armor of the prostrate Goliath, the king had to undergo bitter trials before he won her.

Furthermore, the Bath-sheba episode was a punishment for David's excessive self-consciousness. He had fairly besought God to lead him into temptation, that he might give proof of his constancy. It came about thus: He once complained to God: "O Lord of the world, why do people say God of Abraham, God of Isaac, God of Jacob, and why not God of David?" The answer came: "Abraham, Isaac, and Jacob were tried by me, but thou hast not yet been proved." David entreated: "Then examine me, O Lord, and try me." And God said: "I shall prove thee, and I shall even grant thee what I did not grant the Patriarchs. I shall tell thee beforehand that thou wilt fall into temptation through a woman."

Once Satan appeared to him in the shape of a bird. David threw a dart at him. Instead of striking Satan, it glanced off and broke a wicker screen which hid Bath-sheba combing her hair. The sight of her aroused passion in the king. David realized his transgression, and for twenty-two years he was a penitent. Daily he wept a whole hour and ate his "bread with ashes." But he had to undergo still heavier penance. For a half-year he suffered with leprosy, and even the Sanhedrin, which usually was in close personal attendance upon him, had to leave him. He lived not only in physical, but also in spiritual isolation, for the Shekinah departed from him during that time.

ABSALOM'S REBELLION

Of all the punishments, however, inflicted upon David, none was so severe as the rebellion of his own son.

Absalom was of such gigantic proportions that a man who was himself of extraordinary size, standing in the eye-socket of his skull, sank in down to his nose. As for his marvellous hair, the account of it in the Bible does not convey a notion of its abundance. Absalom had taken the vow of a Nazarite. As his vow was for life, and because the growth of his hair was particularly heavy, the law permitted him to clip it slightly every week. It was of this small quantity that the weight amounted to two hundred shekels.

Absalom arranged for his audacious rebellion with great cunning. He secured a letter from his royal father empowering him to select two elders for his suite in every town he visited. With this document he travelled through the whole of Palestine. In each town he went to the two most distinguished men, and invited them to accompany him, at the same time showing them what his father had written, and assuring them that they had been chosen by him because he had a particular affection for them. So he succeeded in gathering the presidents of two hundred courts about him. This having been accomplished, he arranged a large banquet, at which he seated one of his emissaries between every two of his guests, for the purpose of winning them over to his cause. The plan did not succeed wholly, for, though the elders of the towns stood by Absalom, in their hearts they hoped for David's victory.

The knowledge that a part of Absalom's following sided with him in secret,—that, though he was pursued by his son, his friends remained true to him,—somewhat consoled David in his distress. He thought that in these circumstances, if the worst came to the worst, Absalom would at least feel pity for him. At first, however, the despair of David knew no bounds. He was on the point of worshipping an idol, when his friend Hushai the Archite approached him, saying: "The people will wonder that such a king should serve idols." David replied: "Should a king such as I am be killed by his own son? It is better for me to serve idols than that God should be held responsible for my misfortune, and His Name thus be desecrated." Hushai reproached him: "Why didst thou marry a captive?" "There is no wrong in that," replied David, "it is permitted according to the law." Thereupon Hushai: "But thou didst disregard the connection between the passage permitting it and the one that follows almost immediately after it in the Scriptures, dealing with the disobedient and rebellious son, the natural issue of such a marriage."

Hushai was not the only faithful friend and adherent David had. Some came to his rescue unexpectedly, as, for instance, Shobi, the son of Nahash, who is identical with the Ammonite king Hanun, the enemy of David at first, and later his ally. Barzillai, another one of his friends in need, also surprised him by his loyalty, for on the whole his moral attitude was not the highest conceivable.

Absalom's end was beset with terrors. When he was caught in the branches of the oak-tree, he was about to sever his hair with a sword stroke, but suddenly he saw hell yawning beneath him, and he preferred to hang in the tree to throwing himself into the abyss alive. Absalom's crime was, indeed, of a nature to deserve the supreme torture, for which reason he is one of the few Jews who have no portion in the world to come. His abode is in hell, where he is charged with the control of ten heathen nations in the second division. Whenever the avenging angels sit in judgment on the nations, they desire to visit punishment on Absalom, too, but each time a heavenly voice is heard to call out: "Do not chastise him, do not burn him. He is an Israelite, the son of My servant David." Whereupon Absalom is set upon his throne, and is accorded the treatment due to a king. That the extreme penalties of hell were thus averted from him, was on account of David's eightfold repetition of his son's name in his lament over him. Besides, David's intercession had the effect of re-attaching Absalom's severed head to his body.

At his death Absalom was childless, for all his children, his three sons and his daughter, died before him, as a punishment for his having set fire to a field of grain belonging to Joab.

DAVID'S ATONEMENT

All these sufferings did not suffice to atone for David's sin. God once said to him: "How much longer shall this sin be hidden in thy hand and remain unatoned? On thy account the priestly city of Nob was destroyed, on thy account Doeg the Edomite was cast out of the communion of the pious, and on thy account Saul and his three sons were slain. What dost thou desire now—that thy house should perish, or that thou thyself shouldst be delivered into the hands of thine enemies?" David chose the latter doom.

It happened one day when he was hunting, Satan, in the guise of a deer, enticed him further and further, into the very territory of the Philistines, where he was recognized by Ishbi the giant, the brother of Goliath, his adversary. Desirous of avenging his brother, he seized David, and cast him into a winepress, where the king would have suffered a torturous end, if by a miracle the earth beneath him had not begun to sink, and so saved him from instantaneous death. His plight, however, remained desperate, and it required a second miracle to rescue him.

In that hour Abishai, the cousin of David, was preparing for the advent of the Sabbath, for the king's misfortune happened on Friday as the Sabbath was about to come in. When Abishai poured out water to wash himself, he suddenly caught sight of drops of blood in it. Then he was startled by a dove that came to him plucking out her plumes, and moaning and wailing. Abishai exclaimed: "The dove is the symbol of the people of Israel. It cannot be but that David, the king of Israel, is in distress." Not finding the king at home, he was confirmed in his fears, and he determined to go on a search for David on the swiftest animal at his command, the king's own saddle-beast. But first he had to obtain the permission of the sages to mount the animal ridden by the king, for the law forbids a subject to avail himself of things set aside for the personal use of a king. Only the impending danger could justify the exception made in this case.

Scarcely had Abishai mounted the king's animal, when he found himself in the land of the Philistines, for the earth had contracted miraculously. He met Orpah, the mother of the four giant sons. She was about to kill him, but he anticipated the blow and slew her. Ishbi, seeing that he now had two opponents, stuck his lance into the ground, and hurled David up in the air, in the expectation that when he fell he would be transfixed by the lance. At that moment Abishai appeared, and by pronouncing the Name of God he kept David suspended 'twixt heaven and earth.

Abishai questioned David how such evil plight had overtaken him, and David told him of his conversation with God, and how he himself had chosen to fall into the hands of the enemy, rather than permit the ruin of his house. Abishai replied: "Reverse thy prayer, plead for thyself, and not for thy descendants. Let thy children sell wax, and do thou not afflict thyself about their destiny." The two men joined their prayers, and pleaded with God to avert David's threatening doom. Abishai again uttered the Name of God, and David dropped to earth uninjured. Now both of them ran away swiftly, pursued by Ishbi. When the giant heard of his mother's death, his strength forsook him, and he was slain by David and Abishai.

VISITATIONS

Among the sorrows of David are the visitations that came upon Palestine during his reign, and he felt them all the more as he had incurred them through his own fault. There was first the famine, which was so desolating that it is counted among the ten severest that are to happen from the time of Adam to the time of the Messiah. During the first year that it prevailed, David had an investigation set on foot to discover whether idolatry was practiced in the land, and was keeping back the rain. His suspicion proved groundless. The second year he looked into the moral conditions of his realm, for lewdness can bring about the same punishment as idolatry. Again he was proved wrong. The third year, he turned his attention to the administration of charity. Perhaps the people had incurred guilt in this respect, for abuses in this department also were visited with the punishment of famine. Again his search was fruitless, and he turned to God to inquire of Him the cause of the public distress. God's reply was: "Was not Saul a king anointed with holy oil, did he not abolish idolatry, is he not the companion of Samuel in Paradise? Yet, while you all dwell in the land of Israel, he is 'outside of the land.'" David, accompanied by the scholars and the nobles of his kingdom, at once repaired to Jabesh-gilead, disinterred the remains of Saul and Jonathan, and in solemn procession bore them through the whole land of Israel to the inheritance of the tribe of Benjamin. There they were buried. The tributes of affection paid by the people of Israel to its dead king aroused the compassion of God, and the famine came to an end.

The sin against Saul was now absolved, but there still remained Saul's own guilt in his dealings with the Gibeonites, who charged him with having killed seven of their number. David asked God why He had punished His people on account of proselytes. God's answer to him was: "If thou dost not bring near them that are far off, thou wilt remove them that are near by." To satisfy their vengeful feelings, the Gibeonites demanded the life of seven members of Saul's family. David sought to mollify them, representing to them that they would derive no benefit from the death of their victims, and offering them silver and gold instead. But though David treated with each one of them individually, the Gibeonites were relentless. When he realized their hardness of heart, he cried out: "Three qualities God gave unto Israel; they are compassionate, chaste, and gracious in the service of their fellowmen. The first of these qualities the Gibeonites do not possess, and therefore they must be excluded from communion with Israel."

The seven descendants of Saul to be surrendered to the Gibeonites were determined by letting all his posterity pass by the Ark of the law. Those who were arrested before it were the designated victims. Mephibosheth would have been one of the unfortunates, had he not been permitted to pass by unchecked in answer to the prayer of David, to whom he was dear, not only as the son of his friend Jonathan, but also as the teacher who instructed him in the Torah.

The cruel fate that befell the descendants of Saul had a wholesome effect. All the heathen who saw and heard exclaimed: "There is no God like unto the God of Israel, there is no nation like unto the nation of Israel; the wrong inflicted upon wretched proselytes has been expiated by the sons of kings." So great was the enthusiasm among the heathen over this manifestation of the Jewish sense of justice that one hundred and fifty thousand of them were converted to Judaism.

As for David, his wrong in connection with the famine lay in his not having applied his private wealth to the amelioration of the people's suffering. When David returned victorious from the combat with Goliath, the women of Israel gave him their gold and silver ornaments. He put them aside for use in building the Temple, and even during the three years' famine this fund was not touched. God said: "Thou didst refrain from rescuing human beings from death, in order to save thy money for the Temple. Verily, the Temple shall not be built by thee, but by Solomon."

David is still more blameworthy on account of the census which he took of the Israelites in defiance of the law in the Pentateuch. When he was charged by the king with the task of numbering the people, Joab used every effort to turn him away from his intention. But in vain. Incensed, David said: "Either thou art king and I am the general, or I am king and thou art the general." Joab had no choice but to obey. He selected the tribe of Gad as the first to be counted, because he thought that the Gadites, independent and self-willed, would hinder the execution of the royal order, and David would be forced to give up his plan of taking a census. The Gadites disappointed the expectations of Joab, and he betook himself to the tribe of Dan, hoping that if God's punishment descended, it would strike the idolatrous Danites. Disliking his mission as he did, Joab spent nine months in executing it, though he might have dispatched it in a much shorter time. Nor did he carry out the king's orders to the letter. He himself warned the people of the census. If he saw the father of a family of five sons, he would bid him conceal a few of them. Following the example set by Moses, he omitted the Levites from the enumeration, likewise the tribe of Benjamin, because he entertained particularly grave apprehensions in behalf of this greatly decimated tribe. In the end, David was not informed of the actual number obtained. Joab made two lists, intending to give the king a partial list if he found that he had no suspicion of the ruse.

The prophet Gad came to David and gave him the choice of famine, oppression by enemies, or the plague, as the penalty for the heavy crime of popular census-taking. David was in the position of a sick man who is asked whether he prefers to be buried next to his father or next to his mother. The king considered: "If I choose the calamities of war, the people will say, 'He cares little, he has his warriors to look to.' If I choose famine, they will say, 'He cares little, he has his riches to look to.' I shall choose the plague, whose scourge strikes all alike." Although the plague raged but a very short time, it claimed a large number of victims. The most serious loss was the death of Abishai, whose piety and learning made him the counterpoise of a host of seventy-five thousand.

David raised his eyes on high, and he saw the sins of Israel heaped up from earth to heaven. In the same moment an angel descended, and slew his four sons, the prophet Gad, and the elders who accompanied him. David's terror at this sight, which was but increased when the angel wiped his dripping sword on the king's garments, settled in his limbs, and from that day on they never ceased to tremble.

THE DEATH OF DAVID

David once besought God to tell him when he would die. His petition was not granted, for God has ordained that no man shall foreknow his end. One thing, however, was revealed to David, that his death would occur at the age of seventy on the Sabbath day. David desired that he might be permitted to die on Friday. This wish, too, was denied him, because God said that He delighted more in one day passed by David in the study of the Torah, than in a thousand holocausts offered by Solomon in the Temple. Then David petitioned that life might be vouchsafed him until Sunday; this, too, was refused, because God said it would be an infringement of the rights of Solomon, for one reign may not overlap by a hairbreadth the time assigned to another. Thereafter David spent every Sabbath exclusively in the study of the Torah, in order to secure himself against the Angel of Death, who has no power to slay a man while he is occupied with the fulfillment of God's commandments. The Angel of Death had to resort to cunning to gain possession of David. One Sabbath day, which happened to be also the Pentecost holiday, the king was absorbed in study, when he heard a sound in the garden. He rose and descended the stairway leading from his palace to the garden, to discover the cause of the noise. No sooner had he set foot on the steps than they tumbled in, and David was killed. The Angel of Death had caused the noise in order to utilize the moment when David should interrupt his study. The king's corpse could not be moved on the Sabbath, which was painful to those with him, as it was lying exposed to the rays of the sun. So Solomon summoned several eagles, and they stood guard over the body, shading it with their outstretched pinions.

DAVID IN PARADISE

The death of David did not mean the end of his glory and grandeur. It merely caused a change of scene. In the heavenly realm as on earth David ranks among the first. The crown upon his head outshines all others, and whenever he moves out of Paradise to present himself before God, suns, stars, angels, seraphim, and other holy beings run to meet him. In the heavenly court-room a throne of fire of gigantic dimensions is erected for him directly opposite to the throne of God. Seated on this throne and surrounded by the kings of the house of David and other Israelitish kings, he intones wondrously beautiful psalms. At the end he always cites the verse: "The Lord reigns forever and ever," to which the archangel Metatron and those with him reply: "Holy, holy, holy, is the Lord of hosts!" This is the signal for the holy Hayyot and heaven and earth to join in with praise. Finally the kings of the house of David sing the verse: "And the Lord shall be king over all; in that day shall the Lord be one, and His name one."

The greatest distinction to be accorded David is reserved for the judgment day, when God will prepare a great banquet in Paradise for all the righteous. At David's petition, God Himself will be present at the banquet, and will sit on His throne, opposite to which David's throne will be placed. At the end of the banquet, God will pass the wine cup over which grace is said, to Abraham, with the words: "Pronounce the blessing over the wine, thou who art the father of the pious of the world." Abraham will reply: "I am not worthy to pronounce the blessing, for I am the father also of the Ishmaelites, who kindle God's wrath." God will then turn to Isaac: "Say the blessing, for thou wert bound upon the altar as a sacrifice." "I am not worthy," he will reply, "for the children of my son Esau destroyed the Temple." Then to Jacob: "Do thou speak the blessing, thou whose children were blameless." Jacob also will decline the honor on the ground that he was married to two sisters at the same time, which later was strictly prohibited by the Torah. God will then turn to Moses: "Say the blessing, for thou didst receive the law and didst fulfil its precepts." Moses will answer: "I am not worthy to do it, seeing that I was not found worthy to enter the Holy Land." God will next offer the honor to Joshua, who both led Israel into the Holy Land, and fulfilled the commandments of the law. He, too, will refuse to pronounce the blessing, because he was not found worthy to bring forth a son. Finally God will turn to David with the words: "Take the cup and say the blessing, thou the sweetest singer in Israel and Israel's king. And David will reply: 'Yes, I will pronounce the blessing, for I am worthy of the honor.'" Then God will take the Torah and read various passages from it, and David will recite a psalm in which both the pious in Paradise and the wicked in hell will join with a loud Amen. Thereupon God will send his angels to lead the wicked from hell to Paradise.

THE FAMILY OF DAVID

David had six wives, including Michal, the daughter of Saul, who is called by the pet name Eglah, "Calfkin," in the list given in the Bible narrative. Michal was of entrancing beauty, and at the same time the model of a loving wife. Not only did she save David out of the hands of her father, but also, when Saul, as her father and her king, commanded her to marry another man, she acquiesced only apparently. She entered into a mock marriage in order not to arouse the anger of Saul, who had annulled her union with David on grounds which he thought legal. Michal was good as well as beautiful; she showed such extraordinary kindness to the orphan children of her sister Merab that the Bible speaks of the five sons of Michal "whom she bore to Adriel." Adriel, however, was her brother-in-law and not her husband, but she had raised his children, treating them as though they were her own. Michal was no less a model of piety. Although the law exempted her, as a woman, from the duty, still she executed the commandment of using phylacteries. In spite of all these virtues, she was severely punished by God for her scorn of David, whom she reproached with lack of dignity, when he had in mind only to do honor to God. Long she remained childless, and at last, when she was blessed with a child, she lost her own life in giving birth to it.

But the most important among the wives of David was Abigail, in whom beauty, wisdom, and prophetical gifts were joined. With Sarah, Rahab, and Esther, she forms the quartet of the most beautiful women in history. She was so bewitching that passion was aroused in men by the mere thought of her. Her cleverness showed itself during her first meeting with David, when, though anxious about the life of her husband Nabal, she still, with the utmost tranquility, put a ritual question to him in his rage. He refused to answer it, because, he said, it was a question to be investigated by day, not by night. Thereupon Abigail interposed, that sentence of death likewise may be passed upon a man only during the day. Even if David's judgment were right, the law required him to wait until daybreak to execute it upon Nabal. David's objection, that a rebel like Nabal had no claim upon due process of law, she overruled with the words: "Saul is still alive, and thou art not yet acknowledged king by the world."

Her charm would have made David her captive on this occasion, if her moral strength had not kept him in check. By means of the expression, "And this shall not be unto thee," she made him understand that the day had not yet arrived, but that it would come, when a woman, Bath-sheba, would play a disastrous part in his life. Thus she manifested her gift of prophecy.

Not even Abigail was free from the feminine weakness of coquetry. The words "remember thine handmaid" should never have been uttered by her. As a married woman, she should not have sought to direct the attention of a man to herself. In the women's Paradise she supervises the fifth of the seven divisions into which it is divided, and her domain adjoins that of the wives of the Patriarchs, Sarah, Rebekah, Rachel, and Leah.

Among the sons of David, Adonijah, the son of Haggith, must be mentioned particularly, the pretender to the throne. The fifty men whom he prepared to run before him had fitted themselves for the place of heralds by cutting out their spleen and the flesh of the soles of their feet. That Adonijah was not designated for the royal dignity, was made manifest by the fact that the crown of David did not fit him. This crown had the remarkable peculiarity of always fitting the legitimate king of the house of David.

Chileab was a son worthy of his mother Abigail. The meaning of his name is "like the father," which had been given him because of his striking resemblance to David in appearance, a circumstance that silenced the talk against David's all too hasty marriage with the widow of Nabal. Intellectually, too, Chileab testified to David's paternity. In fact, he excelled his father in learning, as he did even the teacher of David, Mephibosheth, the son of Jonathan. On account of his piety he is one of the few who have entered Paradise alive.

Tamar cannot be called one of the children of David, because she was born before her mother's conversion to Judaism. Consequently, her relation to Amnon is not quite of the grave nature it would have been, had they been sister and brother in the strict sense of the terms.

To the immediate household of David belonged four hundred young squires, the sons of women taken captive in battle. They wore their hair in heathen fashion, and, sitting in golden chariots, they formed the vanguard of the army, and terrified the enemy by their appearance.

HIS TOMB

When David was buried, Solomon put abundant treasures into his tomb. Thirteen hundred years later the high priest Hyrcanus took a thousand talents of the money secreted there to use it in preventing the siege of Jerusalem by the Greek king Antiochus. King Herod also abstracted great sums. But none of the marauders could penetrate to the resting-place of the kings,—next to David his successors were interred,—for it was sunk into the earth so skillfully that it could not be found.

Once on a time, a Moslem pasha visited the mausoleum, and as he was looking through the window in it, a weapon of his ornamented with diamonds and pearls dropped into the tomb. A Mohammedan was lowered through the window to fetch the weapon. When he was drawn up again, he was dead, and three other Mohammedans who tried to enter in the same way met the fate of their comrade. At the instigation of the kadi, the pasha informed the Rabbi of Jerusalem that the Jews would be held responsible for the restoration of the weapon. The Rabbi ordered a three days' fast, to be spent in prayer. Then lots were cast to designate the messenger who was to be charged with the perilous errand. The lot fell upon the beadle of the synagogue, a pious and upright man. He secured the weapon, and returned it to the pasha, who manifested his gratitude by kindly treatment of the Jews thereafter. The beadle later told his adventures in the tomb to the Hakam Bashi. When he had descended, there suddenly appeared before him an old man of dignified appearance, and handed him what he was seeking.

Another miraculous tale concerning the tomb of David runs as follows: A poor but very pious Jewish washerwoman was once persuaded by the keeper of the tomb to enter it. Hardly was she within, when the man nailed up the entrance, and ran to the kadi to inform him that a Jewess had gone in. Incensed, the kadi hastened to the spot, with the intention of having the woman burnt for her presumptuousness. In her terror the poor creature had begun to weep and implore God for help. Suddenly a flood of light illumined the dark tomb, and a venerable old man took her by the hand, and led her downward under the earth until she reached the open. There he parted from her with the words: "Hasten homeward, and let none know that thou wert away from thy house." The kadi had the tomb and its surroundings thoroughly searched by his bailiffs, but not a trace of the woman could be discovered, although the keeper again and again swore by the Prophet that the woman had entered. Now the messengers whom the kadi had sent to the house of the woman returned, and reported they had found her washing busily, and greatly astonished at their question, whether she had been at the tomb of David. The kadi accordingly decided that for his false statements and his perjury, the keeper must die the very death intended for the innocent woman, and so he was burnt. The people of Jerusalem suspected a miracle, but the woman did not divulge her secret until a few hours before her death. She told her story, and then bequeathed her possessions to the congregation, under the condition that a scholar recite Kaddish for her on each anniversary of her death.

V. SOLOMON

SOLOMON PUNISHES JOAB

AT the youthful age of twelve Solomon succeeded his father David as king. His real name was Jedidiah, the "friend of God," but it was superseded by the name Solomon on account of the peace that prevailed throughout the realm during his reign. He bore three other names besides: Ben, Jakeh, and Ithiel. He was called Ben because he was the builder of the Temple; Jakeh, because he was the ruler of the whole world; and Ithiel, because God was with him.

The rebellion Adonijah intended to lead against the future king was suppressed during David's lifetime, by having Solomon anointed in public. On that occasion Solomon rode upon a remarkable she-mule, remarkable because she was not the product of cross-breeding, but of a special act of creation.

As soon as he ascended the throne, Solomon set about executing the instructions his father had given him on his death-bed. The first of them was the punishment of Joab.

Notwithstanding all his excellent qualities, which fitted him to be not only David's first general, but also the president of the Academy, Joab had committed great crimes, which had to be atoned for. Beside the murder of Abner and Amasa of which he was guilty, he had incurred wrong against David himself. The generals of the army suspected him of having had Uriah the Hittite put out of the way for purposes of his own, whereupon he showed them David's letter dooming Uriah. David might have forgiven Joab, but he wanted him to expiate his sins in this world, so that he might be exempt from punishment in the world to come.

When Joab perceived that Solomon intended to have him executed, he sought the protection of the Temple. He knew full well that he could not save his life in this way, for the arm of justice reaches beyond the doors of the sanctuary, to the altar of God. What he wished was to be accorded a regular trial, and not suffer death by the king's order. In the latter case he would lose fortune as well as life, and he was desirous of leaving his children well provided for. Thereupon Solomon sent word to him that he had no intention of confiscating his estates.

Though he was convinced of Joab's guilt, Solomon nevertheless granted him the privilege of defense. The king questioned him: "Why didst thou kill Abner?"

Joab: "I was the avenger of my brother Asahel, whom Abner had slain."

Solomon: "Why, it was Asahel who sought to kill Abner, and Abner acted in self-defense."

Joab: "Abner might have disabled Asahel without going to extremes."

Solomon: "That Abner could not do."

Joab: "What! Abner aimed directly at Asahel's fifth rib, and thou wouldst say he could not have managed to wound him lightly?"

Solomon: "Very well, then, we shall drop Abner's case. But why didst thou slay Amasa?"

Joab: "He acted rebelliously toward King David. He omitted to execute his order to gather an army within three days; for that offense he deserved to suffer the death penalty."

Solomon: "Amasa failed to obey the king's order, because he had been taught by our sages that even a king's injunctions may be set at defiance if they involve neglect of the study of the Torah, which was the case with the order given to Amasa. And, indeed," continued Solomon, "it was not Amasa but thou thyself who didst rebel against the king, for thou wert about to join Absalom, and if thou didst refrain, it was from fear of David's strong-fisted troops."

When Joab saw that death was inevitable, he said to Benaiah, who was charged with the execution of the king's order: "Tell Solomon he cannot inflict two punishments upon me. If he expects to take my life, he must remove the curse pronounced by David against me and my descendants on account of the slaying of Abner. If not, he cannot put me to death." Solomon realized the justness of the plea. By executing Joab, he transferred David's curse to his own posterity: Rehoboam, his son, was afflicted with an issue; Uzziah suffered with leprosy; Asa had to lean on a staff when he walked; the pious Josiah fell by the sword of Pharaoh, and Jeconiah lived off charity. So the imprecations of David were accomplished on his own family instead of Joab's.

THE MARRIAGE OF SOLOMON

The next to suffer Joab's fate was Shimei ben Gera, whose treatment of David had outraged every feeling of decency. His death was of evil portent for Solomon himself. So long as Shimei, who was Solomon's teacher, was alive, he did not venture to marry the daughter of Pharaoh. When, after Shimei's death, Solomon took her to wife, the archangel Gabriel descended from heaven, and inserted a reed in the sea. About this reed more and more earth was gradually deposited, and, on the day on which Jeroboam erected the golden calves, a little hut was built upon the island. This was the first of the dwelling-places of Rome.

Solomon's wedding-feast in celebration of his marriage with the Egyptian princess came on the same day as the consecration of the Temple. The rejoicing over the king's marriage was greater than over the completion of the Temple. As the proverb has it: "All pay flattery to a king." Then it was that God conceived the plan of destroying Jerusalem. It was as the prophet spoke: "This city hath been to me a provocation of mine anger and of my fury from the day that they built it even unto this day."

In the nuptial night Pharaoh's daughter had her attendants play upon a thousand different musical instruments, which she had brought with her from her home, and as each was used, the name of the idol to which it was dedicated was mentioned aloud. The better to hold the king under the spell of her charms, she spread above his bed a tapestry cover studded with diamonds and pearls, which gleamed and glittered like constellations in the sky. Whenever Solomon wanted to rise, he saw these stars, and thinking it was night still, he slept on until the fourth hour of the morning. The people were plunged in grief, for the daily sacrifice could not be brought on this very morning of the Temple dedication, because the Temple keys lay under Solomon's pillow, and none dared awaken him. Word was sent to Bath-sheba, who forthwith aroused her son, and rebuked him for his sloth. "Thy father," she said, "was known to all as a God-fearing man, and now people will say, 'Solomon is the son of Bath-sheba, it is his mother's fault if he goes wrong.' Whenever thy father's wives were pregnant, they offered vows and prayed that a son worthy to reign might be born unto them. But my prayer was for a learned son worthy of the gift of prophecy. Take care, 'give not thy strength unto women nor thy ways to them that destroy kings,' for licentiousness confounds the reason of man. Keep well in mind the things that are necessary in the life of a king. 'Not kings, Lemuel.' Have naught in common with kings who say: 'What need have we of a God?' It is not meet that thou shouldst do like the kings who drink wine and live in lewdness. Be not like unto them. He to whom the secrets of the world are revealed, should not intoxicate himself with wine."

Apart from having married a Gentile, whose conversion to Judaism was not dictated by pure motives, Solomon transgressed two other Biblical laws. He kept many horses, which a Jewish king ought not to do, and, what the law holds in equal abhorrence, he amassed much silver and gold. Under Solomon's rule silver and gold were so abundant among the people that their utensils were made of them instead of the baser metals. For all this he had to atone painfully later on.

HIS WISDOM

But Solomon's wealth and pomp were as naught in comparison with his wisdom. When God appeared to him in Gibeon, in a dream by night, and gave him leave to ask what he would, a grace accorded to none beside except King Ahaz of Judah, and promised only to the Messiah in time to come, Solomon chose wisdom, knowing that wisdom once in his possession, all else would come of itself. His wisdom, the Scriptures testify, was greater than the wisdom of Ethan the Ezrahite, and Heman, and Calcol, and Darda, the three sons of Mahol. This means that he was wiser than Abraham, Moses, Joseph, and the generation of the desert. He excelled even Adam. His proverbs which have come down to us are barely eight hundred in number. Nevertheless the Scripture counts them equal to three thousand, for the reason that each verse in his book admits of a double and a triple interpretation. In his wisdom he analyzed the laws revealed to Moses, and he assigned reasons for the ritual and ceremonial ordinances of the Torah, which without his explanation had seemed strange. The "forty-nine gates of wisdom" were open to Solomon as they had been to Moses, but the wise king sought to outdo even the wise legislator. He had such confidence in himself that he would have dispensed judgment without resort to witnesses, had he not been prevented by a heavenly voice.

The first proof of his wisdom was given in his verdict in the case of the child claimed by two mothers as their own. When the women presented their difficulty, the king said that God in His wisdom had foreseen that such a quarrel would arise, and therefore had created the organs of man in pairs, so that neither of the two parties to the dispute might be wronged. on hearing these words from the king, Solomon's counsellors lamented: "Woe to thee, O land, when thy king is a youth." In a little while they realized the wisdom of the king, and then they exclaimed: "Happy art thou, O land, when thy king is a free man." The quarrel had of set purpose been brought on by God to the end that Solomon's wisdom might be made known. In reality the two litigants were not women at all, but spirits. That all doubt about the fairness of the verdict might be dispelled, a heavenly voice proclaimed: "This is the mother of the child."

During the lifetime of David, when Solomon was still a lad, he had settled another difficult case in an equally brilliant way. A wealthy man had sent his son on a protracted business trip to Africa. On his return he found that his father had died in the meantime, and his treasures had passed into the possession of a crafty slave, who had succeeded in ridding himself of all the other slaves, or intimidating them. In vain the rightful heir urged his claim before King David. As he could not bring witnesses to testify for him, there was no way of dispossessing the slave, who likewise called himself the son of the deceased. The child Solomon heard the case, and he devised a method of arriving at the truth. He had the father's corpse exhumed, and he dyed one of the bones with the blood first of one of the claimants, and then of the other. The blood of the slave showed no affinity with the bone, while the blood of the true heir permeated it. So the real son secured his inheritance.

After his accession to the throne, a peculiar quarrel among heirs was brought before Solomon for adjudication. Asmodeus, the king of demons, once said to Solomon: "Thou art the wisest of men, yet I shall show thee something thou hast never seen." Thereupon Asmodeus stuck his finger in the ground, and up came a double-headed man. He was one of the Cainites, who live underground, and are altogether different in nature and habit from the denizens of the upper world. When the Cainite wanted to descend to his dwelling-place again, it appeared that he could not return thither. Not even Asmodeus could bring the thing about. So he remained on earth, took unto himself a wife, and begot seven sons, one of whom resembled his father in having two heads. When the Cainite died, a dispute broke out among his descendants as to how the property was to be divided. The double-headed son claimed two portions. Both Solomon and the Sanhedrin were at a loss; they could not discover a precedent to guide them. Then Solomon prayed to God: "O Lord of all, when Thou didst appear to me in Gibeon, and didst give me leave to ask a gift of Thee, I desired neither silver nor gold, but only wisdom, that I might be able to judge men in justice."

God heard his prayer. When the sons of the Cainite again came before Solomon, he poured hot water on one of the heads of the double-headed monster, whereupon both heads flinched, and both mouths cried out: "We are dying, we are dying! We are but one, not two." Solomon decided that the double-headed son was after all only a single being.

On another occasion Solomon invented a lawsuit in order to elicit the truth in an involved case. Three men appeared before him, each of whom accused the others of theft. They had been travelling together, and, when the Sabbath approached, they halted and prepared to rest and sought a safe hiding-place for their money, for it is not allowed to carry money on one's person on the Sabbath. They all three together secreted what they had in the same spot, and, when the Sabbath was over, they hastened thither, only to find that it had been stolen. It was clear one of the three must have been the thief, but which one?

Solomon said to them: "I know you to be experienced and thorough business men. I should like you to help me decide a suit which the king of Rome has submitted to me. In the Roman kingdom there lived a maiden and a youth, who promised each other under oath never to enter into a marriage without obtaining each other's permission. The parents of the girl betrothed their daughter to a man whom she loved, but she refused to become his wife until the companion of her youth gave his consent. She took much gold and silver, and sought him out to bribe him. Setting aside his own love for the girl, he offered her and her lover his congratulations, and refused to accept the slightest return for the permission granted. On their homeward way the happy couple were surprised by an old highwayman, who was about to rob the young man of his bride and his money. The girl told the brigand the story of her life, closing with these words: 'If a youth controlled his passion for me, how much more shouldst thou, an old man, be filled with fear of God, and let me go my way.' Her words took effect. The aged highwaymen laid hands neither on the girl nor on the money.

"Now," Solomon continued to the three litigants, "I was asked to decide which of the three persons concerned acted most nobly, the girl, the youth, or the highwayman, and I should like to have your views upon the question."

The first of the three said: "My praise is for the girl, who kept her oath so faithfully." The second: "I should award the palm to the youth, who kept himself in check, and did not permit his passion to prevail." The third said: "Commend me to the brigand, who kept his hands off the money, more especially as he would have been doing all that could be expected of him if he had surrendered the woman he might have taken the money."

The last answer sufficed to put Solomon on the right track. The man who was inspired with admiration of the virtues of the robber, probably was himself filled with greed of money. He had him cross-examined, and finally extorted a confession. He had committed the theft, and he designated the spot where he had hidden the money.

Even animals submitted their controversies to Solomon's wise judgment. A man with a jug of milk came upon a serpent wailing pitifully in a field. To the man's question, the serpent replied that it was tortured with thirst. "And what art thou carrying in the jug?" asked the serpent. When it heard what it was, it begged for the milk, and promised to reward the man by showing him a hidden treasure. The man gave the milk to the serpent, and was then led to a great rock. "Under this rock," said the serpent, "lies the treasure." The man rolled the rock aside, and was about to take the treasure, when suddenly the serpent made a lunge at him, and coiled itself about his neck. "What meanest thou by such conduct?" exclaimed the man. "I am going to kill thee," replied the serpent, "because thou art robbing me of all my money." The man proposed that they put their case to King Solomon, and obtain his decision as to who was in the wrong. So they did. Solomon asked the serpent to state what it demanded of the man. "I want to kill him," answered the serpent, "because the Scriptures command it, saying: 'Thou shalt bruise the heel of man.'" Solomon said: "First release thy hold upon the man's neck and descend; in court neither party to a lawsuit may enjoy an advantage over the other." The serpent glided to the floor, and Solomon repeated his question, and received the same answer as before from the serpent. Then Solomon turned to the man and said: "To thee God's command was to bruise the head of the serpent do it!" And the man crushed the serpent's head.

Sometimes Solomon's assertions and views, though they sprang from profound wisdom, seemed strange to the common run of men. In such cases, the wise king did not disdain to illustrate the correctness of his opinions. For instance, both the learned and the ignorant were stung into opposition by Solomon's saying: "One man among a thousand have I found; but a virtuous woman among all those have I not found." Solomon unhesitatingly pledged himself to prove that he was right. He had his attendants seek out a married couple enjoying a reputation for uprightness and virtue. The husband was cited before him, and Solomon told him that he had decided to appoint him to an exalted office. The king demanded only, as an earnest of his loyalty, that he murder his wife, so that he might be free to marry the king's daughter, a spouse comporting with the dignity of his new station. With a heavy heart the man went home. His despair grew at sight of his fair wife and his little children. Though determined to do the king's bidding, he still lacked courage to kill his wife while she was awake. He waited until she was tight asleep, but then the child enfolded in the mother's arms rekindled his parental and conjugal affection, and he replaced his sword in its sheath, saying to himself: "And if the king were to offer me his whole realm, I would not murder my wife." Thereupon he went to Solomon, and told him his final decision. A month later Solomon sent for the wife, and declared his love for her. He told her that their happiness could be consummated if she would but do away with her husband. Then she should be made the first wife in his harem. Solomon gave her a leaden sword which glittered as though fashioned of steel. The woman returned home resolved to put the sword to its appointed use. Not a quiver of her eyelids betrayed her sinister purpose. On the contrary, by caresses and tender words she sought to disarm any suspicion that might attack to her. In the night she arose, drew forth the sword, and proceeded to kill her husband. The leaden instrument naturally did no harm, except to awaken her husband, to whom she had to confess her evil intent. The next day both man and wife were summoned before the king, who thus convinced his counsellors of the truth of his conviction, that no dependence can be placed on woman.

The fame of Solomon's wisdom spread far and wide. Many entered the service of the king, in the hope of profiting by his wisdom. Three brothers had served under him for thirteen years, and, disappointed at not having learnt anything, they made up their minds to quit his service. Solomon gave them the alternative of receiving one hundred coins each, or being taught three wise saws. They decided to take the money. They had scarcely left the town when the youngest of the three, regardless of the protests of his two brothers, hastened back to Solomon and said to him: "My lord, I did not take service under thee to make money; I wanted to acquire wisdom. Pray, take back thy money, and teach me wisdom instead." Solomon thereupon imparted the following three rules of conduct to him: "When thou travellest abroad, set out on thy journey with the dawn and turn in for the night before darkness falls; do not cross a river that is swollen; and never betray a secret to a woman." The man quickly overtook his brothers, but he confided nothing to them of what he had learned from Solomon. They journeyed on together. At the approach of the ninth hour three hours after noon they reached a suitable spot in which to spend the night. The youngest brother, mindful of Solomon's advice, proposed that they stop there. The others taunted him with his stupidity, which, they said, he had begun to display when he carried his money back to Solomon. The two proceeded on their way, but the youngest arranged his quarters for the night. When darkness came on, and with it nipping cold, he was snug and comfortable, while his brothers were surprised by a snow storm, in which they perished. The following day he continued his journey, and on the road he found the dead bodies of his brothers. Having appropriated their money, he buried them, and went on. When he reached a river that was very much swollen, he bore Solomon's advice in mind, and delayed to cross until the flood subsided. While standing on the bank, he observed how some of the king's servants were attempting to ford the stream with beasts laden with gold, and how they were borne down by the flood. After the waters had abated, he crossed and appropriated the gold strapped to the drowned animals. When he returned home, wealthy and wise, he told nothing of what he had experienced even to his wife, who was very curious to find out where her husband had obtained his wealth. Finally, she plied him so closely with questions that Solomon's advice about confiding a secret to a woman was quite forgotten. Once, when his wife was quarrelling with him, she cried out: "Not enough that thou didst murder thy brothers, thou desirest to kill me, too." Thereupon he was charged with the murder of their husbands by his two sisters-in-law. He was tried, condemned to death, and escaped the hangman only when he told the king the story of his life, and was recognized as his former retainer. It was with reference to this man's adventures that Solomon said: "Acquire wisdom; she is better than gold and much fine gold."

Another of his disciples had a similar experience. Annually a man came from a great distance to pay a visit to the wise king, and when he departed Solomon was in the habit of bestowing a gift upon him. Once the guest refused the gift, and asked the king to teach him the language of the birds and the animals instead. The king was ready to grant his request, but he did not fail to warn him first of the great danger connected with such knowledge. "If thou tellest others a word of what thou hearest from an animal," he said, "thou wilt surely suffer death; thy destruction is inevitable." Nothing daunted, the visitor persisted in his wish, and the king instructed him in the secret art.

Returned home, he overheard a conversation between his ox and his ass. The ass said: "Brother, how farest thou with these people?"

The ox: "As thou livest, brother, I pass day and night in hard and painful toil."

The ass: "I can give thee relief, brother. If thou wilt follow my advice, thou shalt live in comfort, and shalt rid thyself of all hard work."

The ox: "O brother, may thy heart be inclined toward me, to take pity on me and help me. I promise not to depart from thy advice to the right or the left."

The ass: "God knows, I am speaking to thee in the uprightness of my heart and the purity of my thoughts. My advice to thee is not to eat either straw or fodder this night. When our master notices it, he will suppose that thou art sick. He will put no burdensome work upon thee, and thou canst take a good rest. That is the way I did to-day."

The ox followed the advice of his companion. He touched none of the food thrown to him. The master, suspecting a ruse on the part of the ass, arose during the night, went to the stable, and watched the ass eat his fill from the manger belonging to the ox. He could not help laughing out loud, which greatly amazed his wife, who, of course, had noticed nothing out of the way. The master evaded her questions.

Something ludicrous had just occurred to him, he said by way of explanation.

For the sly trick played upon the ox, he determined to punish the ass. He ordered the servant to let the ox rest for the day, and make the ass do the work of both animals. At evening the ass trudged into the stable tired and exhausted. The ox greeted him with the words: "Brother, hast thou heard aught of what our heartless masters purpose?" "Yes," replied the ass, "I heard them speak of having thee slaughtered, if thou shouldst refuse to eat this night, too. They want to make sure of thy flesh at least." Scarcely had the ox heard the words of the ass when he threw himself upon his food like a ravenous lion upon his prey. Not a speck did he leave behind, and the master was suddenly moved to uproarious laughter. This time his wife insisted upon knowing the cause. In vain she entreated and supplicated. She swore not to live with him any more if he did not tell her why he laughed. The man loved her so devotedly that he was ready to sacrifice his life to satisfy her whim, but before taking leave of this world he desired to see his friends and relations once more, and he invited them all to his house.

Meantime his dog was made aware of the master's approaching end, and such sadness took possession of the faithful beast that he touched neither food nor drink. The cock, on the other hand, gaily appropriated the food intended for the dog, and he and his wives enjoyed a banquet. Outraged by such unfeeling behavior, the dog said to the cock: "How great is thy impudence, and how insignificant thy modesty! Thy master is but a step from the grave, and thou eatest and makest merry." The cock's reply was: "Is it my fault if our master is a fool and an idiot? I have ten wives, and I rule them as I will. Not one dares oppose me and my commands. Our master has a single wife, and this one he cannot control and manage." "What ought our master to do?" asked the dog. "Let him take a heavy stick and belabor his wife's back thoroughly," advised the cock, "and I warrant thee, she won't plague him any more to reveal his secrets."

The husband had overheard this conversation, too, and the cock's advice seemed good. He followed it, and death was averted.

On many occasions, Solomon brought his acumen and wisdom to bear upon foreign rulers who attempted to concoct mischief against him. Solomon needed help in building the Temple, and he wrote to Pharaoh, asking him to send artists to Jerusalem. Pharaoh complied with his request, but not honestly. He had his astrologers determine which of his men were destined to die within the year. These candidates for the grave he passed over to Solomon. The Jewish king was not slow to discover the trick played upon him. He immediately returned the men to Egypt, each provided with his grave clothes, and wrote: "To Pharaoh! I suppose thou hadst no shrouds for these people. Herewith I send thee the men, and what they were in need of."

Hiram, king of Tyre, the steadfast friend of the dynasty of David, who had done Solomon such valuable services in connection with the building of the Temple, was desirous of testing his wisdom. He was in the habit of sending catch-questions and riddles to Solomon with the request that he solve them and help him out of his embarrassment about them. Solomon, of course, succeeded in answering them all. Later on he made an agreement with Hiram, that they were to exchange conundrums and riddles, and a money fine was to be exacted from the one of them who failed to find the proper answer to a question propounded by the other. Naturally it was Hiram who was always the loser. The Tyrians maintain that finally Solomon found more than his match in one of Hiram's subjects, one Abdamon, who put many a riddle to Solomon that baffled his wit.

Of Solomon's subtlety in riddle guessing only a few instances have come down to us, all of them connected with riddles put to him by the Queen of Sheba. The story of this queen, of her relation to Solomon, and what induced her to leave her distant home and journey to the court at Jerusalem forms an interesting chapter in the eventful life of the wise king.

THE QUEEN OF SHEBA

Solomon, it must be remembered, bore rule not only over men, but also over the beasts of the field, the birds of the air, demons, spirits, and the spectres of the night. He knew the language of all of them and they understood his language.

When Solomon was of good cheer by reason of wine, he summoned the beasts of the field, the birds of the air, the creeping reptiles, the shades, the spectres, and the ghosts, to perform their dances before the kings, his neighbors, whom he invited to witness his power and greatness. The king's scribes called the animals and the spirits by name, one by one, and they all assembled of their own accord, without fetters or bonds, with no human hand to guide them.

On one occasion the hoopoe was missed from among the birds. He could not be found anywhere. The king, full of wrath, ordered him to be produced and chastised for his tardiness. The hoopoe appeared and said: "O lord, king of the world, incline thine ear and hearken to my words. Three months have gone by since I began to take counsel with myself and resolve upon a course of action. I have eaten no food and drunk no water, in order to fly about in the whole world and see whether there is a domain anywhere which is not subject to my lord the king. and I found a city, the city of Kitor, in the East. Dust is more valuable than gold there, and silver is like the mud of the streets. Its trees are from the beginning of all time, and they suck up water that flows from the Garden of Eden. The city is crowded with men. On their heads they wear garlands wreathed in Paradise. They know not how to fight, nor how to shoot with bow and arrow. Their ruler is a woman, she is called the Queen of Sheba. If, now, it please thee, O lord and king, I shall gird my loins like a hero, and journey to the city of Kitor in the land of Sheba. Its kings I shall fetter with chains and its rulers with iron bands, and bring them all before my lord the king."

The hoopoe's speech pleased the king. The clerks of his land were summoned, and they wrote a letter and bound it to the hoopoe's wing. The bird rose skyward, uttered his cry, and flew away, followed by all the other birds.

And they came to Kitor in the land of Sheba. It was morning, and the queen had gone forth to pay worship to the sun. Suddenly the birds darkened his light. The queen raised her hand, and rent her garment, and was sore astonished. Then the hoopoe alighted near her. Seeing that a letter was tied to his wing, she loosed it and read it. And what was written in the letter? "From me, King Solomon! Peace be with thee, peace with the nobles of thy realm! Know that God has appointed me king over the beasts of the field, the birds of the air, the demons, the spirits, and the spectres. All the kings of the East and the West come to bring me greetings. If thou wilt come and salute me, I shall show thee great honor, more than to any of the kings that attend me. But if thou wilt not pay homage to me, I shall send out kings, legions, and riders against thee. Thou askest, who are these kings, legions, and riders of King Solomon? The beasts of the field are my kings, the birds my riders, the demons, spirit, and shades of the night my legions. The demons will throttle you in your beds at night, while the beasts will slay you in the field, and the birds will consume your flesh."

When the Queen of Sheba had read the contents of the letter, she again rent her garment, and sent word to her elders and her princes: "Know you not what Solomon has written to me?" They answered: "We know nothing of King Solomon, and his dominion we regard as naught." But their words did not reassure the queen. She assembled all the ships of the sea, and loaded them with the finest kinds of wood, and with pearls and precious stones. Together with these she sent Solomon six thousand youths and maidens, born in the same year, in the same month, on the same day, in the same hour all of equal stature and size, all clothed in purple garments. They bore a letter to King Solomon as follows: "From the city of Kitor to the land of Israel is a journey of seven years. As it is thy wish and behest that I visit thee, I shall hasten and be in Jerusalem at the end of three years."

When the time of her arrival drew nigh, Solomon sent Benaiah the son of Jehoiada to meet her. Benaiah was like unto the flush in the eastern sky at break of day, like unto the evening star that outshines all other stars, like unto the lily growing by brooks of water. When the queen caught sight of him, she descended from her chariot to do him honor. Benaiah asked her why she left her chariot. "Art thou not King Solomon?" she questioned in turn. Benaiah replied: "Not King Solomon am I, only one of his servants that stand in his presence." Thereupon the queen turned to her nobles and said: "If you have not beheld the lion, at least you have seen his lair, and if you have not beheld King Solomon, at least you have seen the beauty of him that stands in his presence."

Benaiah conducted the queen to Solomon, who had gone to sit in a house of glass to receive her. The queen was deceived by an illusion. She thought the king was sitting in water, and as she stepped across to him she raised her garment to keep it dry. On her bared feet the king noticed hair, and he said to her: "Thy beauty is the beauty of a woman, but thy hair is masculine; hair is an ornament to a man, but it disfigures a woman."

Then the queen began and said: "I have heard of thee and thy wisdom; if now I inquire of thee concerning a matter, wilt thou answer me?" He replied: "The Lord giveth wisdom, out of His mouth cometh knowledge and understanding." She then said to him:

1. "Seven there are that issue and nine that enter; two yield the draught and

one drinks." Said he to her: "Seven are the days of a woman's defilement, and nine the months of pregnancy; two are the breasts that yield the draught, and one the child that drinks it." Whereupon she said to him: "Thou art wise."

2. Then she questioned him further: "A woman said to her son, thy father is my father, and thy grandfather my husband; thou art my son, and I am thy sister." "Assuredly," said he, "it was the daughter of Lot who spake thus to her son."

3. She placed a number of males and females of the same stature and garb before him and said: "Distinguish between them." Forthwith he made a sign to the eunuchs, who brought him a quantity of nuts and roasted ears of corn. The males, who were not bashful, seized them with bare hands; the females took them, putting forth their gloved hands from beneath their garments. Whereupon he exclaimed: "Those are the males, these the females."

4. She brought a number of men to him, some circumcised and others uncircumcised, and asked him to distinguish between them. He immediately made a sign to the high priest, who opened the Ark of the covenant, whereupon those that were circumcised bowed their bodies to half their height, while their countenances were filled with the radiance of the Shekinah; the uncircumcised fell prone upon their faces. "Those," said he, "are circumcised, these uncircumcised." "Thou art wise, indeed," she exclaimed.

5. She put other questions to him, to all of which he gave replies. "Who is he who neither was born nor has died?" "It is the Lord of the world, blessed be He."

6. "What land is that which has but once seen the sun?" "The land upon which, after the creation, the waters were gathered, and the bed of the Red Sea on the day when it was divided."

7. "There is an enclosure with ten doors, when one is open, nine are shut; when nine are open, one is shut?" "That enclosure is the womb; the ten doors are the ten orifices of man his eyes, ears, nostrils, mouth, the apertures for the discharge of the excreta and the urine, and the navel; when the child is in the embryonic state, the navel is open and the other orifices are closed, but when it issues from the womb, the navel is closed and the others are opened."

8. "There is something which when living moves not, yet when its head is cut off it moves?" "It is the ship in the sea."

9. "Which are the three that neither ate, nor did they drink, nor did they have

bread put into them, yet they saved lives from death?" "The signet, the cord, and the staff are those three."

10. "Three entered a cave and five came forth therefrom?" "Lot and his two daughters and their two children."

11. "The dead lived, the grave moved, and the dead prayed: what is that?" "The dead that lived and prayed, Jonah; and the fish, the moving grave."

12. "Who were the three that ate and drank on the earth, and yet were not born of male and female?" "The three angels who visited Abraham."

13. "Four entered a place of death and came forth alive, and two entered a place of life and came forth dead?" "The four were Daniel, Hananiah, Mishael, and Azariah, and the two were Nadab and Abihu."

14. "Who was he that was born and died not?" "Elijah and the Messiah."

15. "What was that which was not born, yet life was given to it?" "The golden calf."

16. "What is that which is produced from the ground, yet man produces it, while its food is the fruit of the ground?" "A wick."

17. "A woman was wedded to two, and bore two sons, yet these four had one father?" "Tamar."

18. "A house full of dead; no dead one came among them, nor did a living come forth from them?" "It is the story of Samson and the Philistines."

19. The queen next ordered the sawn trunk of a cedar tree to be brought, and she asked Solomon to point out at which end the root had been and at which the branches. He bade her cast it into the water, when one end sank and the other floated upon the surface of the water. That part which sank was the root, and that which remained uppermost was the branch end. Then she said to him: "Thou exceedest in wisdom and goodness the fame which I heard, blessed be thy God!"

The last three riddles which the Queen of Sheba put to Solomon were the following:

20. "What is this? A wooden well with iron buckets, which draw stones and pour out water." The king replied: "A rouge-tube."

21. "What is this? It comes as dust from the earth, its food is dust, it is poured out like water, and lights the house." "Naphtha."

22. "What is this? It walks ahead of all; it cries out loud and bitterly; its head

is like the reed; it is the glory of the noble, the disgrace of the poor; the glory of the dead, the disgrace of the living; the delight of birds, the distress of fishes." He answered: "Flax."

SOLOMON MASTER OF THE DEMONS

Never has there lived a man privileged, like Solomon, to make the demons amenable to his will. God endowed him with the ability to turn the vicious power of demons into a power working to the advantage of men. He invented formulas of incantation by which diseases were alleviated, and others by which demons were exorcised so that they were banished forever. As his personal attendants he had spirits and demons whom he could send hither and thither on the instant. He could grow tropical plants in Palestine, because his ministering spirits secured water for him from India.

As the spirits were subservient to him, so also the animals. He had an eagle upon whose back he was transported to the desert and back again in one day, to build there the city called Tadmor in the Bible. This city must not be confounded with the later Syrian city of Palmyra, also called Tadmor. It was situated near the "mountains of darkness," the trysting-place of the spirits and demons. Thither the eagle would carry Solomon in the twinkling of an eye, and Solomon would drop a paper inscribed with a verse among the spirits, to ward off evil from himself. Then the eagle would reconnoitre the mountains of darkness, until he had spied out the spot in which the fallen angels 'Azza and 'Azzael lie chained with iron fetters a spot which no one, not even a bird, may visit. When the eagle found the place, he would take Solomon under his left wing, and fly to the two angels. Through the power of the ring having the Holy Name graven upon it, which Solomon put into the eagle's mouth, 'Azza and 'Azzael were forced to reveal the heavenly mysteries to the king.

The demons were of greatest service to Solomon during the erection of the Temple. It came about in this wise: When Solomon began the building of the Temple, it once happened that a malicious spirit snatched away the money and the food of one of the king's favorite pages. This occurred several times, and Solomon was not able to lay hold on the malefactor. The king besought God fervently to deliver the wicked spirit into his hands. His prayer was granted. The archangel Michael appeared to him, and gave him a small ring having a seal consisting of an engraved stone, and he said to him: "Take, O Solomon, king, son of David, the gift which the Lord God, the highest Zebaot, hath sent unto thee. With it thou shalt lock up all the demons of the earth, male and female; and with their help thou shalt build up Jerusalem. But thou must wear this seal of God; and this engraving of the seal of the ring sent thee is a Pentalpha." Armed with it, Solomon called up all the demons before him, and he asked of each in turn his or her name, as well as the name of the star or constellation or zodiacal sign and of the particular angel to the influence of which each is subject. One after another the spirits were vanquished, and compelled by Solomon to aid in the construction of the Temple.

Ornias, the vampire spirit who had maltreated Solomon's servant, was the first demon to appear, and he was set to the task of cutting stones near the Temple. And Solomon bade Ornias come, and he gave him the seal, saying: "Away with thee, and bring me hither the prince of all the demons." Ornias took the finger-ring, and went to Beelzeboul, who has kingship over the demons. He said to him: "Hither! Solomon calls thee." But Beelzeboul, having heard, said to him: "Tell me, who is this Solomon of whom thou speakest to me?" Then Ornias threw the ring at the chest of Beelzeboul, saying: "Solomon the king calls thee." But Beelzeboul cried aloud with a mighty voice, and shot out a great, burning flame of fire; and he arose and followed Ornias, and came to Solomon. Brought before the king, he promised him to gather all the unclean spirits unto him. Beelzeboul proceeded to do so, beginning with Onoskelis, that had a very pretty shape and the skin of a fair-hued woman, and he was followed by Asmodeus; both giving an account of themselves.

Beelzeboul reappeared on the scene, and in his conversation with Solomon declared that he alone survived of the angels who had come down from heaven. He reigned over all who are in Tartarus, and had a child in the Red Sea, which on occasion comes up to Beelzeboul and reveals to him what he has done. Next the demon of the Ashes, Tephros, appeared, and after him a group of seven female spirits, who declared themselves to be of the thirty-six elements of the darkness. Solomon bade them dig the foundation of the temple, for the length of it was two hundred and fifty cubits. And he ordered them to be industrious, and with one united murmur of protest they began to perform the tasks enjoined.

Solomon bade another demon come before him. And there was brought to him a demon having all the limbs of a man, but without a head. The demon said to Solomon: "I am called Envy, for I delight to devour heads, being desirous to secure for myself a head; but I do not eat enough, and I am anxious to have such a head as thou hast." A hound-like spirit, whose name was Rabdos, followed, and he revealed to Solomon a green stone, useful for the adornment of the Temple. A number of other male and female demons appeared, among them the thirty-six world-rulers of the darkness, whom Solomon commanded to fetch water to the Temple. Some of these demons he condemned to do the heavy work on the construction of the Temple, others he shut up in prison, and others, again, he ordered to wrestle with fire in the making of gold and silver, sitting down by lead and spoon, and to make ready places for the other demons, in which they should be confined.

After Solomon with the help of the demons had completed the Temple, the rulers, among them the Queen of Sheba, who was a sorceress, came from far and near to admire the magnificence and art of the building, and no less the wisdom of its builder.

One day an old man appeared before Solomon to complain of his son, whom he accused of having been so impious as to raise his hand against his father and give him a blow. The young man denied the charge, but his father insisted that his life be held forfeit. Suddenly Solomon heard loud laughter. It was the demon Ornias, who was guilty of the disrespectful behavior. Rebuked by Solomon, the demon said: "I pray thee, O king, it was not because of thee I laughed, but because of this ill-starred old man and the wretched youth, his son. For after three days his son will die untimely, and, lo, the old man desires to make away with him foully." Solomon delayed his verdict for several days, and when after five days he summoned the old father to his presence, it appeared that Ornias had spoken the truth.

After some time, Solomon received a letter from Adares, the king of Arabia. He begged the Jewish king to deliver his land from an evil spirit, who was doing great mischief, and who could not be caught and made harmless, because he appeared in the form of wind. Solomon gave his magic ring and a leather bottle to one of his slaves, and sent him into Arabia. The messenger succeeded in confining the spirit in the bottle. A few days later, when Solomon entered the Temple, he was not a little astonished to see a bottle walk toward him, and bow down reverently before him;

it was the bottle in which the spirit was shut up. This same spirit once did Solomon a great service. Assisted by demons, he raised a gigantic stone out of the Red Sea. Neither human beings nor demons could move it, but he carried it to the Temple, where it was used as a cornerstone.

Through his own fault Solomon forfeited the power to perform miraculous deed, which the Divine spirit had conferred upon him. He fell in love with the Jebusite woman Sonmanites. The priests of Moloch and Raphan, the false gods she worshiped, advised her to reject his suit, unless he paid homage to these gods. At first Solomon was firm, but, when the woman bade him take five locusts and crush them in his hands in the name of Moloch, he obeyed her. At once he was bereft of the Divine spirit, of his strength and his wisdom, and he sank so low that to please his beloved he built temples to Baal and Raphan.

THE BUILDING OF THE TEMPLE

Among the great achievements of Solomon first place must be assigned to the superb Temple built by him. He was long in doubt as to where he was to build it. A heavenly voice directed him to go to Mount Zion at night, to a field owned by two brothers jointly. One of the brothers was a bachelor and poor, the other was blessed both with wealth and a large family of children. It was harvesting time. Under cover of night, the poor brother kept adding to the other's heap of grain, for, although he was poor, he thought his brother needed more on account of his large family. The rich brother, in the same clandestine way, added to the poor brother's store, thinking that though he had a family to support, the other was without means. This field, Solomon concluded, which had called forth so remarkable a manifestation of brotherly love, was the best site for the Temple, and he bought it.

Every detail of the equipment and ornamentation of the Temple testifies to Solomon's rare wisdom. Next to the required furniture, he planted golden trees, which bore fruit all the time the building stood. When the enemy entered the Temple, the fruit dropped from the trees, but they will put forth blossoms again when it is rebuilt in the days of the Messiah.

Solomon was so assiduous that the erection of the Temple took but seven years, about half the time for the erection of the king's palace, in spite of the greater magnificence of the sanctuary. In this respect, he was the superior of his father David, who first built a house for himself, and then gave thought to a house for God to dwell in. Indeed, it was Solomon's meritorious work in connection with the Temple that saved him from being reckoned by the sages as one of the impious kings, among whom his later actions might properly have put him.

According to the measure of the zeal displayed by Solomon were the help and favor shown him by God. During the seven years it took to build the Temple, not a single workman died who was employed about it, nor even did a single one fall sick. And as the workmen were sound and robust from first to last, so the perfection of their tools remained unimpaired until the building stood complete. Thus the work suffered no sort of interruption. After the dedication of the Temple, however, the workmen died off, lest they build similar structures for the heathen and their gods. Their wages they were to receive from God in the world to come, and the master workman, Hiram, was rewarded by being permitted to reach Paradise alive.

The Temple was finished in the month of Bul, now called Marheshwan, but the edifice stood closed for nearly a whole year, because it was the will of God that the dedication take place in the month of Abraham's birth. Meantime the enemies of Solomon rejoiced maliciously. "Was it not the son of Bath-sheba," they said, "who built the Temple? How, then, could God permit His Shekinah to rest upon it?" When the consecration of the house took place, and "the fire came down from heaven," they recognized their mistake.

The importance of the Temple appeared at once, for the torrential rains which annually since the deluge had fallen for forty days beginning with the month of Marheshwan, for the first time failed to come, and thenceforward appeared no more.

The joy of the people over the sanctuary was so great that they held the consecration ceremonies on the Day of Atonement. It contributed not a little to their ease of mind that a heavenly voice was heard to proclaim: "You all shall have a share in the world to come."

The great house of prayer reflected honor not only on Solomon and the people, but also on King David. The following incident proves it: When the Ark was about to be brought into the Holy of Holies, the door of the sacred chamber locked itself, and it was impossible to open it. Solomon prayed fervently to God, but his entreaties had no effect until he pronounced the words: "Remember the good deeds of David thy servant." The Holy of Holies then opened of itself, and the enemies of David had to admit that God had wholly forgiven his sin.

In the execution of the Temple work a wish cherished by David was fulfilled. He was averse to having the gold which he had taken as booty from the heathen places of worship during his campaigns used for the sanctuary at Jerusalem, because he feared that the heathen would boast, at the destruction of the Temple, that their gods were courageous, and were taking revenge by wrecking the house of the Israelitish God. Fortunately Solomon was so rich that there was no need to resort to the gold inherited from his father, and so David's wish was fulfilled.

THE THRONE OF SOLOMON

Next to the Temple in its magnificence, it is the throne of Solomon that perpetuates the name and fame of the wise king. None before him and none after him could produce a like work of art, and when the kings, his vassals, saw the magnificence of the throne they fell down and praised God. The throne was covered with fine gold from Ophir, studded with beryls, inlaid with marble, and jewelled with emeralds, and rubies, and pearls, and all manner of gems. On each of its six steps there were two golden lions and two golden eagles, a lion and an eagle to the left, and a lion and an eagle to the right, the pairs standing face to face, so that the right paw of the lion was opposite to the left wing of the eagle, and his left paw opposite to the right wing of the eagle. The royal seat was at the top, which was round.

On the first step leading to the seat crouched an ox, and opposite to him a lion; on the second, a wolf and a lamb; on the third, a leopard and a goat; on the fourth perched an eagle and a peacock; on the fifth a falcon and a cock; and on the sixth a hawk and a sparrow; all made of gold. At the very top rested a dove, her claws set upon a hawk, to betoken that the time would come when all peoples and nations shall be delivered into the hands of Israel. Over the seat hung a golden candlestick, with golden lamps, pomegranates, snuff dishes, censers, chains, and lilies. Seven branches extended from each side. On the arms to the right were the images of the seven patriarchs of the world, Adam, Noah, Shem, Job, Abraham, Isaac, and Jacob; and on the arms to the left, the images of the seven pious men of the world,

Kohath, Amram, Moses, Aaron, Eldad, Medad, and the prophet Hur. Attached to the top of the candlestick was a golden bowl filled with the purest olive oil, to be used for the candlestick in the Temple, and below, a golden basin, also filled with the purest olive oil, for the candlestick over the throne. The basin bore the image of the high priest Eli; those of his sons Hophni and Phinehas were on the two faucets protruding from the basin, and those of Nadab and Abihu on the tubes connection the faucets with the basin.

On the upper part of the throne stood seventy golden chairs for the members of the Sanhedrin, and two more for the high priest and his vicar. When the high priest came to do homage to the king, the members of the Sanhedrin also appeared, to judge the people, and they took their seats to the right and to the left of the king. At the approach of the witnesses, the machinery of the throne rumbled the wheels turned, the ox lowed, the lion roared, the wolf howled, the lamb bleated, the leopard growled, the goat cried, the falcon screamed, the peacock gobbled, the cock crowed, the hawk screeched, the sparrow chirped all to terrify the witnesses and keep them from giving false testimony.

When Solomon set foot upon the first step to ascend to his seat, its machinery was put into motion. The golden ox arose and led him to the second step, and there passed him over to the care of the beasts guarding it, and so he was conducted from step to step up to the sixth, where the eagles received him and placed him upon his seat. As soon as he was seated, a great eagle set the royal crown upon his head. Thereupon a huge snake rolled itself up against the machinery, forcing the lions and eagles upward until they encircled the head of the king. A golden dove flew down from a pillar, took the sacred scroll out of a casket, and gave it to the king, so that he might obey the injunction of the Scriptures, to have the law with him and read therein all the days of his life. Above the throne twenty-four vines interlaced, forming a shady arbor over the head of the king, and sweet aromatic perfumes exhaled from two golden lions, while Solomon made the ascent to his seat upon the throne.

It was the task of seven heralds to keep Solomon reminded of his duties as king and judge. The first one of the heralds approached him when he set foot on the first step of the throne, and began to recite the law for kings, "He shall not multiply wives to himself." At the second step, the second herald reminded him, "He shall not multiply horses to himself"; at the third, the next one of the heralds said, "Neither shall he greatly multiply to himself silver and gold." At the fourth step, he was told by the fourth herald, "Thou shalt not wrest judgment"; at the fifth step, by the fifth herald, "Thou shalt not respect persons," and at the sixth, by the sixth herald, "Neither shalt thou take a gift." Finally, when he was about to seat himself upon the throne, the seventh herald cried out: "Know before whom thou standest."

The throne did not remain long in the possession of the Israelites. During the life of Rehoboam, the son of Solomon, it was carried to Egypt. Shishak, the father-in-law of Solomon, appropriated it as indemnity for claims which he urged against the Jewish state in behalf of his widowed daughter. When Sennacherib conquered Egypt, he carried the throne away with him, but, on his homeward march, during the overthrow of his army before the gates of Jerusalem, he had to part with it to Hezekiah. Now it remained in Palestine until the time of Jehoash, when it was once more carried to Egypt by Pharaoh Necho. His possession of the throne brought him little joy. Unacquainted with its wonderful mechanism, he was injured in the side by one of the lions the first time he attempted to mount it, and forever after he limped, wherefore he was given the surname Necho, the hobbler. Nebuchadnezzar was the next possessor of the throne. It fell to his lot at the conquest of Egypt, but when he attempted to use it in Babylonia, he fared no better than his predecessor in Egypt. The lion standing near the throne gave him so severe a blow that he never again dared ascend it. Through Darius the throne reached Elam, but, knowing what its other owners had suffered, he did not venture to seat himself on it, and his example was imitated by Ahasuerus. The latter tried to have his artificers fashion him a like artistic work, but, of course, they failed. The Median rulers parted with the throne to the Greek monarchs, and finally it was carried to Rome.

THE HIPPODROME

The throne was not the only remarkable sight at the court of the magnificent king. Solomon attracted visitors to his capital by means of games and shows. In every month of the year the official who was in charge for the month, was expected to arrange for a horse race, and once a year a race took place in which the competitors were ten thousand youths, mainly of the tribes of Gad and Naphtali, who lived at the court of the king year in, year out, and were maintained by him. For the scholars, their disciples, the priests, and the Levites, the races were held on the last of the month; on the first day of the month the residents of Jerusalem were the spectators, and, on the second day, strangers. The hippodrome occupied an area of three parasangs square, with an inner square measuring one parasang on each side, around which the races were run. Within were two grilles ornamented with all sorts of animals. Out of the jaws of four gilded lions, attached to pillars by twos, perfumes and spices flowed for the people. The spectators were divided into four parties distinguished by the color of their garb: the king and his attendants, the scholars and their disciples, and the priests and Levites were attired in light blue garments; all the rest from Jerusalem wore white; the sight-seers from the surrounding towns and villages wore red, and green marked the heathen hailing from afar, who came laden with tribute and presents. The four colors corresponded to the four seasons. In the autumn the sky is brilliantly blue; in winter the white snow falls; the color of spring is green like the ocean, because it is the season favorable to voyages, and red is the color of summer, when the fruits grow red and ripe.

As the public spectacles were executed with pomp and splendor, so the king's table was royally sumptuous. Regardless of season and climate, it was always laden with the delicacies of all parts of the globe. Game and poultry, even of such varieties as were unknown in Palestine, were not lacking, and daily there came a gorgeous bird from Barbary and settled down before the king's seat at the table. The Scriptures tell us of great quantities of food required by Solomon's household, and yet it was not all that was needed. What the Bible mentions, covers only the accessories, such as spices and the minor ingredients. The real needs were far greater, as may be judged from the custom that all of Solomon's thousand wives arranged a banquet daily, each in the hope of having the king dine with her.

LESSONS IN HUMILITY

Great and powerful as Solomon was, and wise and just, still occasions were not lacking to bring home to him the truth that the wisest and mightiest of mortals may not indulge in pride and arrogance.

Solomon had a precious piece of tapestry, sixty miles square, on which he flew through the air so swiftly that he could eat breakfast in Damascus and supper in Media. To carry out his orders he had at his beck and call Asaph ben Berechiah among men, Ramirat among demons, the lion among beasts, and the eagle among birds. Once it happened that pride possessed Solomon while he was sailing through the air on his carpet, and he said: "There is none like unto me in the world, upon whom God has bestowed sagacity, wisdom, intelligence, and knowledge, besides making me the ruler of the world." The same instant the air stirred, and forty thousand men dropped from the magic carpet. The king ordered the wind to cease from blowing, with the word: "Return!" Whereupon the wind: "If thou wilt return to God, and subdue thy pride, I, too, will return." The king realized his transgression.

On one occasion he strayed into the valley of the ants in the course of his wanderings. He heard one ant order all the others to withdraw, to avoid being crushed by the armies of Solomon. The king halted and summoned the ant that had spoken. She told him that she was the queen of the ants, and she gave her reasons for the order of withdrawal. Solomon wanted to put a question to the ant queen, but she refused to answer unless the king took her up and placed her on his hand. He acquiesced, and then he put his question: "Is there any one greater than I am in all the world?" "Yes," said the ant.

Solomon: "Who?"

Ant: "I am."

Solomon: "How is that possible?"

Ant: "Were I not greater than thou, God would not have led thee hither to put me on thy hand."

Exasperated, Solomon threw her to the ground, and said: "Thou knowest who I am? I am Solomon, the son of David."

Not at all intimidated, the ant reminded the king of his earthly origin, and admonished him to humility, and the king went off abashed.

Next he came to a magnificent building, into which he sought to enter in vain; he could find no door leading into it. After long search the demons came upon an eagle seven hundred years old, and he, unable to give them any information, sent him to his nine hundred years old brother, whose eyrie was higher than his own, and who would probably be in a position to advise them. But he in turn directed them to go to his still older brother. His age counted thirteen hundred years, and he had more knowledge than himself. This oldest one of the eagles reported that he remembered having heard his father say there was a door on the west side, but it was covered up by the dust of the ages that had passed since it was last used. So it turned out to be. They found an old iron door with the inscription: "We, the dwellers in this palace, for many years lived in comfort and luxury; then, forced by hunger, we ground pearls into flour instead of wheat but to no avail, and so, when we were about to die, we bequeathed this palace to the eagles." A second statement contained a detailed description of the wonderful palace, and mentioned where the keys for the different chambers were to be found. Following the directions on the door, Solomon inspected the remarkable building, whose apartments were made of pearls and precious stones. Inscribed on the doors he found the following three wise proverbs, dealing with the vanity of all earthly things, and admonishing men to be humble:

1. O son of man, let not time deceive thee; thou must wither away, and leave thy place, to rest in the bosom of the earth.

2. Haste thee not, move slowly, for the world is taken from one and bestowed upon another.

3. Furnish thyself with food for the journey, prepare thy meal while daylight lasts, for thou wilt not remain on earth forever, and thou knowest not the day of thy death.

In one of the chambers, Solomon saw a number of statues, among them one that looked as though alive. When he approached it, it called out in a loud voice: "Hither, ye satans, Solomon has come to undo you." Suddenly there arose great noise and tumult among the statues. Solomon pronounced the Name, and quiet was restored. The statues were overthrown, and the sons of the satans ran into the sea and were drowned. From the throat of the lifelike statue he drew a silver plate inscribed with characters which he could not decipher, but a youth from the desert told the king: "These letters are Greek, and the words mean: 'I, Shadad ben Ad, ruled over a thousand thousand provinces, rode on a thousand thousand horses, had a thousand thousand kings under me, and slew a thousand thousand heroes, and when the Angel of Death approached me, I was powerless.'"

ASMODEUS

When Solomon in his wealth and prosperity grew unmindful of his God, and, contrary to the injunctions laid down for kings in the Torah, multiplied wives unto himself, and craved the possession of many horses and much gold, the Book of Deuteronomy stepped before God and said: "Lo, O Lord of the world, Solomon is seeking to remove a Yod from out of me, for Thou didst write: 'The king shall not multiply horses unto himself, nor shall he multiply wives to himself, neither shall he greatly multiply to himself silver and gold'; but Solomon has acquired many horses, many wives, and much silver and gold." Hereupon God said: "As thou livest, Solomon and a hundred of his kind shall be annihilated ere a single one of thy letters shall be obliterated."

The charge made against Solomon was soon followed by consequences. He had to pay heavily for his sins. It came about in this way: While Solomon was occupied with the Temple, he had great difficulty in devising ways of fitting the stone from the quarry into the building, for the Torah explicitly prohibits the use of iron tools in erecting an altar. The scholars told him that Moses had used the shamir, the stone that splits rocks, to engrave the names of the tribes on the precious stones of the ephod worn by the high priest. Solomon's demons could give him no information as to where the shamir could be found. They surmised, however, that Asmodeus, king of demons, was in possession of the secret, and they told Solomon the name of the mountain on which Asmodeus dwelt, and described also his manner of life. On this mountain there was a well from which Asmodeus obtained his drinking water. He closed it up daily with a large rock, and sealed it before going to heaven, whither he went every day, to take part in the discussions in the heavenly academy. Thence he would descend again to earth in order to be present, though invisible, at the debates in the earthly houses of learning. Then, after investigating the seal on the well to ascertain if it had been tampered with, he drank of the water.

Solomon sent his chief man, Benaiah the son of Jehoiada, to capture Asmodeus. For this purpose he provided him with a chain, the ring on which the Name of God was engraved, a bundle of wool, and a skin of wine. Benaiah drew the water from the well through a hole bored from below, and, after having stopped up the hole with the wool, he filled the well with wine from above. When Asmodeus descended from heaven, to his astonishment he found wine instead of water in the well, although everything seemed untouched. At first he would not drink of it, and cited the Bible verses that inveigh against wine, to inspire himself with moral courage. At length Asmodeus succumbed to his consuming thirst, and drank till his senses were overpowered, and he fell into a deep sleep. Benaiah, watching him from a tree, then came, and drew the chain about Asmodeus' neck. The demon, on awakening, tried to free himself, but Benaiah called to him: "The Name of thy Lord is upon thee." Though Asmodeus now permitted himself to be led off unresistingly, he acted most peculiarly on the way to Solomon. He brushed against a palm-tree and uprooted it; he knocked against a house and overturned it; and when, at the request of a poor woman, he was turned aside from her hut, he broke a bone. He asked with grim humor: "Is it not written, 'A soft tongue breaketh the bone?'" A blind man going astray he set in the right path, and to a drunkard he did a similar kindness. He wept when a wedding party passed them, and laughed at a man who asked his shoemaker to make him shoes to last for seven years, and at a magician who was publicly showing his skill.

Having finally arrived at the end of the journey, Asmodeus, after several days of waiting, was led before Solomon, who questioned him about his strange conduct on the journey. Asmodeus answered that he judged persons and things according to their real character, and not according to their appearance in the eyes of human beings. He cried when he saw the wedding company, because he knew the bridegroom had not a month to live, and he laughed at him who wanted shoes to last seven years, because the man would not own them for seven days, also at the magician who pretended to disclose secrets, because he did not know that a buried treasure lay under his very feet; the blind man whom he set in the right path was one of the "perfect pious," and he wanted to be kind to him; on the other hand, the drunkard to whom he did a similar kindness was known in heaven as a very wicked man, but he happened to have done a good deed once, and he was rewarded accordingly.

Asmodeus told Solomon that the shamir was given by God to the Angel of the Sea, and that Angel entrusted none with the shamir except the moor-hen, which had taken an oath to watch the shamir carefully. The moor-hen takes the shamir with her to mountains which are not inhabited by men, splits them by means of the shamir, and injects seeds, which grow and cover the naked rocks, and then they can be inhabited. Solomon sent one of his servants to seek the nest of the bird and lay a piece of glass over it. When the moor-hen came and could not reach her young, she flew away and fetched the shamir and placed it on the glass. Then the man shouted, and so terrified the bird that she dropped the shamir and flew away. By this means the man obtained possession of the coveted shamir, and bore it to Solomon. But the moor-hen was so distressed at having broken her oath to the Angel of the Sea that she committed suicide.

Although Asmodeus was captured only for the purpose of getting the shamir, Solomon nevertheless kept him after the completion of the Temple. One day the king told Asmodeus that he did not understand wherein the greatness of the demons lay, if their king could be kept in bonds by a mortal. Asmodeus replied, that if Solomon would remove his chains and lend him the magic ring, he would prove his own greatness. Solomon agreed. The demon stood before him with one wing touching heaven and the other reaching to the earth. Snatching up Solomon, who had parted with his protecting ring, he flung him four hundred parasangs away from Jerusalem, and then palmed himself off as the king.

SOLOMON AS BEGGAR

Banished from his home, deprived of his realm, Solomon wandered about in far-off lands, among strangers, begging his daily bread. Nor did his humiliation end there; people thought him a lunatic, because he never tired of assuring them that he was Solomon, Judah's great and mighty king. Naturally that seemed a preposterous claim to the people. The lowest depth of despair he reached, however, when he met some one who recognized him. The recollections and associations that stirred within him then made his present misery almost unendurable.

It happened that once on his peregrinations he met an old acquaintance, a rich and well-considered man, who gave a sumptuous banquet in honor of Solomon. At the meal his host spoke to Solomon constantly of the magnificence and splendor he had once seen with his own eyes at the court of the king. These reminiscences moved the king to tears, and he wept so bitterly that, when he rose from the banquet, he was satiated, not with the rich food, but with salt tears. The following day it again happened that Solomon met an acquaintance of former days, this time a poor man, who nevertheless entreated Solomon to do him the honor and break bread under his roof. All that the poor man could offer his distinguished guest was a meagre dish of greens. But he tried in every way to assuage the grief that oppressed Solomon. He said: "O my lord and king, God hath sworn unto David He would never let the royal dignity depart from his house, but it is the way of God to reprove those He loves if they sin. Rest assured, He will restore thee in good time to thy kingdom." These words of his poor host were more grateful to Solomon's bruised heart than the banquet the rich man had prepared for him. It was to the contrast between the consolations of the two men that he applied the verse in Proverbs: "Better is a dinner of herbs where love is, than a stalled ox and hatred therewith."

For three long years Solomon journeyed about, begging his way from city to city, and from country to country, atoning for the three sins of his life by which he had set aside the commandment laid upon kings in Deuteronomy not to multiply horses, and wives, and silver and gold. At the end of that time, God took mercy upon him for the sake of his father David, and for the sake of the pious princess Naamah, the daughter of the Ammonite king, destined by God to be the ancestress of the Messiah. The time was approaching when she was to become the wife of Solomon and reign as queen in Jerusalem. God therefore led the royal wanderer to the capital city of Ammon. Solomon took service as an underling with the cook in the royal household, and he proved himself so proficient in the culinary art that the king of Ammon raised him to the post of chief cook. Thus he came under the notice of the king's daughter Naamah, who fell in love with her father's cook. In vain her parents endeavored to persuade her to choose a husband befitting her rank. Not even the king's threat to have her and her beloved executed availed to turn her thoughts away from Solomon. The Ammonite king had the lovers taken to a barren desert, in the hope that they would die of starvation there. Solomon and his wife wandered through the desert until they came to a city situated by the seashore. They purchased a fish to stave off death. When Naamah prepared the fish, she found in its belly the magic ring belonging to her husband, which he had given to Asmodeus, and which, thrown into the sea by the demon, had been swallowed by a fish. Solomon recognized his ring, put it on his finger, and in the twinkling of an eye he transported himself to Jerusalem. Asmodeus, who had been posing as King Solomon during the three years, he drove out, and himself ascended the throne again.

Later on he cited the king of Ammon before his tribunal, and called him to account for the disappearance of the cook and the cook's wife, accusing him of having killed them. The king of Ammon protested that he had not killed, but only banished them. Then Solomon had the queen appear, and to his great astonishment and still greater joy the king of Ammon recognized his daughter.

Solomon succeeded in regaining his throne only after undergoing many hardships. The people of Jerusalem considered him a lunatic, because he said that he was Solomon. After some time, the members of the Sanhedrin noticed his peculiar behavior, and they investigated the matter. They found that a long time had passed since Benaiah, the confidant of the king, had been permitted to enter the presence of the usurper. Furthermore the wives of Solomon and his mother Bath-sheba informed them that the behavior of the king had completely changed it was not befitting royalty and in no respect like Solomon's former manner. It was also very strange that the king never by any chance allowed his foot to be seen, for fear, of course, of betraying his demon origin. The Sanhedrin, therefore, gave the king's magic ring to the wandering beggar who called himself King Solomon, and had him appear before the pretender on the throne. As soon as Asmodeus caught sight of the true king protected by his magic ring, he flew away precipitately.

Solomon did not escape unscathed. The sight of Asmodeus in all his forbidding ugliness had so terrified him that henceforth he surrounded his couch at night with all the valiant heroes among the people.

THE COURT OF SOLOMON

As David had been surrounded by great scholars and heroes of repute, so the court of Solomon was the gathering-place of the great of his people. The most important of them all doubtless was Benaiah the son of Jehoiada, who had no peer for learning and piety either in the time of the first or the second Temple. In his capacity as the chancellor of Solomon, he was the object of the king's special favor. He was frequently invited to be the companion of the king in his games of chess. The wise king naturally was always the winner. One day Solomon left the chess-board for a moment, Benaiah used his absence to remove one of the king's chess-men, and the king lost the game. Solomon gave much thought to the occurrence. He came to the conclusion that his chancellor had dealt dishonestly with him, and he was determined to give him a lesson.

Some days later Solomon noticed two suspicious characters hanging about the palace. Acting at once upon an idea that occurred to him, he put on the clothes of one of his servants and joined the two suspects. The three of them, he proposed, should make the attempt to rob the royal palace, and he drew forth a key which would facilitate their entrance. While the thieves were occupied in gathering booty, the king roused his servants, and the malefactors were taken into custody. Next morning Solomon appeared before the Sanhedrin, which was presided over by Benaiah at the time, and he desired to know from the court what punishment was meted out to a thief. Benaiah, seeing no delinquents before him, and unwilling to believe that the king would concern himself about the apprehension of thieves, was convinced that Solomon was bent on punishing him for his dishonest play. He fell at the feet of the king, confessed his guilt, and begged his pardon. Solomon was pleased to have his supposition confirmed, and also to have Benaiah acknowledge his wrong-doing. he assured him he harbored no evil designs against him, and that when he asked this question of the Sanhedrin, he had had real thieves in mind, who had broken into the palace during the night.

Another interesting incident happened, in which Benaiah played a part. The king of Persia was very ill, and his physician told him he could be cured by nothing but the milk of a lioness. The king accordingly sent a deputation bearing rich presents to Solomon, the only being in the world who might in his wisdom discover means to obtain lion's milk. Solomon charged Benaiah to fulfil the Persian king's wish. Benaiah took a number of kids, and repaired to a lion's den. Daily he threw a kid to the lioness, and after some time the beasts became familiar with him, and finally he could approach the lioness close enough to draw milk from her udders.

On the way back to the Persian king the physician who had recommended the milk cure dreamed a dream. All the organs of his body, his hands, feet, eyes, mouth, and tongue, were quarrelling with one another, each claiming the greatest share of credit in procuring the remedy for the Persian monarch. When the tongue set forth its own contribution to the cause of the king's service, the other organs rejected its claim as totally unfounded. The physician did not forget the dream, and when he appeared before the king, he spoke: "Here is the dog's milk which we went to fetch for you." The king, enraged, ordered the physician to be hanged, because he had brought the milk of a bitch instead of the milk of a lion's dam. During the preliminaries to the execution, all the limbs and organs of the physician began to tremble, whereupon the tongue said: "Did I not tell you that you all are of no good? If you will acknowledge my superiority, I shall even now save you from death." They all made the admission it demanded, and the physician requested the executioner to take him to the king. Once in the presence of his master, he begged him as a special favor to drink of the milk he had brought. The king granted his wish, recovered from his sickness, and dismissed the physician in peace. So it came about that all the organs of the body acknowledge the supremacy of the tongue.

Besides Benaiah, Solomon's two scribes, Elihoreph and Ahijah, the sons of Shisha, deserve mention. They both met their death in a most peculiar way. Solomon once upon a time noticed a care-worn expression on the countenance of the Angel of Death. When he asked the reason, he received the answer, that he had been charged with the task of bringing the two scribes to the next world. Solomon was desirous of stealing a march upon the Angel of Death, as well as keeping his secretaries alive. He ordered the demons to carry Elihoreph and Ahijah to Luz, the only spot on earth in which the Angel of Death has no power. In a jiffy, the demons had done his bidding, but the two secretaries expired at the very moment of reaching the gates of Luz. Next day, the Angel of Death appeared before Solomon in very good humor, and said to him: "Thou didst transport those two men to the very spot in which I wanted them." The fate destined for them was to die at the gates of Luz, and the Angel of Death had been at a loss how to get them there.

A most interesting incident in Solomon's own family circle is connected with one of his daughters. She was of extraordinary beauty, and in the stars he read that she was to marry an extremely poor youth. To prevent the undesirable union, Solomon had a high tower erected in the sea, and to this he sent his daughter. Seventy eunuchs were to guard her, and a huge quantity of food was stored in the tower for her use.

The poor youth whom fate had appointed to be her husband was travelling one cold night. He did not know where to rest his head, when he espied the rent carcass of an ox lying in the field. In this he lay down to keep warm. When he was ensconced in it, there came a large bird, which took the carcass, bore it, together with the youth stretched out in it, to the roof of the tower in which the princess lived, and, settling down there, began to devour the flesh of the ox. In the morning, the princess, according to her wont, ascended to the roof to look out upon the sea, and she caught sight of the youth. She asked him who he was, and who had brought him thither? He told her that he was a Jew from Accho, and had been carried to the tower by a bird. She showed him to a chamber, where he could wash and anoint himself, and array himself in a fresh garb. Then it appeared that he possessed unusual beauty. Besides, he was a scholar of great attainments and of acute mind. So it came about that the princess fell in love with him. She asked him whether he would have her to wife, and he assented gladly. He opened one of his veins, and wrote the marriage contract with his own blood. Then he pronounced the formula of betrothal, taking God and the two archangels Michael and Gabriel as witnesses, and she became his wife, legally married to him.

After some time the eunuchs noticed that she was pregnant. Their questions elicited the suspected truth from the princess, and they sent for Solomon. His daughter admitted her marriage, and the king, though he recognized in her husband the poor man predicted in the constellations, yet he thanked God for his son-in-law, distinguished no less for learning than for his handsome person.

VI. JUDAH AND ISRAEL

THE DIVISION OF THE KINGDOM

THE division of the kingdom into Judah and Israel, which took place soon after the death of Solomon, had cast its shadow before. When Solomon, on the day after his marriage with the Egyptian princess, disturbed the regular course of the Temple service by sleeping late with his head on the pillow under which lay the key of the Temple, Jeroboam with eighty thousand Ephraimites approached the king and publicly called him to account for is negligence. God administered a reproof to Jeroboam; "Why dost thou reproach a prince of Israel? As thou livest, thou shalt have a taste of his rulership, and thou wilt see thou are not equal to its responsibilities."

On another occasion a clash occurred between Jeroboam and Solomon. The latter ordered his men to close the openings David had made in the city wall to facilitate the approach of the pilgrims to Jerusalem. This forced them all the walk through the gates and pay toll. The tax thus collected Solomon gave to his wife, the daughter of Pharaoh, as pin-money. Indignant at this, Jeroboam questioned the king about it in public. In other ways, too, he failed to pay Solomon the respect due to royal position, as his father before him, Sheba the son of Bichri, had rebelled against David, misled by signs and tokens which he had falsely interpreted as pointing to his own elevation to royal dignity, when in reality they concerned themselves with his son.

It was when Jeroboam was preparing to depart from Jerusalem forever, in order to escape the dangers to which Solomon's displeasure exposed him, that Ahijah of Shilo met him with the Divine tidings of his elevation to the kingship. The prophet

Ahijah, of the tribe of Levi, was venerable, not only by reason of his hoary age, his birth occurred at least sixty years before the exodus from Egypt, but because his piety was so profound that a saint of the exalted standing of Simon ben Yohai associated Ahijah with himself. Simon once exclaimed: "My merits and Ahijah together suffice to atone for the iniquity of all sinners from the time of Abraham until the advent of the Messiah."

JEROBOAM

Jeroboam was the true disciple of this great prophet, His doctrine was as pure as the new garment Ahijah wore when he met Jeroboam near Jerusalem, and his learning exceeded that of all the scholars of his time except his own teacher Ahijah alone. The prophet was in the habit of discussing secret love with Jeroboam and subjects in the Torah whose existence was wholly unknown to others.

Had Jeroboam proved himself worthy of his high position, the length of his reign would have equalled David's. It was his pride that led him into destruction. He set up the golden calves as objects to be worshipped by the people, in order to wean them from their habit of going on pilgrimages to Jerusalem. He knew that in the Temple only members of the royal house of David were privileged to sit down. No exception would be made in favor of Jeroboam, and so he would have to stand while Rehoboam would be seated. Rather than appear in public as the subordinate of the Judean king, he introduced the worship of idols, which secured him full royal prerogatives.

In the execution of his plan he proceeded with great cunning, and his reputation as a profound scholar and pious saint stood him in good stead. This was his method: He seated an impious man next to a pious man, and then said to each couple: "Will you put your signature to anything I intend to do?" The two would give an affirmative answer. "Do you want me as king?" he would then ask, only to receive and affirmative answer again. "And you will do whatever I order?" he continued. "Yes," was the reply. "I am to infer, then, that you will even pay worship to idols if I command it?" said Jeroboam. "God forbid !" the pious member of the couple would exclaim, whereupon his impious companion, who was in league with the king, would turn upon him: "Canst thou really suppose for an instant that a man like Jeroboam would serve idols? He only wishes to put our loyalty to the test." Through such machinations he succeeded in obtaining the signatures of the most pious, even the signature of the prophet Ahijah. Now Jeroboam had the people is his power. He could exact the vilest deeds from them.

So entrenched, Jeroboam brought about the division between Judah and Israel, a consummation which his father, Sheba the son of Bichri, had not been able to compass under David, because God desired to have the Temple erected before the split occurred. Not yet satisfied, Jeroboam sought to involve the Ten Tribes in a war against Judah and Jerusalem. But the people of the northern kingdom refused to enter into hostilities with their brethren, and with the ruler of their brethren, a descendant of David. Jeroboam appealed to the elders of the Israelites, and they referred him to the Danites, the most efficient of their warriors; but they swore by the head of Dan, the ancestor of their tribe, that they would never consent to shed blood of their brethren. They were even on the point of rising against Jeroboam, and the clash between them and the followers of Jeroboam was prevented only because God prompted the Danites to leave Palestine.

Their first plan was to journey to Egypt and take possession of the land. They gave it up when their princes reminded them of the Biblical prohibition against dwelling in Egypt. Likewise they were restrained from attacking the Edomites, Ammonites, and Moabites, for the Torah commands considerate treatment of them. Finally they decided to go to Egypt, but not to stay there, only to pass through to Ethiopia. The Egyptians were in great terror of the Danites, and their hardiest warriors occupied the roads travelled by them. Arrived in Ethiopia, the Danites slew a part of the population, and exacted tribute from the rest.

The departure of the Danites relieved Judah from the apprehended invasion by Jeroboam, but danger arose from another quarter. Shishak, the ruler of Egypt, who was the father-in-law of Solomon, came to Jerusalem and demanded his daughter's jointure. He carried off the throne of Solomon, and also the treasure which the Israelites had taken from the Egyptians at the time of the exodus. So the Egyptian money returned to its source.

THE TWO ABIJAHS

Jeroboam did not entirely forego his plan of a campaign against Judah, but it was not executed until Abijah had succeeded his father Rehoboam on the throne of Jerusalem. The Judean king was victorious. However, he could not long enjoy the fruits of his victory. Shortly after occurred his death, brought on by his own crimes. In his war against Jeroboam he had indulged in excessive cruelty; he ordered the corpses of the enemy to be mutilated, and permitted them to be buried only after putrefaction had set in. Such savagery was all the more execrable as it prevented many widows from entering into a second marriage. Mutilating the corpses had made identification impossible, and so it was left doubtful whether their husbands were among the dead.

Moreover, Abijah used most disrespectful language about the prophet Abijah the Shilonite; he called him a "son of Belial" in his address to the people on Mount Zemaraim. That in itself merited severe punishment. Finally, his zeal for true worship of God, which Abijah had urged as the reason of the war between himself and Jeroboam, cooled quickly. When he obtained possession of Beth-el, he failed to do away with the golden calves.

In this respect his namesake, the Israelitish king Abijah, the son of Jeroboam, was by far his superior. By removing the guards stationed at the frontier, he bade defiance to the command of his father, who had decreed the death penalty for pilgrimages to Jerusalem. More than this, he himself ventured to go up to Jerusalem in fulfilment of his religious duty.

ASA

Asa, the son of Abijah of Judah, was a worthier and a more pious ruler than his father had been. He did away with the gross worship of Priapus, to which his mother was devoted. To reward him for his piety, God gave him the victory over Zerah, the king of the Ethiopians. As a result of this victory he came again into possession of the throne of Solomon and of the treasures Shishak had taken from his grandfather, which Zerah in turn had wrested form Shishak. Asa himself did not long keep them. Baasha, the king of Israel, together with Ben-hadad, the Aramean king, attacked Asa, who tried to propitiate Ben-hadad by giving him his lately reacquired treasures. The prophet justly rebuked him for trusting in princes rather than in God, and that in spite of the fact that Divine help had been visible in his conflicts with the Ethiopians and the Lubim; for there had been no need for him to engage in battle with them; in response to his mere prayer God had slain the enemy. In general, Asa showed little confidence in God; he rather trusted his own skill. Accordingly, he made even the scholars of his realm enlist in the army sent out against Baasha. He was punished by being afflicted with gout, he of all men, who was distinguished on account of the strength residing in his feet. Furthermore, the division between Judah and Israel was made permanent, though God had at first intended to limit the exclusion of David's house from Israel to only thirty-six years. Had Asa shown himself deserving, he would have been accorded dominion over the whole of Israel. In point of fact, Asa, through his connection by marriage with the house of Omri, contributed to the stability of the Israelitish dynasty, for as a result of the support given by the southern ruler Omri succeeded in putting his rival Tibni out of the way. Then it was that God resolved that the descendants of Asa should perish simultaneously with the descendants of Omri. This doom was accomplished when Jehu killed the king of Judah on account of his friendship and kinship with Joram the king of Samaria.

JEHOSHAPHAT AND AHAB

The successors of Omri and Asa, each in his way, were worthy of their fathers. Jehoshaphat, the son of Asa, was very wealthy. The treasures which his father had sent to the Aramean ruler reverted to him in consequence of his victory over the Ammonites, themselves the conquerors of the Arameans, whom they had despoiled of their possessions. His power was exceedingly great; each division of his army counted no less than one hundred and sixty thousand warriors. Yet rich and powerful as he was, he was so modest that he refused to don his royal apparel when he went to the house of the prophet Elisha to consult him; he appeared before him in the attire of one of the people. Unlike his father, who had little consideration for scholars, Jehoshaphat was particularly gracious toward them. When a scholar appeared before him, he arose, hastened to meet him, and kissing and embracing him, greeted him with "Rabbi, Rabbi!"

Jehoshaphat concerned himself greatly about the purity and sanctification of the Temple. He was the author of the ordinance forbidding any one to ascend the Temple mount whose term of uncleanness had not expired, even though he had taken the ritual bath. His implicit trust in God made him a complete contrast to his skeptical father. He turned to God and implored His help when to human reason help seemed an utter impossibility. In the war with the Arameans, an enemy held his sword at Jehoshaphat's very throat, ready to deal the fatal blow, but the king entreated help of God, and it was granted.

In power and wealth, Ahab, king of Samaria, outstripped his friend Jehoshaphat, for Ahab is one of that small number of kings who have ruled over the whole world. No less than two hundred and fifty-two kingdoms acknowledged his dominion. As for his wealth, it was so abundant that each of his hundred and forty children possessed several ivory palaces, summer and winter residences. But what gives Ahab his prominence among the Jewish kings is neither his power nor his wealth, but his sinful conduct. For him the gravest transgressions committed by Jeroboam were slight peccadilloes. At his order the gates of Samaria bore the inscription: "Ahab denies the God of Israel." He was so devoted to idolatry, to which he was led astray by his wife Jezebel, that the fields of Palestine were full of idols. But he was not wholly wicked, he possessed some good qualities. He was liberal toward scholars, and he showed great reverence for the Torah, which he studied zealously. When Ben-hadad exacted all he possessed his wealth, his wives, his children he acceded to his demands regarding everything except the Torah; that he refused peremptorily to surrender. In the war that followed between himself and the Syrians, he was so indignant at the presumptuousness of the Aramean upstart that he himself saddled his warhorse for the battle. His zeal was rewarded by God; he gained a brilliant victory in a battle in which no less than a hundred thousand of the Syrians were slain, as the prophet Micaiah had foretold to him. The same seer admonished him not to deal gently with Ben-hadad. God's word to him had been: "Know that I had to set many a pitfall and trap to deliver him into thy hand. If thou lettest him escape, thy life will be forfeit for his."

Nevertheless the disastrous end of Ahab is not to be ascribed to his disregard of the prophet's warning for he finally liberated Ben-hahad, but chiefly to the murder of his kinsman Naboth, whose execution on the charge of treason he had ordered, so that he might put himself in possession of Naboth's wealth. His victim was a pious man, and in the habit of going on pilgrimages to Jerusalem on the festivals. As he was a great singer, his presence in the Holy City attracted many other pilgrims thither. Once Naboth failed to go on his customary pilgrimage. Then it was that his false conviction took place a very severe punishment for the transgression, but not wholly unjustifiable. Under Jehoshaphat's influence and counsel, Ahab did penance for his crime, and the punishment God meted out to him was thereby mitigated to the extent that his dynasty was not cut off from the throne at this death. In the heavenly court of justice, at Ahab's trial, the accusing witnesses and his defenders exactly balanced each other in number and statements, until the spirit of Naboth appeared and turned the scale against Ahab. The spirit of Naboth it had been, too, that had let astray the prophets of Ahab, making them all use the very same words in prophesying a victory at Ramothgilead. This literal unanimity aroused Jehoshaphat's suspicion, and caused him to ask for "a prophet of the Lord," for the rule is: "The same thought is revealed to many prophets, but no two prophets express it in the same words." Jehoshaphat's mistrust was justified by the issue of war. Ahab was slain in a miraculous way by Naaman, at the time only a common soldier of the rank and file. God permitted Naaman's missile to penetrate Ahab's armor, though the latter was harder than the former.

The mourning for Ahab was so great that the memory of it reached posterity. The funeral procession was unusually impressive; no less than thirty-six thousand warriors, their shoulders bared, marched before his bier. Ahab is one of the few in Israel who have no portion in the world to come. He dwells in the fifth division of the nether world, which is under the supervision of the angel Oniel. However, he is exempt from the tortures inflicted upon his heathen associates.

JEZEBEL

Wicked as Ahab was, his wife Jezebel was incomparably worse. Indeed, she is in great part the cause of his suffering, and Ahab realized it. Once Rabbi Levi expounded the Scriptural verse in which the iniquity of Ahab and the influence of his wife over him are discussed, dwelling upon the first half for two months. Ahab visited him in a dream, and reproached him with expatiating on the first half of the verse to the exclusion of the latter half. Thereupon the Rabbi took the second half of the verse as the text of his lectures for the next two months, demonstrating all the time that Jezebel was the instigator of Ahab's sins. Her misdeed are told in the Scriptures. To those there recounted must be added her practice of attaching unchaste images to Ahab's chariot for the purpose of stimulating his carnal desires. Therefore those parts of his chariot were spattered with his blood when he fell at the hand of the enemy. She had her husband weighed every day, and the increase of his weight in gold she sacrificed to the idol. Jezebel was not only the daughter and the wife of a king, she was also co-regent with her husband, the only reigning queen in Jewish history except Athaliah.

Hardened sinner though Jezebel was, even she had good qualities. One of them was her capacity for sympathy with others in joy and sorrow. Whenever a funeral cortege passed the royal palace, Jezebel would descend and join the ranks of the mourners, and, also, when a marriage procession went by, she took part in the merry-making in honor of the bridal couple. By way of reward the limbs and organs with which she had executed these good deeds were left intact by the horses that trampled her to death in the portion of Jezreel.

JORAM OF ISRAEL

Of Joram, the son of Ahab, it can only be said that he had his father's faults without his father's virtues. Ahab was liberal, Joram miserly, nay, he even indulged in usurious practices. From Obadiah, the pious protector of the prophets in hiding, he exacted a high rate of interest on the money needed for their support. As a consequence, at his death he fell pierced between his arms, the arrow going out at his heart, for he had stretched out his arms to receive usury, and had hardened his heart against compassion. In his reign only one event deserves mention, his campaign against Moab, undertaken in alliance with the kings of Judah and Edom, and ending with a splendid victory won by the allied kings. Joram and his people, it need hardly be said, failed to derive the proper lesson from the war. Their disobedience to God's commands went on as before. The king of Moab, on the other hand, in his way sought to come nearer to God. He assembled his astrologers and inquired of them, why it was that the Moabites, successful in their warlike enterprises against other nations, could not measure up to the standard of the Israelites. They explained that God was gracious to Israel, because his ancestor Abraham had been ready to sacrifice Isaac at His bidding. Then the Moabite king reasoned, that if God set so high a value upon mere good intention, how much greater would be the reward for its actual execution, and he, who ordinarily was a sun worshipper, proceeded to sacrifice his son, the successor to the throne, to the God of Israel. God said: "The heathen do not know Me, and their wrong-doing arises from ignorance; but you, Israelites, know Me, and yet you act rebelliously toward Me."

As a result of the seven years' famine, conditions in Samaria were frightful during the great part of Joram's reign. In the first year everything stored in the houses was eaten up. In the second, the people supported themselves with what they could scrape together in the fields. The flesh of the clean animals sufficed for the third year; in the fourth the sufferers resorted to the unclean animals; in the fifth, the reptiles and insects; and in the sixth the monstrous thing happened that women crazed by hunger consumed their own children as food. But the acme of distress was reached in the seventh year, when men sought to gnaw the flesh from their own bones. To these occurrences the prophecies of Joel apply, for he lived in the awful days of the famine in Joram's reign.

Luckily, God revealed to Joel at the same time how Israel would be rescued from the famine. The winter following the seven years of dearth brought no relief, for the rain held back until the first day of the month of Nisan. When it began to fall, the prophet said to the people, "Go forth and sow seed!" But they remonstrated with him, "Shall one who hath saved a measure of wheat or two measures of barely not use his store for food and live, rather than for seed and die?" But the prophet urged them, "Nay, go forth and sow seed." And a miracle happened. In the ant hills and mouse holes, they found enough grain for seed, and they cast it upon the ground on the second, the third, and the fourth day of Nisan. On the fifth day of the month rain fell again. Eleven days later the grain was ripe, and the offering of the 'Omer could be brought at the appointed time, on the sixteenth of the month. Of this the Psalmist was thinking when he said, "They that sow in tears shall reap in joy."

VII. ELIJAH

ELIJAH BEFORE HIS TRANSLATION

THE Biblical account of the prophet Elijah, of his life and work during the reigns of Ahab and his son Joram, gives but a faint idea of a personage whose history begins with Israel's sojourn in Egypt, and will end only when Israel, under the leadership of the Messiah, shall have taken up his abode again in Palestine.

The Scripture tells us only the name of Elijah's home, but it must be added that he was a priest, identical with Phinehas, the priest zealous for the honor of God, who distinguished himself on the journey through the desert, and played a prominent role again in the time of the Judges.

Elijah's first appearance in the period of the Kings was his meeting with Ahab in the house of Hiel, the Beth-elite, the commander-in-chief of the Israelitish army, whom he was visiting to condole with him for the loss of his sons. God Himself had charged the prophet to offer sympathy to Hiel, whose position demanded that honor be paid him. Elijah at first refused to seek out the sinner who had violated the Divine injunction against rebuilding Jericho, for he said that the blasphemous talk of such evil-doers always called forth his rage. Thereupon God promised Elijah that fulfilment should attend whatever imprecation might in his wrath escape him against the godless for their unholy speech. As the prophet entered the general's house, he heard Hiel utter these words: "Blessed be the Lord God of the pious, who grants fulfilment to the words of the pious." Hiel thus acknowledged that he had been justly afflicted with Joshua's curse against him who should rebuild Jericho.

Ahab mockingly asked him: "Was not Moses greater than Joshua, and did he not say that God would let no rain descend upon the earth, if Israel served and worshipped idols? There is not an idol known to which I do not pay homage, yet we enjoy all that is goodly and desirable. Dost thou believe that if the words of Moses remain unfulfilled, the words of Joshua will come true?" Elijah rejoined: "Be it as thou sayest: 'As the Lord, the God of Israel liveth, before whom I stand, there shall not be dew nor rain these years, but according to my word.'" In pursuance of His promise, God could not but execute the words of Elijah, and neither dew nor rain watered the land.

A famine ensued, and Ahab sought to wreak his vengeance upon the prophet. To escape the king's persecutions, Elijah hid himself. He was sustained with food brought from the larder of the pious king Jehoshaphat by ravens, which at the same time would not approach near to the house of the iniquitous Ahab.

God, who has compassion even upon the impious, tried to induce the prophet to release Him from His promise. To influence him He made the brook run dry whence Elijah drew water for his thirst. As this failed to soften the inflexible prophet, God resorted to the expedient of causing him pain through the death of the son of the widow with whom Elijah was abiding, and by whom he had been received with great honor. When her son, who was later to be known as the prophet Jonah, died, she thought God had formerly been gracious to her on account of her great worthiness as compared with the merits of her neighbors and of the inhabitants of the city, and now He had abandoned her, because her virtues had become as naught in the presence of the great prophet. In his distress Elijah supplicated God to revive the child. Now God had the prophet in His power. He could give heed unto Elijah's prayer only provided the prophet released Him from the promise about a drought, for resuscitation from death is brought about by means of dew, and this remedy was precluded so long as Elijah kept God to His word withholding dew and rain from the earth. Elijah saw there was nothing for it but to yield. However, he first betook himself to Ahab with the purpose of overcoming the obduracy of the people, upon whom the famine had made no impression. Manifest wonders displayed before their eyes were to teach them wisdom. The combat between God and Baal took place on Carmel. The mount that had esteemed itself the proper place for the greatest event in Israelitish history, the revelation of the law, was compensated, by the many miracles now performed upon it, for its disappointment at Sinai's having been preferred to it.

The first wonder occurred in connection with the choice of the bullocks. According to Elijah's arrangement with Ahab, one was to be sacrificed to God, and then one to Baal. A pair to twins, raised together, were brought before the contestants, and it was decided by lot which belonged to God and which to Baal. Elijah had no difficulty with his offering; quickly he led it to his altar. But all the priests of Baal, eight hundred and fifty in number, could not make their victim stir a foot. When Elijah began to speak persuasively to the bullock of Baal, urging it to follow the idolatrous priests, it opened its mouth and said: "We two, yonder bullock and myself, came forth from the same womb, we took our food from the same manger, and now he has been destined for God, as an instrument for the glorification of the Divine Name, while I am to be used for Baal, as an instrument to enrage my Creator." Elijah urged: "Do thou but follow the priests of Baal that they may have no excuse, and then thou wilt have a share in that glorification of God for which my bullock will be used." The bullock: "So dost thou advise, but I swear I will not move from the spot, unless thou with thine own hands wilt deliver me up." Elijah thereupon led the bullock to the priests of Baal.

In spite of this miracle, the priests sought to deceive the people. They undermined the altar, and Hiel hid himself under it with the purpose of igniting a fire at the mention of the word Baal. But God sent a serpent to kill him. In vain the false priests cried and called, Baal! Baal! the expected flame did not shoot up. To add to the confusion of the idolaters, God had imposed silence upon the whole world. The powers of the upper and of the nether regions were dumb, the universe seemed deserted and desolate, as if without a living creature. If a single sound had made itself heard, the priests would have said, "It is the voice of Baal."

That all preparations might be completed in one day, the erection of the altar, the digging of the trench, and whatever else was necessary, Elijah commanded the sun to stand still. "For Joshua," he said, "thou didst stand still that Israel might conquer his enemies; now stand thou still, neither for my sake, nor for the sake of Israel, but that the Name of God may be exalted." And the sun obeyed his words.

Toward evening Elijah summoned his disciple Elisha, and bade him pour water over his hands. A miracle happened. Water flowed out from Elijah's fingers until the whole trench was filled. Then the prophet prayed to God to let fire descend, but in such wise that the people would know it to be a wonder from heaven, and not think it a magician's trick. He spoke: "Lord of the world, Thou wilt send me as a messenger 'at the end of time,' but if my words do not meet with fulfilment now, the Jews cannot be expected to believe me in the latter days." His pleading was heard on high, and fire fell from heaven upon the altar, a fire that not only consumed what it touched, but also licked up the water. Nor was that all; his prayer for rain was also granted. Scarcely had these words dropped from his lips, "Though we have no other merits, yet remember the sign of the covenant which the Israelites bear upon their bodies," when the rain fell to earth.

In spite of all these miracles, the people persisted in their idolatrous ways and thoughts. Even the seven thousand who had not bowed down unto Baal were unworthy sons of Israel, for they paid homage to the golden calves of Jeroboam.

The misdeeds of the people had swelled to such number that they could no longer reckon upon "the merits of the fathers" to intercede for them; they had overdrawn their account. When they sank to the point of degradation at which they gave up the sign of the covenant, Elijah could control his wrath no longer, and he accused Israel before God. In the cleft of the rock in which God had once aforetimes appeared to Moses, and revealed Himself as compassionate and long-suffering, He now met with Elijah, and conveyed to him, by various signs, that it had been better to defend Israel than accuse him. But Elijah in his zeal for God was inexorable. Then God commanded him to appoint Elisha as his successor, for He said: "I cannot do as thou wouldst have me." Furthermore God charged him: "Instead of accusing My children, journey to Damascus, where the Gentiles have an idol for each day of the year. Though Israel hath thrown down My altars and slain My prophets, what concern is it of thine?"

The four phenomena that God sent before His appearance wind, earthquake, fire, and a still small voice were to instruct Elijah about the destiny of man. God told Elijah that these four represent the worlds through which man must pass: the first stands for this world, fleeting as the wind; the earthquake is the day of death, which makes the human body to tremble and quake; fire is the tribunal in Gehenna, and the still small voice is the Last Judgment, when there will be none but God alone. later, Elijah was taken up into heaven, but not without first undergoing a struggle with the Angel of Death. He refused to let Elijah enter heaven at his translation, on the ground that he exercised jurisdiction over all mankind, Elijah not excepted. God maintained that at the creation of heaven and earth He had explicitly ordered the Angel of Death to grant entrance to the living prophet, but the Angel of Death insisted that by Elijah's translation God had given just cause for complaint to all other men, who could not escape the doom of death. Thereupon God: "Elijah is not like other men. He is able to banish thee from the world, only thou dost not recognize his strength." With the consent of God, a combat took place between Elijah and the Angel of Death. The prophet was victorious, and, if God had not restrained him, he would have annihilated his opponent. Holding his defeated enemy under his feet, Elijah ascended heavenward.

In heaven he goes on living for all time. There he sits recording the deeds of men and the chronicles of the world. He has another office besides. He is the Psychopomp, whose duty is to stand at the cross-ways in Paradise and guide the pious to their appointed places; who brings the souls of sinners up from Gehenna at the approach of the Sabbath, and leads them back again to their merited punishment when the day of rest is about to depart; and who conducts these same souls, after they have atoned for their sins, to the place of everlasting bliss.

Elijah's miraculous deeds will be better understood if we remember that he had been an angel from the very first, even before the end of his earthly career. When God was about to create man, Elijah said to Him: "Master of the world! If it be pleasing in Thine eyes, I will descend to earth, and make myself serviceable to the sons of men." Then God changed his angel name, and later, under Ahab, He permitted him to abide among men on earth, that he might convert the world to the belief that "the Lord is God." His mission fulfilled, God took him again into heaven, and said to him: "Be thou the guardian spirit of My children forever, and spread the belief in Me abroad in the whole world."

His angel name is Sandalphon, one of the greatest and mightiest of the fiery angel host. As such it is his duty to wreathe garlands for God out of the prayers sent aloft by Israel. Besides, he must offer up sacrifices in the invisible sanctuary, for the Temple was destroyed only apparently; in reality, it went on existing, hidden from the sight of ordinary mortals.

AFTER HIS TRANSLATION

Elijah's removal from earth, so far being an interruption to his relations with men, rather marks the beginning of his real activity as a helper in time of need, as a teacher and as a guide. At first his intervention in sublunar affairs was not frequent. Seven years after his translation, he wrote a letter to the wicked king Jehoram, who reigned over Judah. The next occasion on which he took part in an earthly occurrence was at the time of Ahasuerus, when he did the Jews a good turn by assuming the guise of the courtier Harbonah, in a favorable moment inciting the king against Haman.

It was reserved for later days, however, for Talmudic times, the golden age of the great scholars, the Tannaim and the Amoraim, to enjoy Elijah's special vigilance as protector of the innocent, as a friend in need, who hovers over the just and the pious, ever present to guard them against evil or snatch them out of danger. With four strokes of his wings Elijah can traverse the world. Hence no spot on earth is too far removed for his help. As an angel he enjoys the power of assuming the most various appearances to accomplish his purposes. Sometimes he looks like an ordinary man, sometimes he takes the appearance of an Arab, sometimes of a horseman, now he is a Roman court-official, now he is a harlot.

Once upon a time it happened that when Nahum, the great and pious teacher, was journeying to Rome on a political mission, he was without knowledge robbed of the gift he bore to the Emperor as an offering from the Jews. When he handed the casket to the ruler, it was found to contain common earth, which the thieves had substituted for the jewels they had abstracted. The Emperor thought the Jews were mocking at him, and their representative, Nahum, was condemned to suffer death. In his piety the Rabbi did not lose confidence in God; he only said: "This too is for good." And so it turned out to be. Suddenly Elijah appeared, and, assuming the guise of a court-official, he said: "Perhaps the earth in this casket is like that used by Abraham for purposes of war. A handful will do the work of swords and bows." At his instance the virtues of the earth were tested in the attack upon a city that had long resisted Roman courage and strength. His supposition was verified. The contents of the casket proved more efficacious than all the weapons of the army, and the Romans were victorious. Nahum was dismissed, laden with honors and treasures, and the thieves, who had betrayed themselves by claiming the precious earth, were executed, for, naturally enough, Elijah works no wonder for evil-doers.

Another time, for the purpose of rescuing Rabbi Shila, Elijah pretended to be a Persian. An informer had announced the Rabbi with the Persian Government, accusing him of administering the law according to the Jewish code. Elijah appeared as witness for the Rabbi and against the informer, and Shila was honorably dismissed.

When the Roman bailiffs were pursuing Rabbi Meir, Elijah joined him in the guise of a harlot. The Roman emissaries desisted from their pursuit, for they could not believe that Rabbi Meir would choose such a companion.

A contemporary of Rabbi Meir, Rabbi Simon ben Yohai, who spent thirteen years in a cave to escape the vengeance of the Romans, was informed by Elijah of the death of the Jew-baiting emperor, so that he could leave his hiding-place.

Equally characteristic is the help Elijah afforded the worthy poor. Frequently he brought them great wealth. Rabbi Kahana was so needy that he had to support himself by peddling with household utensils. Once a lady of high standing endeavored to force him to commit an immoral act, and Kahana, preferring death to iniquity, threw himself from a loft. Though Elijah was at a distance of four hundred parasangs, he hastened to the post in time to catch the Rabbi before he touched the ground. Besides, he gave him means enough to enable him to abandon an occupation beset with perils.

Rabba bar Abbahu likewise was a victim of poverty. He admitted to Elijah that on account of his small means he had no time to devote to his studies. Thereupon Elijah led him into Paradise, bade him remove his mantle, and fill it with leaves grown in the regions of the blessed. When the Rabbi was about to quit Paradise, his garment full of leaves, a voice was heard to say: "Who desires to anticipate his share in the world to come during his earthly days, as Rabba bar Abbahu is doing?" The Rabbi quickly cast the leaves away; nevertheless he received twelve thousand denarii for his upper garment, because it retained the wondrous fragrance of the leaves of Paradise.

Elijah's help was not confined to poor teachers of the law; all who were in need, and were worthy of his assistance, had a claim upon him. A poor man, the father of a family, in his distress once prayed to God: "O Lord of the world, Thou knowest, there is none to whom I can tell my tale of woe, none who will have pity upon me. I have neither brother nor kinsman nor friend, and my starving little ones are crying with hunger. Then do Thou have mercy and be compassionate, or let death come and put an end to our suffering." His words found a hearing with God, for, as he finished, Elijah stood before the poor man, and sympathetically inquired why he was weeping. When the prophet had heard the tale of his troubles, he said: "Take me and sell me as a slave; the proceeds will suffice for thy needs." At first the poor man refused to accept the sacrifice, but finally yielded, and Elijah was sold to a prince for eighty denarii. This sum formed the nucleus of the fortune which the poor man amassed and enjoyed until the end of his days. The prince who had purchased Elijah intended to build a palace, and he rejoiced to hear that his new slave was an architect. He promised Elijah liberty if within six months he completed the edifice. After nightfall of the same day, Elijah offered a prayer, and instantaneously the palace stood in its place in complete perfection. Elijah disappeared. The next morning the prince was not a little astonished to see the palace finished. But when he sought his slave to reward him, and sought him in vain, he realized that he had had dealings with an angel. Elijah meantime repaired to the man who had sold him, and related his story to him, that he might know he had not cheated the purchaser out of his price; on the contrary, he had enriched him, since the palace was worth a hundred times more than the money paid for the pretended slave.

A similar thing happened to a well-to-do man who lost his fortune, and became so poor that he had to do manual labor in the field of another. Once, when he was at work, he was accosted by Elijah, who had assumed the appearance of an Arab: "Thou art destined to enjoy seven good years. When dost thou want them now, or as the closing years of thy life?" The man replied: "Thou art a wizard; go in peace, I have nothing for thee." Three times the same question was put, three times the same reply was given. Finally the man said: "I shall ask the advice of my wife." When Elijah came again, and repeated his question, the man, following the counsel of his wife, said: "See to it that seven good years come to us at once." Elijah replied: "Go home. Before thou crossest thy threshold, thy good fortune will have filled thy house." And so it was. His children had found a treasure in the ground, and, as he was about to enter his house, his wife met him and reported the lucky find. His wife was an estimable, pious woman, and she said to her husband: "We shall enjoy seven good years. Let us use this time to practice as much charity as possible; perhaps God will lengthen out our period of prosperity." After the lapse of seven years, during which man and wife used every opportunity of doing good, Elijah appeared again, and announced to the man that the time had come to take away what he had given him. The man responded: "When I accepted thy gift, it was after consultation with my wife. I should not like to return it without first acquainting her with what is about to happen." His wife charged him to say to the old man who had come to resume possession of his property: "If thou canst find any who will be more conscientious stewards of the pledges entrusted to us than we have been, I shall willingly yield them up to thee." God recognized that these people had made a proper use of their wealth, and He granted it to them as a perpetual possession.

If Elijah was not able to lighten the poverty of the pious, he at least sought to inspire them with hope and confidence. Rabbi Akiba, the great scholar, lived in dire poverty before he became the famous Rabbi. His rich father-in-law would have nothing to do with him or his wife, because the daughter had married Akiba against her father's will. On a bitter cold winter night, Akiba could offer his wife, who had been accustomed to the luxuries wealth can buy, nothing but straw as a bed to sleep upon, and he tried to comfort her with assurances of his love for the privations she was suffering. At that moment Elijah appeared before their hut, and cried out in supplicating tones: "O good people, give me, I pray you, a little bundle of straw. My wife has been delivered of a child, and I am so poor I haven't even enough straw to make a bed for her." Now Abika could console his wife with the fact that their own misery was not so great as it might have been, and thus Elijah had attained his end, to sustain the courage of the pious.

In the form of an Arab, he once appeared before a very poor man, whose piety equalled his poverty. He gave him two shekels. These two coins brought him such good fortune that he attained great wealth. But in his zeal to gather worldly treasures, he had no time for deeds of piety and charity. Elijah again appeared before him and took away the two shekels. In a short time the man was as poor as before. A third time Elijah came to him. He was crying bitterly and complaining of his misfortune, and the prophet said: "I shall make thee rich once more, if thou wilt promise me under oath thou wilt not let wealth ruin they character." He promised, the two shekels were restored to him, he regained his wealth, and he remained in possession of it for all time, because his piety was not curtailed by his riches.

Poverty was not the only form of distress Elijah relieved. He exercised the functions of a physician upon Rabbi Shimi bar Ashi, who had swallowed a noxious reptile. Elijah appeared to him as an awe-inspiring horseman, and forced him to apply the preventives against the disease to be expected in these circumstances.

He also cured Rabbi Judah ha-Nasi of long-continued toothache by laying his hand on the sufferer, and at the same time he brought about the reconciliation of Rabbi Judan with Rabbi Hayyah, whose form he had assumed. Rabbi Judah paid the highest respect to Rabbi Hayyah after he found out that Elijah had considered him worthy of taking his appearance.

On another occasion, Elijah re-established harmony between a husband and his wife. The woman had come home very late on Friday evening, having allowed herself to be detained by the sermon preached by Rabbi Meir. Her autocratic husband swore she should not enter the house until she had spat in the very face of the highly-esteemed Rabbi. Meantime Elijah went to Rabbi Meir, and told him a pious woman had fallen into a sore predicament on his account. To help the poor woman, the Rabbi restored to a ruse. He announced that he was looking for one who knew how to cast spells, which was done by spitting into the eye of the afflicted one. When he caught sight of the woman designated by Elijah, he asked her to try her power upon him. Thus she was able to comply with her husband's requirement without disrespect to the Rabbi; and through the instrumentality of Elijah conjugal happiness was restored to an innocent wife.

Elijah's versatility is shown in the following occurrence. A pious man bequeathed a spice-garden to his three sons. They took turns in guarding it against thieves. The first night the oldest son watched the garden. Elijah appeared to him and asked him: "My son, what wilt thou have knowledge of the Torah, or great wealth, or a beautiful wife?" He chose wealth, great wealth. Accordingly Elijah gave him a coin, and he became rich. The second son, to whom Elijah appeared the second night, chose knowledge of the Torah. Elijah gave him a book, and "he knew the whole Torah." The third son, on the third night, when Elijah put the same choice before him as before his brothers, wished for a beautiful wife. Elijah invited this third brother to go on a journey with him. Their first night was passed at the house of a notorious villain, who had a daughter. During the night Elijah overheard the chickens and the geese say to one another: "What a terrible sin that young may must have committed, that he should be destined to marry the daughter of so great a villain!" The two travellers journeyed on. The second night the experiences of the first were repeated. The third night they lodged with a man who had a very pretty daughter. During the night Elijah heard the chickens and the geese say to one another: "How great must be the virtues of this young man, if he is privileged to marry so beautiful and pious a wife." In the morning, when Elijah arose, he at once became a matchmaker, the young man married the pretty maiden, and husband and wife journeyed homeward in joy.

If it became necessary, Elijah was ready to do even the services of a sexton. When Rabbi Akiba died in prison, Elijah betook himself to the dead man's faithful disciple, Rabbi Joshua, and the two together went to the prison. There was none to forbid their entrance; a deep sleep had fallen upon the turnkeys and the prisoners alike. Elijah and Rabbi Joshua took the corpse with them, Elijah bearing it upon his shoulder. Rabbi Joshua in astonishment demanded how he, a priest, dared defile himself upon a corpse. The answer was: "God forbid! the pious can never cause defilement." All night the two walked on with their burden. At break of day they found themselves near Caesarea. A cave opened before their eyes, and within they saw a bed, a chair, a table, and a lamp. They deposited the corpse upon the bed, and left the cave, which closed up behind them. Only the light of the lamp, which had lit itself after they left, shone through the chinks. Whereupon Elijah said: "Hail, ye just, hail to you who devote yourselves to the study of the law. Hail to you, ye God-fearing men, for your places are set aside, and kept, and guarded, in Paradise, for the time to come. Hail to thee, Rabbi Akiba, that thy lifeless body found lodgment for a night in a lovely spot."

CENSOR AND AVENGER

Helpfulness and compassion do not paint the whole of the character of Elijah. He remained the stern and inexorable censor whom Ahab feared. The old zeal for the true and the good he never lost, as witness, he once struck a man dead because he failed to perform his devotions with due reverence.

There were two brothers, one of them rich and miserly, the other poor and kind-hearted. Elijah, in the garb of an old beggar, approached the rich man, and asked him for alms. Repulsed by him, he turned to the poor brother, who received him kindly, and shared his meagre supper with him. On bidding farewell to him and his equally hospitable wife, Elijah said: "May God reward you! The first thing you undertake shall be blessed, and shall take no end until you yourselves cry out Enough!" Presently the poor man began to count the few pennies he had, to convince himself that they sufficed to purchase bread for his next meal. But the few became many, and he counted and counted, and still their number increased. He counted a whole day, and the following night, until he was exhausted, and had to cry out Enough! And, indeed, it was enough, for he had become a very wealthy man. His brother was not a little astonished to see the fortunate change in his kinsman's circumstances, and when he heard how it had come about, he determined, if the opportunity should present itself again, to show his most amiable side to the old beggar with the miraculous power of blessing. He had not long to wait. A few days later he saw the old man pass by. He hastened to accost him, and, excusing himself for his unfriendliness at their former meeting, begged him to come into his house. All that the larder afforded was put before Elijah, who pretended to eat of the dainties. At his departure, he pronounced a blessing upon his hosts: "May the first thing you do have no end, until it is enough." The mistress of the house thereupon said to her husband: "That we may count gold upon gold undisturbed, let us first attend to our most urgent physical needs." So they did and they had to continue to do it until life was extinct.

The extreme of his rigor Elijah displayed toward teachers of the law. From them he demanded more than obedience to the mere letter of a commandment. For instance, he pronounced severe censure upon Rabbi Ishmael ben Jose because he was willing to act as bailiff in prosecuting Jewish thieves and criminals. He advised Rabbi Ishmael to follow the example of his father and leave the country.

His estrangement from his friend Rabbi Joshua ben Levi is characteristic. One who was sought by the officers of the law took refuge with Rabbi Joshua. His pursuers were informed of his place of concealment. Threatening to put all the inhabitants of the city to the sword if he was not delivered up, they demanded his surrender. The Rabbi urged the fugitive from justice to resign himself to his fate.

Better for one individual to die, he said, than for a whole community to be exposed to peril. The fugitive yielded to the Rabbi's argument, and gave himself up to the bailiffs. Thereafter Elijah, who had been in the habit of visiting Rabbi Joshua frequently, stayed away from his house, and he was induced to come back only by the Rabbi's long fasts and earnest prayers. In reply to the Rabbi's question, why he had shunned him, he said: "Dost thou suppose I care to have intercourse with informers?" The Rabbi quoted a passage from the Mishnah to justify his conduct, but Elijah remained unconvinced. "Dost thou consider this a law for a pious man?" he said. "Other people might have been right in doing as thou didst; thou shouldst have done otherwise."

A number of instances are known which show how exalted a standard Elijah set up for those who would be considered worthy of intercourse with him. Of two pious brothers, one provided for his servants as for his own table, while the other permitted his servants to eat abundantly only of the first course; of the other courses they could have nothing but the remnants. Accordingly, with the second brother Elijah would have nothing to do, while he often honored the former with his visits.

A similar attitude Elijah maintained toward another pair of pious brothers. One of them was in the habit of providing for his servants after his own needs were satisfied, while the other of them attended to the needs of his servants first. To the latter it was that Elijah gave the preference.

He dissolved an intimacy of many years' standing, because his friend built a vestibule which was so constructed that the supplications of the poor could be heard but faintly by those within the house.

Rabbi Joshua ben Levi incurred the displeasure of Elijah a second time, because a man was torn in pieces by a lion in the vicinity of his house. In a measure Elijah held Rabbi responsible, because he did not pray for the prevention of such misfortunes.

The story told of Elijah and Rabbi Anan forms the most striking illustration of the severity of the prophet. Someone brought Rabbi Anan a mess of little fish as a present, and at the same time asked the Rabbi to act as judge in a lawsuit he was interested in. Anan refused in these circumstances to accept a gift from the litigant. To demonstrate his single-mindedness, the applicant urged the Rabbi to take the fish and assign the case to another judge. Anan acquiesced, and he requested one of his colleagues to act for him, because he was incapacitated from serving as a judge. His legal friend drew the inference, that the litigant introduced to him was a kinsman of Rabbi Anan's, and accordingly he showed himself particularly complaisant toward him. As a result, the other party to the suit was intimidated. He failed to present his side as convincingly as he might otherwise have done, and so lost the case. Elijah, who had been the friend of Anan and his teacher as well, thenceforth shunned his presence, because he considered that the injury done the second party to the suit was due to Anan's carelessness. Anan in his distress kept many fasts, and offered up many prayers, before Elijah would return to him. Even then the Rabbi could not endure the sight of him; he had to content himself with listening to Elijah's words without looking upon his face.

Sometimes Elijah considered it his duty to force people into abandoning a bad habit. A rich man was once going to a cattle sale, and he carried a snug sum of money to buy oxen. He was accosted by a stranger none other than Elijah who inquired the purpose of his journey. "I go to buy cattle," replied the would-be purchaser. "Say, it if please God," urged Elijah. "Fiddlesticks! I shall buy cattle whether it please God or not! I carry the money with me, and the business will be dispatched." "But not with good fortune," said the stranger, and went off. Arrived at the market, the cattle-buyer discovered the loss of his purse, and he had to return home to provide himself with other money. He again set forth on his journey, but this time he took another road to avoid the stranger of ill omen. To his amazement he met an old man with whom he had precisely the same adventure as with the first stranger. Again he had to return home to fetch money. By this time had learned his lesson. When a third stranger questioned him about the object of his journey, he answered: "If it please God, I intend to buy oxen." The stranger wished him success, and the wish was fulfilled. To the merchant's surprise, when a pair of fine cattle were offered him, and their price exceeded the sum of money he had about his person, he found the two purses he had lost on his first and second trips. Later he sold the same pair of oxen to the king for a considerable price, and he became very wealthy.

As Elijah coerced this merchant into humility toward God, so he carried home a lesson to the great Tanna Eliezer, the son of Rabbi Simon ben Yohai. This Rabbi stood in need of correction on account of his overweening conceit. Once, on returning from the academy, he took a walk on the sea-beach, his bosom swelling with pride at the thought of his attainments in the Torah. He met a hideously ugly man, who greeted him with the words: "Peace be with thee, Rabbi." Eliezer, instead of courteously acknowledging the greeting, said: "O thou wight, how ugly thou art! Is it possible that all the residents of thy town are as ugly as thou?" "I know not," was the reply, "but it is the Master Artificer who created me that thou shouldst have said: 'How ugly is this vessel which Thou hast fashioned.'" The Rabbi realized the wrong he had committed, and humbly begged pardon of the ugly man another of the protean forms adopted by Elijah. The latter continued to refer him to the Master Artificer of the ugly vessel. The inhabitants of the city, who had hastened to do honor to the great Rabbi, earnestly urged the offended man to grant pardon, and finally he declared himself appeased, provided the Rabbi promised never again to commit the same wrong.

The rigor practiced by Elijah toward his friends caused one of them, the Tanna Rabbi Jose, to accuse him of being passionate and irascible. As a consequence, Elijah would have nothing to do with him for a long time. When he reappeared, and confessed the cause of his withdrawal, Rabbi Jose said he felt justified, for his charge could not have received a more striking verification.

INTERCOURSE WITH THE SAGES

Elijah's purely human relations to the world revealed themselves in their fulness, neither in his deeds of charity, nor in his censorious rigor, but rather in his gentle and scholarly intercourse with the great in Israel, especially the learned Rabbis of the Talmudic time. He is at once their disciple and their teacher. To one he resorts for instruction on difficult points, to another he himself dispenses instruction. As a matter of course, his intimate knowledge of the supernatural world makes him appear more frequently in the role of giver than receiver. Many a bit of secret lore the Jewish teachers learnt from Elijah, and he it was who, with the swiftness of lightning, carried the teachings of one Rabbi to another sojourning hundreds of miles away.

Thus it was Elijah who taught Rabbi Jose the deep meaning hidden in the Scriptural passage in which woman is designated as the helpmeet of man. By means of examples he demonstrated to the Rabbi how indispensable woman is to man.

Rabbi Nehorai profited by his exposition of why God created useless, even noxious insects. The reason for their existence is that the sight of superfluous and harmful creatures prevents God from destroying His world at times when, on account of the wickedness and iniquity prevailing in it, it repents Him of having created it. If He preserves creatures that at their best are useless, and at their worst injurious, how much more should He preserve human beings with all their potentialities for good.

The same Rabbi Nehorai was told by Elijah, that God sends earthquakes and other destructive phenomena when He sees places of amusement prosperous and flourishing, while the Temple lies a heap of dust and ashes.

To Rabbi Judah he communicated the following three maxims: Let not anger master thee, and thou wilt not fall into sin; let not drink master thee, and thou wilt be spared pain; before thou settest out on a journey, take counsel with thy Creator.

In case of a difference of opinion among scholars, Elijah was usually questioned as to how the moot point was interpreted in the heavenly academy. Once, when the scholars were not unanimous in their views as to Esther's intentions when she invited Haman to her banquets with the king, Elijah, asked by Rabba bar Abbahu to tell him her real purpose, said that each and every one of the motives attributed to her by various scholars were true, for her invitations to Haman had many a purpose.

A similar answer he gave the Amora Abiathar, who disputed with his colleagues as to why the Ephraimite who cause the war against the tribe of Benjamin first cast off his concubine, and then became reconciled to her. Elijah informed Rabbi Abiathar that in heaven the cruel conduct of the Ephraimite was explained in two ways, according to Abiathar's conception and according to his opponent Jonathan's as well.

Regarding the great contest between Rabbi Eliezer ben Hyrcanus and the whole body of scholars, in which the majority maintained the validity of its opinion, though a heavenly voice pronounced Rabbi Eliezer's correct, Elijah told Rabbi Nathan, that God in His heaven had cried out: "My children have prevailed over Me!"

On one occasion Elijah fared badly for having betrayed celestial events to his scholars. He was a daily attendant at the academy of Rabbi Judah ha-Nasi. One day, it was the New Moon Day, he was late. The reason for his tardiness, he said, was that it was his daily duty to awaken the three Patriarchs, wash their hands for them, so that they might offer up their prayers, and after their devotions lead them back to their resting-places. On this day their prayers took very long, because they were increased by the Musaf service on account of the New Moon celebration, and hence he did not make his appearance at the academy in good time. Elijah did not end his narrative at this point, but went on to tell the Rabbi, that this occupation of his was rather tedious, for the three Patriarchs were not permitted to offer up their payers at the same time. Abraham prayed first, then came Isaac, and finally Jacob. If they all were to pray together, the united petitions of three such paragons of piety would be so efficacious as to force God to fulfil them, and He would be induced to bring the Messiah before his time. Then Rabbi Judah wanted to know whether there were any among the pious on earth whose prayer possessed equal efficacy. Elijah admitted that the same power resided in the prayers of Rabbi Hayyah and his two sons. Rabbi Judah lost no time in proclaiming a day of prayer and fasting and summoning Rabbi Hayyah and his sons to officiate as the leaders in prayer. They began to chant the Eighteen Benedictions. Then they uttered the word for wind, a storm arose; when they continued and made petition for rain, the rain descended at once. But as the readers approached the passage relating to the revival of the dead, great excitement arose in heaven, and when it became known that Elijah had revealed the secret of the marvellous power attaching to the prayers of the three men, he was punished with fiery blows. To thwart Rabbi Judah's purpose, Elijah assumed the form of a bear, and put the praying congregation to flight.

Contrariwise, Elijah was also in the habit of reporting earthly events in the celestial regions. He told Rabba bar Shila that the reason Rabbi Meir was never quoted in the academy on high was because he had had so wicked a teacher as Elisha ben Abuyah. Rabba explained Rabbi Meir's conduct by an apologue. "Rabbi Meir," he said, "found a pomegranate; he enjoyed the heart of the fruit, and cast the skin aside." Elijah was persuaded of the justness of this defense, and so were all the celestial powers. Thereupon one of Rabbi Meir's interpretations was quoted in the heavenly academy.

Elijah was no less interested in the persons of the learned than in their teachings, especially when scholars were to be provided with the means of devoting themselves to their studies. It was he who, when Rabbi Eliezer ben Hyrcanus, later a great celebrity, resolved to devote himself to the law, advised him to repair to Jerusalem and sit at the feet of Rabban Johanan ben Zakkai.

He once met a man who mocked at his exhortations to study, and he said that on the great day of reckoning he would excuse himself for his neglect of intellectual pursuits by the fact that he had been granted neither intelligence nor wisdom. Elijah asked him what his calling was. "I am a fisherman," was the reply. "Well, my son," questioned Elijah, "who taught thee to take flax and make nets and throw them into the sea to catch fish?" He replied: "For this heaven gave me intelligence and insight." Hereupon Elijah: "If thou possessest intelligence and insight to cast nets and catch fish, why should these qualities desert thee when thou dealest with the Torah, which, thou knowest, is very nigh unto man that he may do it?" The fisherman was touched, and he began to weep. Elijah pacified him by telling him that what he had said applied to many another beside him.

In another way Elijah conveyed the lesson of the great value residing in devotion to the study of the Torah. Disguised as a Rabbi, he was approached by a man who promised to relieve him of all material cares if he would but abide with him. Refusing to leave Jabneh, the centre of Jewish scholarship, he said to the tempter: "Wert thou to offer me a thousand million gold denarii, I would not quit the abode of the law, and dwell in a place in which there is no Torah."

By Torah, of course, is meant the law as conceived and interpreted by the sages and the scholars, for Elijah was particularly solicitous to establish the authority of the oral law, as he was solicitous to demonstrate the truth of Scriptural promises that appeared incredible at first sight. For instance, he once fulfilled Rabbi Joshua ben Levi's wish to see the precious stones which would take the place of the sun in illuminating Jerusalem in the Messianic time. A vessel in mid-ocean was nigh unto shipwreck. Among a large number of heathen passengers there was a single Jewish youth. To him Elijah appeared and said, he would rescue the vessel, provided the boy went to Rabbi Joshua ben Levi, and took him to a certain place far removed from the town and from human habitation, and showed him the gems. The boy doubted that so great a man would consent to follow a mere slip of a youth to a remote spot, but, reassured by Elijah, who told him of Rabbi Joshua's extraordinary modesty, he undertook the commission, and the vessel with its human freight was saved. The boy came to the Rabbi, besought him to go whither he would lead, and Joshua, who was really possessed of great modesty, followed the boy three miles without even inquiring the purpose of the expedition. When they finally reached the cave, the boy said: "See, here are the precious stones!" The Rabbi grasped them, and a flood of light spread as far as Lydda, the residence of Rabbi Joshua. Startled, he cast the precious stones away from him, and they disappeared.

This Rabbi was a particular favorite of Elijah, who even secured him an interview with the Messiah. The Rabbi found the Messiah among the crowd of afflicted poor gathered near the city gates of Rome, and he greeted him with the words: "Peace be with thee, my teacher and guide!" Whereunto the Messiah replied: "Peace be with thee, thou son of Levi!" The Rabbi then asked him when he would appear, and the Messiah said, "To-day." Elijah explained to the Rabbi later that what the Messiah meant by "to-day" was, that he for his part was ready to bring Israel redemption at any time. If Israel but showed himself worthy, he would instantly fufil his mission.

Elijah wanted to put Rabbi Joshua into communication with the departed Rabbi Simon ben Yohai also, but the later did not consider him of sufficient importance to honor him with his conversation. Rabbi Simon had addressed a question to him, and Rabbi Joshua in his modesty had made a reply not calculated to give one a high opinion of him. In reality Rabbi Joshua was the possessor of such sterling qualities, that when he entered Paradise Elijah walked before him calling out: "Make room for the son of Levi."

GOD'S JUSTICE VINDICATED

Among the many and various teachings dispensed by Elijah to his friends, there are none so important as his theodicy, the teachings vindicating God's justice in the administration of earthly affairs. He used many an opportunity to demonstrate it by precept and example. Once he granted his friend Rabbi Joshua ben Levi the fulfilment of any wish he might express, and all the Rabbi asked for was, that he might be permitted to accompany Elijah on his wanderings through the world. Elijah was prepared to gratify this wish. He only imposed the condition, that, however odd the Rabbi might think Elijah's actions, he was not to ask any explanation of them. If ever he demanded why, they would have to part company. So Elijah and the Rabbi fared forth together, and they journeyed on until they reached the house of a poor man, whose only earthly possession was a cow. The man and his wife were thoroughly good-hearted people, and they received the two wanderers with a cordial welcome. They invited the strangers into their house, set before them food and drink of the best they had, and made up a comfortable couch for them for the night. When Elijah and the Rabbi were ready to continue their journey on the following day, Elijah prayed that the cow belonging to his host might die. Before they left the house, the animal had expired. Rabbi Joshua was so shocked by the misfortune that had befallen the good people, he almost lost consciousness. He thought: "Is that to be the poor man's reward for all his kind services to us?" And he could not refrain from putting the question to Elijah. But Elijah reminded him of the condition imposed and accepted at the beginning of their journey, and they travelled on, the Rabbi's curiosity unappeased. That night they reached the house of a wealthy man, who did not pay his guest the courtesy of looking them in the face. Though they passed the night under his roof, he did not offer them food or drink. This rich man was desirous of having a wall repaired that had tumbled down. There was no need for him to take any steps to have it rebuilt, for, when Elijah left the house, he prayed that the wall might erect itself, and, lo! it stood upright. Rabbi Joshua was greatly amazed, but true to his promise he suppressed the question that rose to his lips. So the two travelled on again, until they reached an ornate synagogue, the seats in which were made of silver and gold. But the worshippers did not correspond in character to the magnificence of the building, for when it came to the point of satisfying the needs of the way-worn pilgrims, one of those present said: "There is not dearth of water and bread, and the strange travellers can stay in the synagogue, whither these refreshments can be brought to them." Early the next morning, when they were departing, Elijah wished those present in the synagogue in which they had lodged, that God might raise them all to be "heads." Rabbi Joshua again had to exercise great self-restraint, and not put into words the question that troubled him profoundly. In the next town, they were received with great affability, and served abundantly with all their tired bodies craved. On these kind hosts Elijah, on leaving, bestowed the wish that God might give them but a single head. Now the Rabbi could not hold himself in check any longer, and he demanded an explanation of Elijah's freakish actions. Elijah consented to clear up his conduct for Joshua before they separated from each other. He spoke as follows: "The poor man's cow was killed, because I knew that on the same day the death of his wife had been ordained in heaven, and I prayed to God to accept the loss of the poor man's property as a substitute for the poor man's wife. As for the rich man, there was a treasure hidden under the dilapidated wall, and, if he had rebuilt it, he would have found the gold; hence I set up the wall miraculously in order to deprive the curmudgeon of the valuable find. I wished that the inhospitable people assembled in the synagogue might have many heads, for a place of numerous leaders is bound to be ruined by reason of multiplicity of counsel and disputes. To the inhabitants of our last sojourning place, on the other hand, I wished a 'single head,' for the one to guide a town, success will attend all its undertakings. Know, then, that if thou seest an evil-doer prosper, it is not always unto his advantage, and if a righteous man suffers need and distress, think not God is unjust." After these words Elijah and Rabbi Joshua separated from each other, and each went his own way.

How difficult it is to form a true judgment with nothing but external appearances as a guide, Elijah proved to Rabbi Baroka. They were once waling in a crowded street, and the Rabbi requested Elijah to point out any in the throng destined to occupy places in Paradise. Elijah answered that there was none, only to contradict himself and point to a passer-by the very next minute. His appearance was such that in him least of all the Rabbi would have suspected a pious man. His garb did not even indicate that he was a Jew. Later Rabbi Baroka discovered by questioning him that he was a prison guard. In the fulfilment of his duties as such he was particularly careful that the virtue of chastity should not be violated in the prison, in which both men women were kept in detention. Also, his position often brought him into relations with the heathen authorities, and so he was enabled to keep the Jews informed of the disposition entertained toward them by the powers that be. The Rabbi was thus taught that no station in life precluded its occupant from doing good and acting nobly.

Another time Elijah designated two men to whom a great future was assigned in Paradise. Yet these men were nothing more than clowns! They made it their purpose in life to dispel discontent and sorrow by their jokes and their cheery humor, and they used the opportunities granted by their profession to adjust the difficulties and quarrels that disturb the harmony of people living in close contact with each other.

ELIJAH AND THE ANGEL OF DEATH

Among the many benevolent deeds of Elijah, special mention ought to be made of his rescue of those doomed by a heavenly decree to fall into the clutches of the Angel of Death. He brought these rescues about by warning the designated victims of their impending fate, and urging them to do good deeds, which would prove protection against death.

There was once a pious and rich man with a beautiful and saintly daughter. She had had the misfortune of losing three husbands in succession, each on the day after the wedding. These sorrows determined her never again to enter into the marriage state. A cousin of hers, the nephew of her father, induced by the poverty of his parents, journeyed from his distant home to apply for help to his rich uncle. Scarcely had he laid eyes upon his lovely cousin when he fell victim to her charms. In vain her father sought to dissuade his nephew from marrying his daughter. But the fate of his predecessors did not affright him, and the wedding took place. While he was standing under the wedding canopy, Elijah came to him in the guise of an old man, and said: "My son, I want to give thee a piece of advice. While thou are seated at the wedding dinner, thou wilt be approached by a ragged, dirty beggar, with hair like nails. As soon as thou catchest sight of him, hasten to seat him beside thee, set food and drink before him, and be ready to grant whatever he may ask of thee. Do as I say, and thou wilt be protected against harm. Now I shall leave thee and go my way." At the wedding feast, a stranger as described by Elijah appeared, and the bridegroom did according to Elijah's counsel. After the wedding the stranger revealed his identity, introducing himself as the messenger of the Lord sent to take the young husband's life. The supplications of the bridegroom failed to move him; he refused to grant a single day's respite. All he yielded was permission to the young husband to bid farewell to his newly-wed wife. When the bride saw that what she had feared was coming to pass, she repaired to the Angel of Death and argued with him: "The Torah distinctly exempts the newly-wed from all duties for a whole year. If thou deprivest my husband of life, thou wilt give the lie to the Torah." Thereupon God commanded the Angel of Death to desist, and, when the relatives of the bride came to prepare the grave of the groom, they found him well and unharmed.

A similar thing befell the son of the great and extremely pious scholar Rabbi Reuben. To him came the Angel of Death and announced that his only son would have to die. The pious man was resigned: "We mortals can do nothing to oppose a Divine decree," he said, "but I pray there, give him thirty days' respite, that I may see him married." The Angel of Death acquiesced. The Rabbi told no one of this encounter, waited until the appointed time was drawing to a close, and, on the very last day, the thirtieth, he arranged his son's wedding feast. On that day, the bridegroom-to-be met Elijah, who told him of his approaching death. A worthy son of his father, he said: "Who may oppose God? And am I better than Abraham, Isaac, and Jacob? They, too, had to die." Elijah told him furthermore, that the Angel of Death would appear to him in the guise of a ragged, dirty beggar, and he advised him to receive him in the kindliest possible manner, and in particular he was to insist upon his taking food and drink from him. All happened as Elijah had predicted, and his advice, too, proved efficacious, for the heart of the Angel of Death, who finally revealed his identity with the beggar, was softened by the entreaties of the father, combined with the tears of the young wife, who resorted to the argument cited above, of the year of exemption from duty granted to the newly-married. The Angel of Death, disarmed by the amiable treatment accorded to him, himself went before the throne of God and presented the young wife's petition. The end was God added seventy years to the life of Rabbi Reuben's son.

TEACHER OF THE KABBALAH

The frequent meetings between Elijah and the teachers of the law of the Talmudic time were invested with personal interest only. Upon the development of the Torah they had no influence whatsoever. His relation to the mystic science was of quite other character. It is safe to say that what Moses was to the Torah, Elijah was to the Kabbalah.

His earliest relation to it was established through Rabbi Simon ben Yohai and his son Rabbi Eliezer. For thirteen years he visited them twice daily in their subterranean hiding-place, and imparted the secrets of the Torah to them. A thousand years later, Elijah again gave the impetus to the development of the Kabbalah, for it was he that revealed mysteries, first to the Nazarite Rabbi Jacob, then to his disciple of the latter, Abraham ben David. The mysteries in the books "Peliah" and "Kanah," the author Elkanah owed wholly to Elijah. He had appeared to him in the form of a venerable old man, and had imparted to him the secret lore taught in the heavenly academy. Besides, he led him to a fiery rock whereon mysterious characters were engraved, which were deciphered by Elkanah.

After his disciple had thus become thoroughly impregnated with mystical teachings, Elijah took him to the tomb of the Patriarchs, and thence to the heavenly academy. But the angels, little pleased by the intrusion of one "born of woman," inspired him with such terror that he besought Elijah to carry him back to earth. His mentor allayed his fears, and long continued to instruct him in the mystical science, according to the system his disciple has recorded in his two works.

The Kabbalists in general were possessed of the power to cite Elijah, to conjure him up by means of certain formulas. One of them, Rabbi Joseph della Reyna, once called upon Elijah in this way, but it proved his own undoing. He was a saintly scholar, and he had conceived no less a purpose than to bring about the redemption of man by the conquest of the angel Samael, the Prince of Evil. After many prayers and vigils and long indulgence in fasting, and other ascetic practices, Rabbi Joseph united himself with his five disciples for the purpose of conjuring up Elijah. When the prophet, obeying the summons, suddenly stood before him, Rabbi Joseph spoke as follows: "Peace be with thee, our master! True prophet, bearer of salvation, be not displeased with me that I have troubled thee to come hither. God knows, I have not done it for myself, and not for mine own honor. I am zealous for the name and the honor of God, and I know thy desire is the same as mine, for it is thy vocation to make the glory of God to prevail on earth. I pray thee, therefore, to grant my petition, tell me with what means I can conquer Satan." Elijah at first endeavored to dissuade the Rabbi from his enterprise. He described the great power of Satan, ever growing as it feeds upon the sins of mankind. But Rabbi Joseph could not be made to desist. Elijah then enumerated what measures and tactics he would have to observe in his combat with the fallen angel. He enumerated the pious, saintly deeds that would win the interest of the archangel Sandalphon in his undertaking, and from this angel he would learn the method of warfare to be pursued. The Rabbi followed out Elijah's directions carefully, and succeeded in summoning Sandalphon to his assistance. If he had continued to obey instructions implicitly, and had carried out all Sandalphon advised, the Rabbi would have triumphed over Satan and hastened the redemption of the world. Unfortunately, at one point the Rabbi committed an indiscretion, and he lost the great advantages he had gained over Satan, who used his restored power to bring ruin upon him and his disciples.

The radical transformation in the character of Kabbalistic teaching which is connected with the name of Rabbi Isaac Loria likewise is an evidence of Elijah's activity. Elijah sought out this "father of the Kabbalistic Renaissance," and revealed the mysteries of the universe to him. Indeed, he had shown his interest in him long before any one suspected the future greatness of Rabbi Isaac. Immediately after his birth, Elijah appeared to the father of the babe, and enjoined him not to have the rite of circumcision performed until he should be told by Elijah to proceed. The eighth day of the child's life arrived, to witness the solemn ceremonial, but to the great astonishment of his fellow-townsmen the father delayed it. The people naturally did not know he was waiting for Elijah to appear, and he was called upon once and again to have the ceremony take place. But he did not permit the impatience of the company to turn him from his purpose. Suddenly, Elijah, unseen, of course, by the others, appeared to him, and bade him have the ceremony performed. Those present were under the impression that the father was holding the child on his knees during the circumcision; in reality, however it was Elijah. After the rite was completed, Elijah handed the infant back to the father with the words: "Here is thy child. Take good care of it, for it will spread a brilliant light over the world."

It was also Elijah who in a similar way informed Rabbit Eliezer, the father of Rabbi Israel Baal Shem Tob, the father of him whose name is unrivalled in the annals of the Hasidic Kabbalah that a son would be born to him who should enlighten the eyes of Israel. This Rabbi Eliezer was justly reputed to be very hospitable. He was in the habit of stationing guards at the entrances to the village in which he lived, and they were charged to bring all strangers to his house. In heaven it was ordained that Rabbi Eliezer's hospitable instincts should be put to a test. Elijah was chosen for the experiment. On a Sabbath afternoon, arrayed in the garb of a beggar, he entered the village with knapsack and staff. Rabbi Eliezer, taking no notice of the fact that the beggar was desecrating the Sabbath, received him kindly, attended to his bodily wants, and the next morning, on parting with him, gave him some money besides. Touched by his kind-heartedness, Elijah revealed his identity and the purpose of his disguise, and told him that, as he had borne the trial so well, he would be rewarded by the birth of a son who should "enlighten the eyes of Israel."

FORERUNNER OF THE MESSIAH

Many-sided though Elijah's participation in the course of historical events is, it cannot be compared with what he is expected to do in the days of the Messiah. He is charged with the mission of ordering the coming time aright and restoring the tribes of Jacob. His Messianic activity thus is to be twofold: he is to be the forerunner of the Messiah, yet in part he will himself realize the promised scheme of salvation. His first task will be to induce Israel to repent when the Messiah is about to come, and to establish peace and harmony in the world. Hence he will have to settle all legal difficulties, and solve all legal problems, that have accumulated since days immemorial, and decide vexed questions of ritual concerning which authors entertain contradictory views. In short, all difference of opinion must be removed from the path of the Messiah. This office of expounder of the law Elijah will continue to occupy even after the reign of peace has been established on earth, and his relation to Moses will be the same Aaron once held.

Elijah's preparatory work will be begun three days before the advent of the Messiah. Then he will appear in Palestine, and will utter a lament over the devastation of the Holy Land, and his wail will be heard throughout the world. The last words of his elegy will be: "Now peace will come upon earth!" When the evildoers hear this message, they will rejoice. On the second day, he will appear again and proclaim: "Good will come upon earth!" And on the third his promise will be heard: "Salvation will come upon earth." Then Michael will blow the trumpet, and once more Elijah will make his appearance, this time to introduce the Messiah. To make sure of the identity of the Messiah, the Jews will demand that he perform the miracle of resurrection before their eyes, reviving such of the dead as they had known personally. But the Messiah will do the following seven wonders: He will bring Moses and the generation of the desert to life; Korah and his band he will raise from out of the earth; he will revive the Ephraimitic Messiah, who was slain; he will show the three holy vessels of the Temple, the Ark, the flask of manna, and the cruse of sacred oil, all three of which disappeared mysteriously; he will wave the sceptre given him by God; he will grind the mountains of the Holy Land into powder like straw, and he will reveal the secret of redemption. Then the Jews will believe that Elijah is the Elijah promised to them, and the Messiah introduced by him is the true Messiah.

The Messiah will have Elijah blow the trumpet, and, at the first sound, the primal light, which shone before the week of Creation, will reappear; at the second sound the dead will arise, and with the swiftness of wind assemble around the Messiah from all corners of the earth; at the third sound, the Shekinah will become visible to all; the mountains will be razed at the fourth sound, and the Temple will stand in complete perfection as Ezekiel described it.

During the reign of peace, Elijah will be one of the eight princes forming the cabinet of the Messiah. Even the coming of the great judgment day will not end his activity. On that day the children of the wicked who had to die in infancy on account of the sins of their fathers will be found among the just, while their fathers will be ranged on the other side. The babes will implore their fathers to come to them, but God will not permit it. Then Elijah will go to the little ones, and teach them how to plead in behalf of their fathers. They will stand before God and say: "Is not the measure of good, the mercy of God, larger than the measure of chastisements? If, then, we died for the sins of our fathers, should they not now for our sakes be granted the good, and be permitted to join us in Paradise?" God will give assent to their pleadings, and Elijah will have fulfilled the word of the prophet Malachi; he will have brought back the fathers to the children.

The last act of Elijah's brilliant career will be the execution of God's command to slay Samael, and so banish evil forever.

VIII. ELISHA AND JONAH

ELISHA THE DISCIPLE OF ELIJAH

THE voices of the thousands of prophets of his time were stilled when Elijah was translated from earth to heaven. With him vanished the prophetical spirit of those who in former times had in no wise been his inferiors. Elisha was the only one among them whose prophetical powers were not diminished. On the contrary, they were strengthened, as a reward for the unhesitating readiness with which he obeyed Elijah's summons, and parted with the field he was ploughing, and with all else he possessed, in favor of the community. Thenceforward he remained Elijah's unwearying companion. When the angel descended from heaven to take Elijah from earth, he found the two so immersed in a learned discussion that he could not attract their attention, and he had to return, his errand unfulfilled.

Elijah's promise to bestow a double portion of his wondrous spirit upon his disciple was realized instantaneously. During his life Elisha performed sixteen miracles, and eight was all his master had performed. The first of them, the crossing of the Jordan, was more remarkable than the corresponding wonder done by Elijah, for Elisha traversed the river alone, and Elijah had been accompanied by Elisha. Two saints always have more power than one by himself.

His second miracle, the "healing" of the waters of Jericho, so that they became fit to drink, resulted in harm to himself, for the people who had earned their livelihood by the sale of wholesome water were very much incensed against the prophet for having spoiled their trade. Elisha, whose prophetic powers enabled him to read both the past and the future of these tradesmen, knew that they , their ancestors, and their posterity had "not even the aroma of good about them." Therefore he cursed them. Suddenly a forest sprang up and the bears that infested it devoured the murmuring traders. The wicked fellows were not undeserving of the punishment they received, yet Elisha was made to undergo a very serious sickness, by way of correction for having yielded to passion. In this he resembled his master Elijah; he allowed wrath and zeal to gain the mastery over him. God desired that the two great prophets might be purged of this fault. Accordingly, when Elisha rebuked King Jehoram of Israel, the spirit of prophecy forsook him, and he had to resort to artificial means to re-awaken it within himself.

Like his teacher, Elisha was always ready to help the poor and needy, as witness his sympathy with the widow of one of the sons of the prophets, and the effective aid he extended to her. Her husband had been none other than Obadiah, who, though a prophet, had at the same time been one of the highest officials at the court of the sinful king Ahab. By birth an Edomite, Obadiah had been inspired by God to utter the prophecy against Edom. In his own person he embodied the accusation against Esau, who had lived with his pious parents without following their example, while Obadiah, on the contrary, lived in constant intercourse with the iniquitous King Ahab and his still more iniquitous spouse Jezebel without yielding to the baneful influence they exercised. This same Obadiah not only used his own fortune, but went to the length of borrowing money on interest from the future king, in order to have the wherewithal to support the prophets who were in hiding. On his death, the king sought to hold the children responsible for the debt of the father. In her despair the pious wife of Obadiah went to the graveyard, and there she cried out: "O thou God-fearing man!" At once a heavenly voice was heard questioning her: "There are four God-fearing men, Abraham, Joseph, Job, and Obadiah. To which of them does thou desire to speak?" "To him of whom it is said, 'He feared the Lord greatly.'"

She was led to the grave of the prophet Obadiah, where she poured out the tale of her sorrow. Obadiah told her to take the small remnant of oil she still had to the prophet Elisha and request him to intercede for him with God, "for God," he said, "is my debtor, seeing that I provided a hundred prophets, not only with bread and water, but also with oil to illuminate their hiding-place, for do not the Scriptures say: 'He that hath pity upon the poor lendeth unto the Lord'?" Forthwith the woman carried out his behest. She went to Elisha, and he helped her by making her little cruse of oil fill vessels upon vessels without number, and when the vessels gave out, she fetched potsherds, saying, "May the will that made empty vessels full, make broken vessels perfect." So it was. The oil ceased to flow only when the supply of potsherds as well as vessels gave out. In her piety the woman wanted to pay her tithe-offering, but Elisha was of the opinion that, as the oil had been bestowed upon her miraculously, she could keep it wholly and entirely for her own use. Furthermore, Elisha reassured her as to the power of the royal princes to do her harm: "The God who will close the jaws of the lions set upon Daniel, and who did close the jaws of the dogs in Egypt, the same God will blind the eyes of the sons of Ahab, and deafen their ears, so that they can do thee no harm." Not only was the poor widow helped out of her difficulties, her descendants unto all times were provided for. The oil rose in price, and it yielded so much profit that they never suffered want.

THE SHUNAMMITE

The great woman of Shunem, the sister of Abishag and wife of the prophet Iddo, also had cause to be deeply grateful to Elisha. When Elisha came to Shunem on his journey through the land of Israel, his holiness made a profound impression upon the Shunammite. Indeed, the prophet's eye was so awe-inspiring that now woman could look him in the face and live. Contrary to the habit of most women, who are intent upon diminishing their expenses and their toil, the Shunammite took delight in the privilege of welcoming the prophet to her house as a guest. She observed that not even a fly dared approach close to the holy man, and a grateful fragrance exhaled from his person. "If he were not so great a saint," she said, "and the holiness of the Lord did not invest him, there were no such pleasant fragrance about him." That he might be undisturbed, she assigned the best chambers in the house to the prophet. He on his part, desiring to show his appreciation of her hospitality, knew no better return for her kindness than to promise that she should be blessed with a child within a year. The woman protested: "O, my husband is an old man, nor am I of an age to bear children; the promise cannot be fulfilled." Yet it happened as the prophet had foretold. Before a twelvemonth had passed, she was a mother.

A few years later her child died a sudden death. The mother repaired to the prophet, and lamented before him: "O that the vessel had remained empty, rather than it should be filled first, and then be left void." The prophet admitted that, though as a rule he was acquainted with all things that were to happen, God had left him in the dark about the misfortune that had befallen her. With trust in God, he gave his staff to his disciple Gehazi, and sent him to bring the boy back to life. But Gehazi was unworthy of his master. His conduct toward the Shunammite was not becoming a disciple of the prophet, and, above all, he had no faith in the possibility of accomplishing the mission entrusted to him. Instead of obeying the behest of Elisha, not to speak a word on his way to the child of the Shunammite, Gehazi made sport of the task laid upon him. To whatever man he met he addressed the questions: "Dost thou suppose this staff can bring the dead back to life?" The result was that he forfeited the power of executing the errand with which he had been charged. Elisha himself had to perform the miracle. The prophet uttered the prayer: "O Lord of the world! As Thou didst wonders through my master Elijah, and didst permit him to bring the dead to life, so, I pray Thee, do Thou perform a wonder through me, and let me restore life to this lad." The prayer was granted, and the child was revived. The act of the prophet proves the duty of gratitude in return for hospitality. Elisha did not attempt to resuscitate his own kith and kin who had been claimed by death; he invoked a miracle for the sake of the woman who had welcomed him kindly to her house.

GEHAZI

Gehazi, proved untrustworthy by his conduct on this occasion, again aroused the ire of the prophet when he disregarded the order not to accept money from Naaman, the Syrian captain. He did not succeed in deceiving the prophet. On his return from Naaman he found Elisha occupied with the study of the chapter in the Mishnah Shabbat which deals with the eight reptiles. The prophet Elisha greeted him with the rebuke: "Thou villain! the time has come for me to be rewarded for the study of the Mishnah about the eight reptiles. May my reward be that the disease of Naaman afflict thee and thy descendants for evermore." Scarcely had these words escaped his lips, when he saw the leprosy come out on Gehazi's face. Gehazi deserved the punishment on account of his base character. He was sensual and envious, and did not believe in the resurrection of the dead. His unworthy qualities were displayed in his conduct toward the Shunammite and toward the disciples of Elisha. When the pretty Shunammite came to the prophet in her grief over the death of her child, Gehazi took her passionately in his arms, under the pretext of forcing her away from the prophet, on whom she had laid hold in her supplications.

As for the other disciples of Elisha, he endeavored to keep them away from the house of the prophet. He was in the habit of standing without the door. This induced many to turn away and go home, for they reasoned that, if the house were not full to overflowing, Gehazi would not be standing outside. Only after Gehazi's dismissal did the disciples of Elisha increase marvellously. That Gehazi had no faith in the resurrection of the dead, is shown by his incredulity with regard to the child of the Shunammite.

In spite of all these faults, Elisha regretted that he had cast off his disciple, who was a great scholar in the law, especially as Gehazi abandoned himself to a sinful life after leaving the prophet. By means of magnetism he made the golden calves at Beth-el float in the air, and many were brought to believe in the divinity of these idols. Moreover, he engraved the great and awful Name of God in their mouth. Thus they were enabled to speak, and they gave forth the same words God had proclaimed from Sinai: "I am the Lord thy God Thou shalt have no other gods before Me." Elisha accordingly repaired to Damascus to lead Gehazi back to the paths of righteousness. But he remained impenitent, for he said: "From thyself I have learned that there is no return for him who not only sins himself, but also induces others to sin." So Gehazi died without having done aught to atone for his transgressions, which were so great that he is one of the few Jews who have no share in Paradise. His children inherited his leprosy. He and his three sons are the four leprous men who informed the king of Israel of the precipitate flight of the Syrian host.

Elisha's excessive severity toward his servant Gehazi and toward the mocking boys of Jericho did not go unpunished. He had to endure two periods of disease, and the third sickness that befell him cause his death. He is the first known to history who survived a sickness. Before him death had been the inevitable companion of disease. A great miracle marked the end of a life rich in miraculous deeds: a dead man revived at the touch of Elisha's bier, and stood on his feet. It was a worthy character for whom the wonder was accomplished Shallum the son of Tikvah, the husband of Huldah the prophetess, a man of noble descent, who had led a life of lovingkindness. He was in the habit of going daily beyond the city bearing the pitcher of water, from which he gave every traveller to drink, a good deed that received a double reward. His wife became a prophetess, and when he died and his funeral, attended by a large concourse of people, was disturbed by the invasion of the Arameans, he was given new life by contact with the bones of Elisha. He lived to have a son, Hanamel by name.

The death of Elisha was a great misfortune for the Israelites. So long as he was alive, no Aramean troops entered Palestine. The first invasion by them happened on the day of his burial.

THE FLIGHT OF JONAH

Among the many thousands of disciples whom Elisha gathered about him during the sixty years and more of his activity, the most prominent was the prophet Jonah. While the master was still alive, Jonah was charged with the important mission of anointing Jehu king. The next task laid upon him was to proclaim their destruction to the inhabitants of Jerusalem. The doom did not come to pass, because they repented of their wrong-doing, and God had mercy upon them. Among the Israelites Jonah was, therefore, known as "the false prophet." When he was sent to Nineveh to prophesy the downfall of the city, he reflected: "I know to a certainly that the heathen will do penance, the threatened punishment will not be executed, and among the heathen, too, I shall gain the reputation of being a false prophet." To escape this disgrace, he determined to take up his abode on the sea, where there were none to whom prophecies never to be fulfilled would have to be delivered.

On his arrival at Joppa, there was no vessel in port. To try him, God cause a storm to arise, and it carried a vessel back to Joppa, which had made a two days' journey away from the harbor. The prophet interpreted this chance to mean that God approved his plan. He was so rejoiced at the favorable opportunity for leaving land that he paid the whole amount for the entire cargo in advance, no less a sum than four thousand gold denarii. After a day's sailing out from shore, a terrific storm broke loose. Wonderful to relate, it injured no vessel but Jonah's. Thus he was taught the lesson that God is Lord over heaven and earth and sea, and man can hide himself nowhere from His face.

On the same vessel were representatives of the seventy nations of the earth, each with his peculiar idols. They all resolved to entreat their gods for succor, and the god from whom help would come should be recognized and worshipped at the only one true God. But help came from none. Then it was that the captain of the vessel approached Jonah where he lay asleep, and said to him: "We are suspended 'twixt life and death, and thou liest here asleep. Pray, tell me, to what nation dost thou belong?" "I am a Hebrew," replied Jonah. "We have heard," said the captain, "that the God of the Hebrews is the most powerful. Cry to Him for help. Perhaps He will perform such miracles for us as He did in days of old for the Jews at the Red Sea."

Jonah confessed to the captain that he was to blame for the whole misfortune, and he besought him to cast him adrift, and appease the storm. The other passengers refused to consent to so cruel an act. Though the lot decided against Jonah, they first tried to save the vessel by throwing the cargo overboard. Their efforts were in vain. Then they placed Jonah at the side of the vessel and spoke: "O Lord of the world, reckon this not up against us as innocent blood, for we know not the case of this man, and he himself bids us throw him into the sea." Even then they could not make up their minds to let him drown. First they immersed him up to his knees in the water of the sea, and the storm ceased; they drew him back into the vessel, and forthwith the storm raged in its old fury. Two more trials they made. They lowered him into the water up to his navel, and raised him out of the depths when the storm was assuaged. Again, when the storm broke out anew, they lowered him to his neck, and a second time they took him back into the vessel when the wind subsided. But finally the renewed rage of the storm convinced them that their danger was due to Jonah's transgressions, and they abandoned him to his fate. He was thrown into the water, and on the instant the sea grew calm.

JONAH IN THE WHALE

At the creation of the world, God made a fish intended to harbor Jonah. He as so large that the prophet was as comfortable inside of him as in a spacious synagogue. The eyes of the fish served Jonah as windows, and, besides, there was a diamond, which shone as brilliantly as the sun at midday, so that Jonah could see all things in the sea down to its very bottom.

It is a law that when their time has come, all the fish of the sea must betake themselves to leviathan, and let the monster devour them. The life term of Jonah's fish was about to expire, and the fish warned Jonah of what was to happen. When he, with Jonah in his belly, came to leviathan, the prophet said to the monster: "For thy sake I came hither. It was meet that I should know thine abode, for it is my appointed task to capture thee in the life to come and slaughter thee for the table of the just and pious." When leviathan observed the sign of the covenant on Jonah's body, he fled affrighted, and Jonah and the fish were saved. To show his gratitude, the fish carried Jonah whithersoever there was a sight to be seen. He showed him the river from which the ocean flows, showed him the spot at which the Israelites crossed the Red Sea, showed him Gehenna and Sheol, and many other mysterious and wonderful place.

Three days Jonah had spent in the belly of the fish, and he still felt so comfortable that he did not think of imploring God to change his condition. But God sent a female fish big with three hundred and sixty-five thousand little fish to Jonah's host, to demand the surrender of the prophet, else she would swallow both him and the guest he harbored. The message was received with incredulity, and leviathan had to come and corroborate it; he himself had heard God dispatch the female fish on her errand. So it came about that Jonah was transferred to another abode. His new quarters, which he had to share with all the little fish, were far from comfortable, and from the bottom of his heart a prayer for deliverance arose to God on high. The last words of his long petition were, "I shall redeem my vow," whereupon God commanded the fish to spew Jonah out. At a distance of nine hundred and sixty-five parasangs from the fish he alighted on dry land. These miracles induced the ship's crew to abandon idolatry, and they all became pious proselytes in Jerusalem.

THE REPENTANCE OF NINEVEH

Jonah went straightway to Nineveh, the monster city covering forty square parasangs and containing a million and half of human beings. He lost no time in proclaiming their destruction to the inhabitants. The voice of the prophet was so sonorous that it reached to every corner of the great city, and all who heard his words resolved to turn aside from their ungodly ways. At the head of the penitents was King Osnappar of Assyria. He descended from his throne, removed his crown, strewed ashes on his head instead, took off his purple garments, and rolled about in the dust of the highways. In all the streets royal heralds proclaimed the king's decree bidding the inhabitants fast three days, wear sackcloth, and supplicate God with tears and prayers to avert the threatened doom. The people of Nineveh fairly compelled to God's mercy to descend upon them. They held their infants heavenward, and amid streaming tears they cried: "For the sake of these innocent babes, hear our prayers." The young of their stalled cattle they separated from the mother beasts, the young were left within the stable, the old were put without. So parted from one another, the young and the old began to bellow aloud. Then the Ninevites cried: "If Thou wilt not have mercy upon us, we will not have mercy upon these beasts."

The penance of the Ninevites did not stop at fasting and praying. Their deeds showed that they had determined to lead a better life. If a man had usurped another's property, he sought to make amends for his iniquity; some went so far as to destroy their palaces in order to be able to give back a single brick to the rightful owner. Of their own accord others appeared before the courts of justice, and confessed their secret crimes and sins, known to none beside themselves, and declared themselves ready to submit to well-merited punishment, though it be death that was decreed against them.

One incident that happened at the time will illustrate the contrition of the Ninevites. A man found a treasure in the building lot he had acquired from his neighbor. Both buyer and seller refused to assume possession of the treasure. The seller insisted that the sale of the lot carried with it the sale of all it contained. The buyer held that he had bought the ground, not the treasure hidden therein.

Neither rested satisfied until the judge succeeded in finding out who had hidden the treasure and where were his heirs, and the joy of the two was great when they could deliver the treasure up to its legitimate owners. Seeing that the Ninevites had undergone a real change of heart, God took mercy upon them, and pardoned them. Thereupon Jonah likewise felt encouraged to plead for himself with God, that He forgive him for his flight. God spoke to him: "Thou wast mindful of Mine honor," the prophet had not wanted to appear a liar, so that men's trust in God might not be shaken "and for this reason thou didst take to sea. Therefore did I deal mercifully with thee, and rescue thee from the bowels of Sheol."

His sojourn in the inside of the fish the prophet could not easily dismiss from his mind, nor did it remain without visible consequences. The intense heat in the belly of the fish had consumed his garments, and made his hair fall out, and he was sore plagued by swarms of insects. To afford Jonah protection, God caused the kikayon to grow up. When he opened his eyes one morning, he saw a plant with two hundred and seventy-five leaves, each leaf measuring more than a span, so that it afforded relief from the heat of the sun. But the sun smote the gourd that it withered, and Jonah was again annoyed by the insects. He began to weep and wish for death to release him from his troubles. But when God led him to the plant, and showed him what lesson he might derive from it, how, though he had not labored for the plant, he had pity on it, he realized his wrong in desiring God to be relentless toward Nineveh, the great city, with its many inhabitants, rather than have his reputation as a prophet suffer taint. He prostrated himself and said: "O God, guide the world according to Thy goodness."

God was gracious to the people of Nineveh so long as they continued worthy of His lovingkindness. But at the end of forty days they departed from the path of piety, and they became more sinful than ever. Then the punishment threatened by Jonah overtook them, and they were swallowed up by the earth.

Jonah's suffering in the watery abyss had been so severe that by way of compensation of God exempted him from death: living he was permitted to enter Paradise. Like Jonah, his wife was known far and wide for her piety. She had gained fame particularly through her pilgrimage to Jerusalem, a duty which, by reason of her sex, she was not obliged to fulfil. On one of these pilgrimages it was that the prophetical spirit first descended upon Jonah.

IX. THE LATER KINGS OF JUDAH

JOASH

WHEN the prophet Jonah, doing the behest of his master Elisha, anointed Jehu king over Israel, he poured the oil out of a pitcher, not out of a horn, to indicate that the dynasty of Jehu would not occupy the throne long. At first Jehu, though a somewhat foolish king, was at least pious, but he abandoned his God-fearing ways from the moment he saw the document bearing the signature of the prophet Ahijah of Shilo, which bound the signers to pay implicit obedience to Jeroboam. The king took this as evidence that the prophet had approved the worship of the golden calves. So it came to pass that Jehu, the destroyer of Baal worship, did nothing to oppose the idolatrous service established by Jeroboam at Beth-el. The successors of Jehu were not better; on the contrary, they were worse, and therefore in the fifth generation an end was put to the dynasty of Jehu by the hand of the assassin.

The kings of Judah differed in no essential particular from their colleagues in the north. Ahaziah, whom Jehu killed, was a shameless sinner; he had the Name of God expurged from every passage in which it occurred in the Holy Scriptures, and the names of idols inserted in its place.

Upon the death of Ahaziah followed the reign of terror under the queen Athaliah, when God exacted payment from the house of David for his trespass in connection with the extermination of the priest at Nob. As Abiathar had been the only male descendant of Abimelech to survive the persecution of Saul, so the sole representative of the house of David to remain after the sword of Athaliah had raged was Joash, the child kept in hiding, in the Holy of Holies in the Temple, by the high priest Jehoiada and his wife Jehosheba. Later Jehoiada vindicated the right of Joash upon the throne, and installed him as king of Judah. The very crown worn by the rulers of the house of David testified to the legitimacy of the young prince, for it possessed the peculiarity of fitting none but the rightful successors to David.

At the instigation of Jehoiada, King Joash undertook the restoration of the Temple. The work was completed so expeditiously that one living at the time the Temple was erected by Solomon was permitted to see the new structure shortly before his death. This good fortune befell Jehoiada himself, the son of Benaiah, commander-in-chief of the army under Solomon. So long as Joash continued under the tutelage of Jehoiada, he was a pious king. When Jehoiada departed this life, the courtiers came to Joash and flattered him: "If thou wert not a god, thou hadst not been able to abide for six years in the Holy of Holies, a spot which even the high priest is permitted to enter but once a year." The king lent ear to their blandishments, and permitted the people to pay him Divine homage. But when the folly of the king went to the extreme of prompting him to set up an idol in the Temple, Zechariah, the son of Jehoiada, placed himself at the entrance, and barring the way said: "Thou shalt not do it so long as I live." High priest, prophet, and judge though Zechariah was, and son-in-law of Joash to boot, the king still did not shrink from having him killed for his presumptuous words, not was he deterred by the fact that it happened on a Day of Atonement which fell on the Sabbath. The innocent blood crimsoning the hall of the priests did not remain unavenged. For two hundred and fifty-two years it did not leave off seething and pulsating, until, finally, Nebuzaradan, captain of Nebuchadnezzar's guard, ordered a great carnage among the Judeans, to avenge the death of Zechariah.

Joash himself, the murderer of Zechariah, met with an evil end. He fell into the hands of the Syrians, and they abused him in their barbarous, immoral way. Before he could recover from the suffering inflicted upon him, his servants slew him.

Amaziah, the son and successor of Joash, in many respects resembled his father. At the beginning of his reign he was God-fearing, but when, through the aid of God, he had gained a brilliant victory over the Edomites, he knew no better way of manifesting his gratitude than to establish in Jerusalem the cult of the idol worshipped by his conquered enemies. To compass his chastisement, God inspired Amaziah with the idea of provoking a war with Joash, the ruler of the northern kingdom. Amaziah demanded that Joash should either recognize the suzerainty of the southern realm voluntarily, or let the fate of battle decide the question. At first Joash sought to turn Amaziah aside from his purpose by a parable reminding him of the fate of Shechem, which the sons of Jacob had visited upon him for having done violence to their sister Dinah. Amaziah refused to be warned. He persisted in his challenge, and a war ensued. The fortune of battle decided against Amaziah. He suffered defeat, and later he was tortured to death by his own subjects.

THREE GREAT PROPHETS

The reign of Uzziah, who for a little while occupied the throne during his father Amaziah's lifetime, is notable particularly because it marks the beginning of the activity of three of the prophets, Hosea, Amos, and Isaiah. The oldest of the three was Hosea, the son of the prophet and prince Beeri, the Beeri who later was carried away captive by Tiglath-pileser, the king of Assyria. Of Beeri's prophecies we have but two verses, preserved for us by Isaiah.

The peculiar marriage contracted by Hosea at the command of God Himself was not without a good reason. When God spoke to the prophet about the sins of Israel, expecting him to defend or excuse his people, Hosea said severely: "O Lord of the world! Thine is the universe. In place of Israel choose another as Thy peculiar people from among the nations of the earth." To make the true relation between God and Israel known to the prophet, he was commanded to take to wife a woman with a dubious past. After she had borne him several children, God suddenly put the question to him: "Why followest thou not the example of thy teacher Moses, who denied himself the joys of family life after his call to prophecy?" Hosea replied: "I can neither send my wife away nor divorce her, for she has borne me children." "If, now," said God to him, "thou who hast a wife of whose honesty thou art so uncertain that thou canst not even be sure that her children are thine, and yet thou canst not separate from her, how, then can I separate Myself from Israel, from My children, the children of My elect, Abraham, Isaac, and Jacob!" Hosea entreated God to pardon him. But God said: "Better were it that thou shouldst pray for the welfare of Israel, for thou art the cause that I issued three fateful decrees against them." Hosea prayed as he was bidden, and his prayer averted the impending threefold doom.

Hosea died at Babylon at a time in which a journey thence to Palestine was beset with many perils. Desirous of having his earthly remains rest in sacred ground, he requested before his death that his bier be loaded upon a camel, and the animal permitted to make its way as it would. Wherever it stopped, there his body was to be buried. As he commanded, so it was done. Without a single mishap the camel arrived at Safed. In the Jewish cemetery of the town it stood still, and there Hosea was buried in the presence of a large concourse.

The prophetical activity of Amos commenced after Hosea's had closed, and before Isaiah's began. Though he had an impediment in his speech, he obeyed the call of God, and betook himself to Beth-el to proclaim to the sinful inhabitants thereof the Divine message with which he had been charged. The denunciation of the priest Amaziah, of Beth-el, who informed against the prophet before King Jeroboam of Israel, did him no harm, for the king, idolater though he was, entertained profound respect for Amos. He said to himself: "God forbid I should think the prophet guilty of cherishing traitorous plans, and if he were, it would surely be at the bidding of God." For this pious disposition Jeroboam was rewarded; never had the northern kingdom attained to such power as under him.

However, the fearlessness of Amos finally caused his death. King Uzziah inflicted a mortal blow upon his forehead with a red-hot iron.

Two years after Amos ceased to prophesy, Isaiah was favored with his first Divine communication. It was the day on which King Uzziah, blinded by success and prosperity, arrogated to himself the privileges of the priesthood. He tried to offer sacrifices upon the altar, and when the high priest Azariah ventured to restrain him, he threatened to slay him and any priest sympathizing with him unless they kept silent. Suddenly the earth quaked so violently that a great breach was torn in the Temple, through which a brilliant ray of sunlight pierced, falling upon the forehead of the king and causing leprosy to break forth upon him. Nor was that all the damage done by the earthquake. On the west side of Jerusalem, half of the mountain was split off and hurled to the east, into a road, at a distance of four stadia. And not heaven and earth alone were outraged by Uzziah's atrocity and sought to annihilate him; even the angels of fire, the seraphim, were on the point of descending and consuming him, when a voice from on high proclaimed, that the punishment appointed for Uzziah was unlike that meted out to Korah and his company despite the similarity of their crimes.

When Isaiah beheld the august throne of God on this memorable day, he was sorely affrighted, for he reproached himself with not having tried to turn the king away from his impious desire. Enthralled he hearkened to the hymns of praise sung by the angels, and lost in admiration he failed to join his voice with theirs. "Woe is me," he cried out, "that I was silent! Woe is me that I did not join the chorus of the angels praising God! Had I done it, I, too, like the angels, would have become immortal, seeing I was permitted to look upon sights to behold which had brought death to other men." Then he began to excuse himself: "I am a man of unclean lips, and I dwell in the midst of people of unclean lips." At once resounded the voice of God in rebuke: "Of thyself thou art the master, and of thyself thou mayest say what thou choosest, but who gave thee the right to calumniate My children of Israel and call them 'a people of unclean lips'?" And Isaiah heard God bid one of the seraphim touch his lips with a live coal as a punishment for having slandered Israel. Though the coal was so hot that the seraph needed tongs to hold the tongs with which he had taken the coal from the altar, the prophet yet escaped unscathed, but he learned the lesson, that it was his duty to defend Israel, not traduce him. Thenceforth the championship of his people was the mainspring of the prophet's activity, and he was rewarded by having more revelations concerning Israel and the other nations vouchsafed him than any other prophet before or after him. Moreover God designated Isaiah to be "the prophet of consolation." Thus it happened that the very Isaiah whose early prophecies foretold the exile and the destruction of the Temple, later described and proclaimed, in plainer terms than any other prophet, the brilliant destiny in store for Israel.

THE TWO KINGDOMS CHASTISED

Afflicted with leprosy, Uzziah was unfit to reign as king, and Jotham administered the affairs of Judah for twenty-five years before the death of his father. Jotham possessed so much piety that his virtues added to those of two other very pious men suffice to atone for all the sins of the whole of mankind committed from the hour of creation until the end of all time.

Ahaz, the son of Jotham; was very unlike him. "From first to last he was a sinner." He abolished the true worship of God, forbade the study of the Torah, set up an idol in the upper room of the Temple, and disregarded the Jewish laws of marriage. His transgressions are the less pardonable, because he sinned against God knowing His grandeur and power, as appears from his reply to the prophet. Isaiah said to him: "Ask a sign of God, as, for instance, that the dead should arise, Korah come up from Sheol, or Elijah descend from heaven." The king's answer was: "I know thou hast the power to do any of these, but I do not wish the Name of God to be glorified through me."

The only good quality possessed by Ahaz was respect for Isaiah. To avoid his reproaches, Ahaz would disguise himself when he went abroad, so that the prophet might not recognize him. Only to this circumstance, joined to the fact he was the father of a pious son and the son of an equally pious father, is it to be ascribed that, in spite of his wickedness, Ahaz is not one of those who have forfeited their portion in the world to come. But he did not escape punishment; on the contrary, his chastisement was severe, not only as king but also as man. In the ill-starred war against Pekah, the king of the northern kingdom, he lost his first-born son, a great hero.

Pekah, however, was not permitted to enjoy the fruits of his victory, for the king of Assyria invaded his empire, captured the golden calf at Dan, and led the tribes on the east side of Jordan away into exile. The dismemberment of the Israelitish kingdom went on apace for some years. Then the Assyrians, in the reign of Hoshea, carried off the second golden calf together with the tribes of Asher, Issachar, Zebulon, and Naphtali, leaving but one-eighth of the Israelites in their own land. The larger portion of the exiles was taken to Damascus. After that Israel's doom overtook it with giant strides, and the last ruler of Israel actually hastened the end of his kingdom by a pious deed. After the golden calves were removed by the Assyrians, Hoshea, the king of the north, abolished the institution of stationing the guards on the frontier between Judah and Israel to prevent pilgrimages to Jerusalem. But the people made no use of the liberty granted them. They persisted in their idolatrous cult, and this quickened their punishment. So long as their kings had put obstacles in their path, they could excuse themselves before God for not worshipping Him in the true way. The action taken by their king Hoshea left them no defense. When the Assyrians made their third incursion into Israel, the kingdom of the north was destroyed forever, and the people, one and all, were carried away into exile.

The heathen nations settled in Samaria by the Assyrians instead of the deported Ten Tribes were forced by God to accept the true religion of the Jews. Nevertheless they continued to worship their olden idols: the Babylonians paid devotion to a hen, the people of Cuthah to a cock, those of Hamath to a ram, the dog and the ass were the gods of the Avvites, and the mule and the horse the gods of the Sepharvites.

HEZEKIAH

While the northern kingdom was rapidly descending into the pit of destruction, a mighty upward impulse was given to Judah, both spiritually and materially, by its king Hezekiah. In his infancy the king had been destined as a sacrifice to Moloch. His mother had saved him from death only by rubbing him with the blood of a salamander, which made him fire-proof. In every respect he was the opposite of his father. As the latter is counted among the worst of sinners, so Hezekiah is counted among the most pious of Israel. His first act as king is evidence that he held the honor of God to be his chief concern, important beyond all else. He refused to accord his father regal obsequies; his remains were buried as though he had been poor and of plebeian rank. Impious as he was, Ahaz deserved nothing more dignified. God had Himself made it known to Hezekiah, by a sign, that his father was to have no consideration paid him. On the day of the dead king's funeral daylight lasted but two hours, and his body had to be interred when the earth was enveloped in darkness.

Throughout his reign, Hezekiah devoted himself mainly to the task of dispelling the ignorance of the Torah which his father had caused. While Ahaz had forbidden the study of the law, Hezekiah's orders read: "Who does not occupy himself with the Torah, renders himself subject to the death penalty." The academies closed under Ahaz were kept open day and night under Hezekiah. The king himself supplied the oil needed for illuminating purposes. Gradually, under this system, a generation grew up so well trained that one could search the land from Dan even to Beer-sheba and not find a single ignoramus. The very women and the children, both boys and girls, knew the laws of "clean and unclean." By way of rewarding his piety, God granted Hezekiah a brilliant victory over Sennacherib.

This Assyrian king, who had conquered the whole world, equipped an army against Hezekiah like unto which there is none, unless it be the army of the four kings whom Abraham routed, or the army to be raised by God and Magog in the Messianic time. Sennacherib's army consisted of more than two millions and a half of horsemen, among them forty-five thousand princes sitting in chariots and surrounded by their paramours, by eighty thousand armor-clad soldiers, and sixty thousand swordsmen. The camp extended over a space of four hundred parasangs, and the saddle-beasts standing neck to neck formed a line forty parasangs long. The host was divided into four divisions. After the first of them had passed the Jordan, it was well nigh dry, for the soldiers had all slaked their thirst with water of the river. The second division found nothing to quench their thirst except the water gathered under the hoofs of the horses. The third division was forced to dig wells, and when the fourth division crossed the Jordan, they kicked up great clouds of dust.

With this vast army Sennacherib hastened onward, in accordance with the disclosures of the astrologers, who warned him that he would fail in his object of capturing Jerusalem, if he arrived there later than the day set by them. His journey having lasted but one day instead of ten, as he had expected, he rested at Nob. A raised platform was there erected for Sennacherib, whence he could view Jerusalem. On first beholding the Judean capital, the Assyrian king exclaimed: "What! Is this Jerusalem, the city for whose sake I gathered together my whole army, for whose sake I first conquered all other lands? Is it not smaller and weaker than all the cities of the nations I subdued with my strong hand?" He stretched himself and shook his head, and waved his hand contemptuously toward the Temple mount and the sanctuary crowning it. When his warriors urged him to make his attack upon Jerusalem, he bade them take their ease for one night, and be prepared to storm the city the next day. It seemed no great undertaking. Each warrior would but have to pick up as much mortar from the wall as is needed to seal a letter and the whole city would disappear. But Sennacherib made the mistake of not proceeding directly to the attack upon the city. If he had made the assault at once, it would have been successful, for the sin of Saul against the priest at Nob had not yet been wholly expiated; on that very day it was fully atoned for. In the following night, which was the Passover night, when Hezekiah and the people began to sing the Hallel Psalms, the giant host was annihilated. The archangel Gabriel sent by God to ripen the fruits of the field, was charged to address himself to the task of making away with the

Assyrians, and he fulfilled his mission so well that of all the millions of the army, Sennacherib alone was saved with his two sons, his son-in-law Nebuchadnezzar, and Nebuzaradan. The death of the Assyrians happened when the angel permitted them to hear the "song of the celestials." Their souls were burnt, though their garments remained intact. Such an end was too good for Sennacherib. To him a disgraceful death was apportioned. On his flight away from Jerusalem, he met a Divine apparition in the guise of an old man. He questioned Sennacherib as to what he would say to the kings allied with him, in reply to their inquiry about the fate of their sons at Jerusalem. Sennacherib confessed his dread of a meeting with those kings. The old man advised him to have his hair cut off, which would change his appearance beyond recognition. Sennacherib assented, and his advisor sent him to a house in the vicinity to fetch a pair of shears. Here he found some people angels in disguise busying themselves with a hand-mill. They promised to give him the shears, provided he ground a measure of grain for them. So it grew late and dark by the time Sennacherib returned to the old man, and he had to procure a light before his hair could be cut. As he fanned the fire into a flame, a spark flew into his beard and singed it, and he had to sacrifice his beard as well as his hair. On his return to Assyria, Sennacherib found a plank, which he worshipped as an idol, because it was part of the ark which had saved Noah from the deluge. He vowed that he would sacrifice his sons to this idol if he prospered in his next ventures. But his sons heard his vows, and they killed their father, and fled to Kardu where they released the Jewish captives confined there in great numbers. With these they marched to Jerusalem, and became proselytes there. The famous scholars Shemaiah and Abtalion were the descendants of these two sons of Sennacherib.

MIRACLES WROUGHT FOR HEZEKIAH

The destruction of the Assyrian host delivered Hezekiah from an inner as well as an outer enemy, for he had opponents in Jerusalem, among them the high priest Shebnah. Shebnah had a more numerous following in the city than the king himself, and they and their leader had favored peace with Sennacherib. Supported by Joah, another influential personage, Shebnah had fastened a letter to a dart, and shot the dart into the Assyrian camp. The contents of the letter were: "We and the whole people of Israel wish to conclude peace with thee, but Hezekiah and Isaiah will not permit it." Shebnah's influence was so powerful that Hezekiah began to show signs of yielding. Had it not been for the prophet Isaiah, the king would have submitted to Sennacherib's demands.

Shebnah's treachery and his other sins did not go unpunished. When he and his band of adherents left Jerusalem to join the Assyrians, the angel Gabriel closed the gate as soon as Shebnah had passed beyond it, and so he was separated from his followers. To the inquiry of Sennacherib about the many sympathizers he had written of, he could give no reply but that they had changed their mind. The Assyrian king thought Shebnah had made sport of him. He, therefore, ordered his attendants to bore a hole through his heels, tie him to the tail of a horse by them, and spur the horse on to run until Shebnah was dragged to death.

The unexpected victory won by Hezekiah over the Assyrians, to whom the kingdom of Samaria had fallen a prey but a short time before, showed how wrong they had been who had mocked at Hezekiah for his frugal ways. A king whose meal consisted of a handful of vegetables could hardly be called a dignified ruler, they had said. These critics would gladly have seen his kingdom pass into the hands of Pekah, the king of Samaria, whose dessert, to speak of nothing else, consisted of forty seim of young pigeons.

In view of all the wonders God had done for him, it was unpardonable that Hezekiah did not feel himself prompted at least to sing a song of praise to God. Indeed, when the prophet Isaiah urged him to it, he refused, saying that the study of the Torah, to which he devoted himself with assiduous zeal, was a substitute for direct expressions of gratitude. Besides, he thought God's miracles would become known to the world without action on his part, in such ways as these: After the destruction of the Assyrian army, when the Jews searched the abandoned camps, they found Pharaoh the king of Egypt and the Ethiopian king Tirhakah. These kings had hastened to the aid of Hezekiah, and the Assyrians had taken them captive and clapped them in irons, in which they were languishing when the Jews came upon them. Liberated by Hezekiah, the two rulers returned to their respective realms, spreading the report of the greatness of God everywhere. And again, all the vassal troops in Sennacherib's army, set free by Hezekiah, accepted the Jewish faith, and on their way home they proclaimed the kingdom of God in Egypt and in many other lands.

By failing in gratitude Hezekiah lost a great opportunity. The Divine plan had been to make Hezekiah the Messiah, and Sennacherib was to be God and Magog. Justice opposed this plan, addressing God thus: "O Lord of the world! David, king of Israel, who sang so many songs and hymns of praise to Thee, him Thou didst not make the Messiah, and now Thou wouldst confer the distinction upon Hezekiah, who has no word of praise for Thee in spite of the manifold wonders Thou hast wrought for him?" Then the earth appeared before God, and said: "Lord of the world! I will song Thee a song in place of this righteous man; make him to be the Messiah," and the earth forthwith intoned a song of praise. Likewise spake the Prince of the World: "Lord of the world! Do the will of this righteous man." But a voice from heaven announced: "This is my secret, this is my secret." And again, when the prophet exclaimed sorrowfully, "Woe is me! How long, O Lord, how long!" the voice replied: "The time of the Messiah will arrive when the 'treacherous dealers and the treacherous dealers' shall have come."

The sin committed by Hezekiah asleep, he had to atone for awake. If he refused to devote a song of praise to God for his escape from the Assyrian peril, he could not refrain from doing it after his recovery from the dangerous sickness that befell him. This sickness was a punishment for another sin beside ingratitude. He had "peeled off" the gold from the Temple, and sent it to the king of the Assyrians; therefore the disease that afflicted him caused his skin to "peel off." Moreover, this malady of Hezekiah's was brought upon him by God, to afford an opportunity for the king and the prophet Isaiah to come close to each other. The two had had a dispute on a point of etiquette. The king adduced as a precedent the action of Elijah, who "went to show himself unto Ahab," and demanded that Isaiah, too, should appear before him. The prophet, on the other hand, modelled his conduct after Elisha's, who permitted the kings of Israel, and Judah, and Edom, to come to him. But God settled the dispute by afflicting Hezekiah with sickness, and then He bade Isaiah go to the king and pay the visit due to the sick. The prophet did the bidding of God. When he appeared in the presence of the ailing king, he said: "Set thine house in order, for thou wilt die in this world and not live in the next" a fate which Hezekiah incurred because he had failed to take unto himself a wife and bring forth posterity. The king's defense, that he had preferred a celibate's life because he had seen in the holy spirit that he was destined to have impious children, the prophet did not consider valid. He rebutted it with the words: "Why does thou concern thyself with the secrets of the All-Merciful? Thou hast but to do thy duty. God will do whatsoever it pleases Him." Thereupon Hezekiah asked the daughter of the prophet in marriage, saying: "Perchance my merits joined to thine will cause my children to be virtuous." But Isaiah rejected the proposal of marriage, because he knew that the decree of God ordaining the king's death was unalterable. Whereupon the king: "Thou son of thus has it been transmitted to me from the house of my ancestor: Even if a sharp sword rests at the very throat of a man, he may yet not refrain from uttering a prayer for mercy."

And the king was right. Though death had been decreed against him, his prayer averted it. In his prayer he supplicated God to keep him alive for the sake of the merits of his ancestors, who had built the Temple and brought many proselytes into the Jewish fold, and for the sake of his own merits, for, he said, "I searched out all the two hundred and forty-eight members of my body which Thou didst give me, and I found none which I had used in a manner contrary to Thy will."

His prayer was heard. God added fifteen years to his life, but He made him understand very clearly, that he owed the mercy solely to the merits of David, not at all to his own, as Hezekiah fondly believed. Before Isaiah left the court of the palace, God instructed him to return to the king, and announce his recovery to him. Isaiah feared lest Hezekiah should place little trust in his words, as he had but a short while before predicted his swiftly approaching end. But God reassured the prophet. In his modesty and piety, the king would harbor no doubt derogatory to the prophet's trustworthiness. The remedy employed by Isaiah, a cake of figs applied to the boil, increased the wonder of Hezekiah's recovery, for it was apt to aggravate the malady rather than alleviate it.

A number of miracles besides were connected with the recovery of Hezekiah. In itself it was remarkable, as being the first case of a recovery on record. Previously illness had been inevitably followed by death. Before he had fallen sick, Hezekiah himself had implored God to change this order of nature. He held that sickness followed by restoration to health would induce men to do penance. God had replied: "Thou art right, and the new order shall be begun with thee." Furthermore, the day of Hezekiah's recovery was marked by the great miracle that the sun shone ten hours longer than its wonted time. The remotest lands were amazed thereat, and Baladan, the ruler of Babylon, was prompted by it to send an embassy to Hezekiah, which was to carry his felicitations to the Jewish king upon his recovery. Baladan, it should be said by the way, was not the real king of Babylon. The throne was occupied by his father, whose face had changed into that of a dog. Therefore the son had to administer the affairs of state, and he was known by his father's name as well as his own. This Baladan was in the habit of dining at noon, and then he took a nap until three o'clock of the afternoon. On the day of Hezekiah's recovery, when he awoke from his sleep, and saw the sun overhead, he was on the point of having his guards executed, because he thought they had permitted him to sleep a whole afternoon and the night following it. He desisted only when he was informed of Hezekiah's miraculous recovery, and realised that the God of Hezekiah was greater than his own god, the sun. He at once set about sending greetings to the Jewish king. His letter read as follows: "Peace be with Hezekiah, peace with his great God, and peace with Jerusalem." After the letter was dispatched, it occurred to Baladan that it had not been composed properly. Mention of Hezekiah had been made before mention of God. He had the messengers called back, and ordered another letter to be written, in which the oversight was made good. As a reward for his punctiliousness, three of his descendants, Nebuchadnezzar, Evil-merodach, and Belshazzar, were appointed by God to be world monarchs. God said: "Thou didst arise from thy throne, and didst take three steps to do Me honor, by having thy letter re-written, therefore will I grant thee three descendants who shall be known from one end of the world to the other."

The embassy sent by the Babylonian monarch was an act of homage to God for his miracle-working power. Hezekiah, however, took it to be an act of homage toward himself, and it had the effect of making him arrogant. Not only did he eat and drink with the heathen who made up the embassy, but also, in his haughtiness of mind, he displayed before them all the treasures which he had captured from Sennacherib, and many other curiosities besides, among them magnetic iron, a peculiar sort of ivory, and honey as solid as stone.

What was worse, he had his wife partake of the meal in honor of the embassy, and, most heinous crime of all, he opened the holy Ark, and pointing to the tables of law within it, said to the heathen: "With the help of these we undertake wars and win victories." God sent Isaiah to reproach Hezekiah for these acts. The king, instead of confessing his wrong at once, answered the prophet haughtily. would revert to Babylon some time in the future, and his descendants, Daniel and the three companions of Daniel, would serve the Babylonia ruler as eunuchs.

Despite his pride in this case, Hezekiah was one of the most pious kings of Judah. Especially he is deserving of praise for his efforts to have Hebrew literature put into writing, for it was Hezekiah who had copies made of the books of Isaiah, Ecclesiastes, Song of Songs, and Proverbs. On the other hand, he had concealed the books containing medical remedies.

Great was the mourning over him at his death. No less than thirty-six thousand men with bared shoulders marched before his bier, and, rarer distinction still, a scroll of the law was laid upon his bier, for it was said: "He who rests in this bier, has fulfilled all ordained in this book." He was buried next to David and Solomon.

MANASSEH

Hezekiah had finally yielded to the admonitions of Isaiah, and had taken a wife unto himself, the daughter of the prophet. But he entered upon marriage with a heavy heart. His prophetic spirit foretold to him that the impiousness of the sons he would beget would make their death to be preferable to their life. These fears were confirmed all too soon. His two sons, Rabshakeh and Manasseh, showed their complete unlikeness to their parents in early childhood. Once, when Hezekiah was carrying his two little ones on his shoulders to the Bet ha-Midrash, he overheard their conversation. The one said: "Our father's bald head might do for frying fish." The other rejoined: "It would do well for offering sacrifices to idols." Enraged by these words, Hezekiah let his sons slip from his shoulders. Rabshakeh was killed by the fall, but Manasseh escaped unhurt. Better had it been if Manasseh had shared his brother's untimely fate. He was spared for naught but murder, idolatry, and other abominable atrocities.

After Hezekiah had departed this life, Manasseh ceased to serve the God of his father. He did whatever his evil imagination prompted. The altar was destroyed, and in the inner space of the Temple he set up an idol with four faces, copied from the four figures on the throne of God. It was so placed that from whatever direction one entered the Temple, a face of the idol confronted him.

As Manasseh was sacrilegious toward God, he was malevolent toward his fellows. He had fashioned an image so large that it required a thousand men to carry it. Daily a new force was employed on this task, because Manasseh had each set of porters killed off at the end of the day's work. All his acts were calculated to cast contempt upon Judaism and its tenets. It did not satisfy his evil desire to obliterate the name of God from the Holy Scriptures; he went so far as to deliver public lectures whose burden was to ridicule the Torah. Isaiah and the other prophets, Micah, Joel, and Habakkuk, left Jerusalem and repaired to a mountain in the desert, that they might be spared the sight of the abominations practiced by the king. Their abiding-place was disclosed to the king. A Samaritan, a descendant of the false prophet Zedekiah, had taken refuge in Jerusalem after the destruction of the Temple. But he did not remain there long; charges were made against him before the pious king Hezekiah, and he withdrew to Bethlehem, where he gathered hangers-on about him. This Samaritan it was who traced the prophets to their retreat, and lodged accusations against them before Manasseh. The impious king sat in judgment on Isaiah, and condemned him to death. The indictment against him was that his prophecies contained teachings in contradiction with the law of Moses. God said unto Moses: "Thou canst not see My face; for man shall not see Me and live"; while Isaiah said: "I saw the Lord sitting upon a throne, high and lifted up." Again, Isaiah compared the princes of Israel and the people with the impious inhabitants of Sodom and Gomorrah, and he prophesied the downfall of Jerusalem and the destruction of the Temple. The prophet offered no explanation. He was convinced of the uselessness of defending himself, and he preferred Manasseh should act from ignorance rather than from wickedness. However, he fled for safety. When he heard the royal bailiffs in pursuit of him, he pronounced the Name of God, and a cedar-tree swallowed him up. The king ordered the tree to be sawn in pieces. When the saw was applied to the portion of the bark under which the mouth of Isaiah lay concealed, he died. His mouth was the only vulnerable part of his body, because at the time when he was called to his prophetical mission, it had made use of the contemptuous words "a people of unclean lips," regarding Israel. Isaiah died at the age of one hundred and twenty years, by the hands of his own grandchild.

God is long-suffering, but in the end Manasseh received the deserved punishment for his sins and crimes. In the twenty-second year of his rulership, the Assyrians came and carried him off to Babylon in fetters, him together with the old Danite idol, Micah's image. In Babylonia, the king was put into an oven which was heated from below. Finding himself in this extremity, Manasseh began to call upon god after god to help him out of his straits. As this proved inefficacious, he resorted to other means. "I remember," he said, "my father taught me the verse: 'When thou art in tribulation, if in the latter days thou shalt return to the Lord thy God, and hearken unto His voice, He will not fail thee.' Now I cry to God. If He inclines His ear unto me, well and good; if not, then all kinds of god are alike." The angels stopped up the windows of heaven, that the prayer of Manasseh might not ascend to God, and they said: "Lord of the world! Art Thou willing to give gracious hearing to one who has paid worship to idols, and set up an idol in the Temple?" "If I did not accept the penance of this man," replied God, "I should be closing the door in the face of all repentant sinners." God made a small opening under the Throne of His Glory, and received the prayer of Manasseh through it. Suddenly a wind arose, and carried Manasseh back to Jerusalem. His return to God not only helped him in his distress, but also brought him pardon for all his sins, so that not even his share in the future world was withdrawn from him.

The people of this time were attracted to idolatry with so irresistible a force that the vast learning of Manasseh, who knew fifty-two different interpretations of the Book of Leviticus, did not give him enough moral strength to withstand its influence. Rab Ashi, the famous compiler of the Talmud, once announced a lecture on Manasseh with the words: "To-morrow I shall speak about our colleague Manasseh." At night the king appeared to Ashi in a dreams, and put a ritual question to him, which the Rabbi could not answer. Manasseh told him the solution, and Ashi, in amazement at the king's scholarship, asked why one so erudite had served idols. Manasseh's reply was: "Hadst thou lived at my time, thou wouldst have caught hold of the hem of my garment and run after me."

Amon, the son of Manasseh, surpassed his father in wickedness. He was in the habit of saying: "My father was a sinner from early childhood, and in his old age he did penance. I shall do the same. First I shall satisfy the desires of my heart, and afterward I shall return to God." Indeed, he was guilty of more grievous sins than his predecessor; he burned the Torah; under him the place of the altar was covered with spiderwebs; and, as though of purpose to set at naught the Jewish religion, he committed the worst sort of incest, a degree more heinous than his father's crime of a similar nature. Thus he executed the first half of his maxim literally. For repentance, however, he was given no time; death cut him off in the fulness of his sinful ways.

JOSIAH AND HIS SUCCESSORS

That the full measure of punishment was not meted out to Amon his evil deeds were such that he should have forfeited his share in the world to come was due to the circumstance that he had a pious and righteous son. Josiah offers a shining model of true, sincere repentance. Though at first he followed in the footsteps of his father Amon, he soon gave up the ways of wickedness, and became one of the most pious kings of Israel, whose chief undertaking was the effort to bring the whole people back to the true faith. It dates from the time when a copy of the Torah was found in the Temple, a copy that had escaped the holocaust kindled by his father and predecessor Amon for the purpose of exterminating the Holy Scriptures. When he opened the Scriptures, the first verse to strike his eye was the one in Deuteronomy: "The Lord shall bring thee and thy king into exile, unto a nation which thou hast not known." Josiah feared this doom of exile was impending, and he sought to conciliate God through the reform of his people.

His first step was to enlist the intercession of the prophets in his behalf. He addressed his request, not to Jeremiah, but to the prophetess Huldah, knowing that women are more easily moved to compassion. As Jeremiah was a kinsman of the prophetess their common ancestors were Joshua and Rahab the king felt no apprehension that the prophet take his preference for Huldah amiss. The proud, dignified answer of the prophetess was, that the misfortune could not be averted from Israel, but the destruction of the Temple, she continued consolingly, would not happen until after the death of Josiah. In view of the imminent destruction of the Temple, Josiah hid the holy Ark and all its appurtenances, in order to guard them against desecration at the hands of the enemy.

The efforts of the king in behalf of God and His law found no echo with the great majority of the people. Though the king was successful in preventing the worship of idols in public, his subjects knew how to deceive him. Josiah sent out his pious sympathizers to inspect the houses of the people, and he was satisfied with their report, that they had found no idols, not suspecting that the recreant people has fastened half an image on each wing of the doors, so that the inmates faced their household idols as they closed the door upon Josiah's inspectors.

This godless generation contemporaneous with Josiah was to blame for his death. When King Pharaoh, in his campaign against the Assyrians, wanted to travel through Palestine, Jeremiah advised the king not to deny the Egyptians the passage through his land. He cited a prophecy by his teacher Isaiah, who had foreseen the war between Assyria and Egypt. But Josiah retorted: "Moses, thy teacher's teacher, spake: 'I will give peace in the land, and no sword shall go through your land,' not even the sword that is not raised against Israel with hostile intent." The king, innocent of the deception practiced by the people, knew not that they were idol worshippers, to whom the promises of the Torah have no application. In the engagement that ensued between the Jews and the Egyptians, no less than three hundred darts struck the king. In his death agony he uttered no word of complaint; he only said: "The Lord is righteous, for I have rebelled against His commandment," thus admitting his guilt in not having heeded the advice of the prophet.

So ended the days of this just king after a brilliant career, the only king since Solomon to rule over both Judah and Israel, for Jeremiah had brought back to Palestine the ten exiled tribes of the north, and made them subject to Josiah. The mourning for him was profound. Even Jeremiah perpetuated his memory in his Lamentations.

Pharaoh of Egypt was not permitted to enjoy the results of his victory to the full, for it was soon after this that, in attempting to ascend the wondrous throne of Solomon, he was stuck down by the lions and rendered lame by the blow.

The people put Jehoahaz on the throne of Judah to succeed Josiah, though his brother Jehoiakim was the older by two years. To silence the legitimate claims of Jehoiakim, the new king underwent the ceremony of anointing. But his reign was very brief. At the end of three months Pharaoh carried him off into exile in Egypt, and Jehoiakim ruled in his stead.

Jehoiakim was another of the sinful monarchs of the Jews, uncharitable toward men and disobedient to God and the laws of God. His garments were of two kinds of stuff mingled together, his body was tattooed with the names of idols, and in order that he might appear as a non-Jew, he performed the operation of an epipost upon himself. Various forms of incest were committed by him, and, besides, he was in the habit of putting men to death that he might violate their wives, and confiscate their possessions. Blasphemous as he was, he spoke: "My predecessors did not know how to provoke the wrath of God. As for me, I say frankly, we have no need whatsoever of Him; the very light He gives us we can dispense with, for the gold of Parvaim can well replace it."

Seeing such abominations, God desired to resolve the world into its original chaos. If He desisted from His purpose, it was only because the people led a God-fearing life during the time of Jehoiakim. After he had reigned eleven years, Nebuchadnezzar put an end to his dominion. Advancing with his army, the Babylonian king halted at Daphne, a suburb of Antioch. Here he was met by the Sanhedrin of Jerusalem, who desired to know whether he was coming with the purpose of destroying the Temple. Nebuchadnezzar assured them, that all he wanted was the surrender of Jehoiakim, who had rebelled against his authority. Returned to Jerusalem, the Sanhedrin informed Jehoiakim of Nebuchadnezzar's intention. The king asked the elders, whether it was ethical to purchase their lives by sacrificing his. For answer they referred him to the story of the way Joab dealt with the city of Abel of Beth-maacah, which had saved itself by surrendering the rebel Sheba, the son of Bichri. The king's objections did not deter the Sanhedrin from following the example of Joab acting under the direction of David. They made Jehoiakim glide down from the city walls of Jerusalem by a chain. Below, the Babylonians stood ready to receive him. Nebuchadnezzar took Jehoiakim in fetters to all the cities of Judah, then he slew him, and, his rage still unabated, threw his corpse to the dogs after having stuck it into the carcass of an ass. The dogs left nothing of Jehoiakim's body over except his skull, on which were written the words: "This and something besides." Many centuries later it was found by a Rabbi near the gates of Jerusalem. He tried in vain to give it burial; the earth refused to retain it, and the Rabbi concluded therefrom that it belonged to the corpse of Jehoiakim. He wrapped the skull in a cloth, and laid it in a closet. One day the wife of the Rabbi discovered it there, and she burnt it, thinking the skull belonged to a former wife of her husband, so dear to him even after her death that he could not separate himself from this relic.

When Nebuchadnezzar returned to Babylonia from his Palestinian expedition, the people received him with great pomp and solemnity. He announced to them that in place of Jehoiakim, whom he had slain, he had installed Mattaniah, the rebel's son, called Jehoiachin, as king over Judah, and the people uttered the warning: "One cannot educate a well-behaved puppy whose dam was ill-conditioned; let alone an ill-conditioned puppy whose dam was ill-conditioned."

Nebuchadnezzar returned to Daphne, and informed the Sanhedrin, who hastened from Jerusalem to meet him, that he desired the surrender of Jehoiachin. If they refused to satisfy his demand, he would destroy the Temple. When the Jewish king was told the threat of his Babylonian adversary, he mounted upon the roof of the Temple, and, holding all the keys of its chambers in his hand, he spoke thus to God: "Until now Thou didst consider us worthy of confidence, and Thou didst entrust Thy keys to us. Since Thou no longer dost esteem us trustworthy, here, take back Thy keys." He was held to his word: a hand was stretched forth from heaven, and it received the keys.

Jehoiachin, good and pious, did not desire the city of Jerusalem to be exposed to peril for his sake. So he delivered himself to the Babylonian leaders, after they swore that neither city nor people should suffer harm. But the Babylonians did not keep their oath. A short while thereafter they carried into exile, not only the king, but also his mother, of the Jewish nobility and of the great scholars. This was the second attempt made by Nebuchadnezzar to deport the Jews. On taking the former king Jehoiakim captive, he had exiled three hundred of the noblest of the people, among them the prophet Ezekiel.

The king Jehoiachin was incarcerated for life, a solitary prisoner, separated from his wife and his family. The Sanhedrin, who were among those deported with the king, feared that the house of David die out. They therefore besought Nebuchadnezzar not to separate Jehoiachin from his wife. They succeeded in enlisting the sympathy of the queen's hairdresser, and through her of the queen herself, Semiramis, the wife of Nebuchadnezzar, who in turn prevailed upon the king to accord mild treatment to the unfortunate prince exiled from Judea. Suffering had completely changed the once sinful king, so that, in spite of his great joy over his reunion with his wife, he still paid regard to the prescriptions of the Jewish law regulating conjugal life. He was prepared to deny himself every indulgence, when the purchase price was an infringement of the word of God. Such steadfastness pleaded with God to pardon the king for his sins, and the heavenly Sanhedrin absolved God from His oath, to crush Jehoiachin and deprive his house of sovereignty. By way of reward for his continence he was blessed with distinguished posterity. Not only was Zerubbabel, the first governor of Palestine after the destruction of the Temple, a grandson of Jehoiachin's, but also the Messiah himself will be a descendant of his.

X. THE EXILE

ZEDEKIAH

THE execution of one king and the deportation of another were but preludes to the great national catastrophe in the time of Zedekiah, the destruction of the Temple and the exile of the whole people. After Nebuchadnezzar had led Jehoiachin and a portion of the people into banishment, his commiseration was aroused for the Jews, and he inquired, whether any other sons of Josiah were still living. Only Mattaniah was left. He was re-named Zedekiah, in the hope that he would be the father of pious sons. In reality the name became the omen of the disasters to happen in the time of this king.

Nebuchadnezzar, who invested Zedekiah with the royal office, demanded that he swear fealty to him. Zedekiah was about to swear by his own soul, but the Babylonian king, not satisfied, brought a scroll of the law, and made his Jewish vassal take the oath upon that. Nevertheless he did not keep faith with Nebuchadnezzar for long. Nor was this his only treachery toward his suzerain. He had once surprised Nebuchadnezzar in the act of cutting a piece from a living hare and eating it, as is the habit of barbarians. Nebuchadnezzar was painfully embarrassed, and he begged the Jewish king to promise under oath not to mention what he had seen. Though Nebuchadnezzar treated him with great friendliness, even making him sovereign lord over five vassal kings, he did not justify the trust reposed in him. To flatter Zedekiah, the five kings once said: "If all were as it should be, thou wouldst occupy the throne of Nebuchadnezzar." Zedekiah could not refrain from exclaiming: "O yes, Nebuchadnezzar, whom I once saw eating a live hare!"

The five kings at once repaired to Nebuchadnezzar, and reported what Zedekiah had said. Thereupon the king of Babylonia marched to Daphne, near Antioch, with the purpose of chastising Zedekiah. At Daphne he found the Sanhedrin of Jerusalem, who had hastened thither to receive him. Nebuchadnezzar met the Sanhedrin courteously, ordered his attendants to bring state chairs for all the members, and requested them to read the Torah to him and explain it. When they reached the passage in the Book of Numbers dealing with the remission of vows, the king put the question: "If a man desires to be released from a vow, what steps must he take?" The Sanhedrin replied: "He must repair to a scholar, and he will absolve him from his vow." Whereupon Nebuchadnezzar exclaimed: "I verily believe it was you who released Zedekiah from the vow he took concerning me." And he ordered the members of the Sanhedrin to leave their state chairs and sit on the ground. They were forced to admit, that they had not acted in accordance with the law, for Zedekiah's vow affected another beside himself, and without the acquiescence of the other party, namely, Nebuchadnezzar, the Sanhedrin had no authority to annul the vow.

Zedekiah was duly punished for the grievous crime of perjury. When Jerusalem was captured, he tried to escape through a cave extending from his house to Jericho. God sent a deer into the camp of the Chaldeans, and in their pursuit of this game, the Babylonian soldiers reached the farther opening of the cave at the very moment when Zedekiah was leaving it. The Jewish king together with his ten sons was brought before Nebuchadnezzar, who addressed Zedekiah thus: "Were I to judge thee according to the law of thy God, thou wouldst deserve the death penalty, for thou didst swear a false oath by the Name of God; no less wouldst thou deserve death, if I were to judge thee according to the law of the state, for thou didst fail in thy sworn duty to thy overlord."

Zedekiah requested the grace that his execution take place before his children's, and he be spared the sight of their blood. His children, on the other hand, besought Nebuchadnezzar to slay them before he slew their father, that they might be spared the disgrace of seeing their father executed. In his heartlessness Nebuchadnezzar had resolved worse things than Zedekiah anticipated. In the sight of their father, the children of Zedekiah were killed, and then Zedekiah himself was deprived of sight; his eyes were blinded. He had been endowed with eyes of superhuman strength, they were the eyes of Adam, and the iron lances forced into them were powerless to destroy his sight. Vision left him only because of the tears he shed over the fate of his children. Now he realized how true Jeremiah had spoken when he had prophesied his exile to Babylonia. Though he should live there until his death, he would never behold the land with his eyes. On account of its seeming contradictoriness, Zedekiah had thought the prophecy untrue. For this reason he had not heeded Jeremiah's advice to make peace with Nebuchadnezzar. Now it had all been verified; he was carried to Babylonia a captive, yet, blind as he was, he did not see the land of his exile.

JEREMIAH

Though Zedekiah besmirched his career by perjury, he was nevertheless so good and just a king that for his sake God relinquished his purpose of returning the world to its original chaos, as a punishment for the evil-doing of a wicked generation. In this depraved time, it was first and foremost Jeremiah to whom was delegated the task of proclaiming the word of God. He was a descendant of Joshua and Rahab, and his father was the prophet Hilkiah. He was born while his father was fleeing from the persecution of Jezebel, the murderess of prophets. At his very birth he showed signs that he was destined to play a great part. He was born circumcised, and scarcely had he left his mother's womb when he broke into wailing, and his voice was the voice, not of a babe, but of a youth. He cried: "My bowels, my bowels tremble, the walls of my heart they are disquieted, my limbs quake, destruction upon destruction I bring upon earth." In this strain he continued to moan and groan, complaining of the faithlessness of his mother, and when she expressed her amazement at the unseemly speech of her new-born son, Jeremiah said: "Not thee do I mean, my mother, not to thee doth my prophecy refer; I speak of Zion, and against Jerusalem are my words directed. She adorns her daughters, arrays them in purple, and puts golden crowns upon their heads. Robbers will come and strip them of their ornaments."

As a lad he received the call to be a prophet. But he refused to obey, saying: "O Lord, I cannot go as a prophet to Israel, for when lived there a prophet whom Israel did not desire to kill? Moses and Aaron they sought to stone with stones; Elijah the Tishbite they mocked at because his hair was grown long; and they called after Elisha, 'Go up, thou bald head' no, I cannot go to Israel, for I am still naught but a lad." God replied: "I love youth, for it is innocent. When I carried Israel out of Egypt, I called him a lad, and when I think of Israel lovingly, I speak of him as a lad. Say not, therefore, thou art only a lad, but thou shalt go on whatsoever errand I shall send thee. Now, then," God, continued, "take the 'cup of wrath,' and let the nations drink of it." Jeremiah put the question which land was to drink first from the "cup of wrath," and the answer of God was: "First Jerusalem is to drink, the head of all earthly nations, and then the cities of Judah." When the prophet heard this, he began to curse the day of his birth. "I am like the high priest," he said, "who has to administer the 'water of bitterness' to a woman who is held under the suspicion of adultery, and when he approaches the woman with the cup, lo, he beholds his own mother. And I, O Mother Zion, thought, when I was called to prophesy, that I was appointed to proclaim prosperity and salvation to thee, but now I see that my message forebodes thee evil."

Jeremiah's first appearance in public was during the reign of Josiah, when he announced to the people in the streets: "If ye will give up your wicked doings, God will raise you above all nations; if not, He will deliver His house into the hands of the enemies, and they will deal with it as seemeth best to them."

The prophets contemporary with Jeremiah in his early years were Zechariah and Huldah. The province of the latter was among women, while Zechariah was active in the synagogue. Later, under Jehoiakim, Jeremiah was supported by the prophets of his relative Uriah of Kiriathjearim, a friend of the prophet Isaiah. But Uriah was put to death by the ungodly king, the same who had the first chapter of Lamentations burnt after obliterating the Name of God wherever it occurs in the whole book. But Jeremiah added four chapters.

The prophet fell upon evil times under Zedekiah. He had both the people and the court against him. Nor was that surprising in a day when not even the high priests in the Temple bore the sign of the covenant upon their bodies. Jeremiah had called forth general hostility by condemning the alliance with Egypt against Babylonia, and favoring peace with Nebuchadnezzar; and this though to all appearances the help of the Egyptians would prove of good effect for the Jews. The hosts of Pharaoh Necho had actually set forth from Egypt to join the Jews against Babylon. But when they were on the high seas, God commanded the waters to cover themselves with corpses. Astonished, the Egyptians asked each other, whence the dead bodies. Presently the answer occurred to them: they were the bodies of their ancestors drowned in the Red Sea on account of the Jews, who had shaken off Egyptian rule. "What," said the Egyptians thereupon, "shall we bring help to those who drowned our fathers?" So they returned to their own country, justifying the warning of Jeremiah, that no dependence could be put upon Egyptian promises.

A little while after this occurrence, when Jeremiah wanted to leave Jerusalem to go to Anathoth and partake of his priestly portion there, the watchman at the gate accused him of desiring to desert to the enemy. He was delivered to his adversaries at court, and they confined him in prison. The watchman knew full well that it was a trumped up charge he was bringing against Jeremiah, and the intention attributed to him was as far as possible from the mind of the prophet, but he took this opportunity to vent an old family grudge. For this gateman was a grandson of the false prophet Hananiah, the enemy of Jeremiah, the one who had prophesied complete victory over Nebuchadnezzar within two years. It were proper to say, he calculated the victory rather than prophesied it. He reasoned: "If unto Elam, which is a mere ally of the Babylonians against the Jews, destruction has been appointed by God through Jeremiah, so much the more will the extreme penalty fall upon the Babylonians themselves, who have inflicted vast evil upon the Jews." Jeremiah's prophecy had been the reverse: so far from holding forth any hope that a victory would be won over Nebuchadnezzar, the Jewish state, he said, would suffer annihilation. Hananiah demanded a sign betokening the truth of Jeremiah's prophecy. But Jeremiah contended there could be no sign for such a prophecy as his, since the Divine determination to do evil can be annulled. On the other hand, it was the duty of Hananiah to give a sign, for he was prophesying pleasant things, and the Divine resolution for good is executed without. Finally, Jeremiah advanced the clinching argument: "I, a priest, may be well content with the prophecy; it is to my interest that the Temple should continue to stand. As for thee, thou art a Gibeonite, thou wilt have to do a slave's service in it so long as there is a Temple. But instead of troubling thy mind with the future in store for others, thou shouldst rather have thought of thine own future, for this very year thou wilt die." Hananiah, in very truth, died on the last day of the year set as his term of life, but before his death he ordered that it should be kept secret for two days, so to give the lie to Jeremiah's prophecy. With his last words, addressed to his son Shelemiah, he charged him to seek every possible way of taking revenge upon Jeremiah, to whose curse his death was to be ascribed. Shelemiah had no opportunity of fulfilling his father's last behest, but it did not pass from his mind, and when he, in turn, lay upon his deathbed, he impressed the duty of revenge upon his son Jeriah. It was the grandson of Hananiah who, when he saw Jeremiah leaving the city, hastened to take the opportunity of accusing the prophet of treason. His purpose prospered. The aristocratic enemies of Jeremiah, enraged against him, welcomed the chance to put him behind prison bars, and gave him in charge of a jailer, Jonathan, who had been a friend of the false prophet Hananiah. Jonathan pleased himself by mocking at his prisoner: "See," he would say, "see what honor thy friend does thee, to put thee in so fine a prison as this; verily, it is a royal palace."

Despite his suffering, Jeremiah did not hold back the truth. When the king inquired of him, whether he had a revelation from God, he replied: "Yes, the king of Babylonia will carry thee off into exile." To avoid irritating the king, he went into no further detail. He only prayed the king to liberate him from prison, saying: "Even wicked men like Hananiah and his descendants at least cast about for a pretext when they desire to take revenge, and their example ought not to be lost upon thee who art called Zedekiah, 'just man.'" The king granted his petition, but Jeremiah did not enjoy liberty for long. Hardly out of prison, he again advised the people to surrender, and the nobility seized him and cast him into a lime pit filled with water, where they hoped he would drown. But a miracle happened. The water sank to the bottom, and the mud rose to the surface, and supported the prophet above the water. Help came to him from Ebed-melech, a "white raven," the only pious man at court. Ebed-melech hastened to the king and spoke: "Know, if Jeremiah perishes in the lime pit, Jerusalem will surely be captured." With the permission of the king, Ebed-melech went to the pit, and cried out aloud several times, "O my lord Jeremiah," but no answer came. Jeremiah feared the words were spoken by his former jailer Jonathan, who had not given up his practice of mocking at the prophet. He would come to the edge of the pit and call down jeeringly: "Do not rest thy head on the mud, and take a little sleep, Jeremiah." To such sneers Jeremiah made no reply, and hence it was that Ebed-melech was left unanswered. Thinking the prophet dead, he began to lament and tear his clothes. Then Jeremiah, realizing that it was a friend, and not Jonathan, asked: "Who is it that is calling my name and weeps therewith?" and he received the assurance that Ebed-melech had come to rescue him from his perilous position.

NEBUCHADNEZZAR

The suffering to which Jeremiah was exposed was finally ended by the capture of Jerusalem by Nebuchadnezzar. This Babylonian king was a son of King Solomon and the Queen of Sheba. His first contact with the Jews happened in the time of his father-in-law Sennacherib, whom he accompanied on his campaign against Hezekiah. The destruction of the Assyrian army before the walls of Jerusalem, the great catastrophe from which only Nebuchadnezzar and four others escaped with their life, inspired him with fear of God. Later, in his capacity as secretary to the Babylonian king Merodach-baladan, it was he who called his master's notice to the mention of the Jewish king's name before the Name of God. "Thou callest Him 'the great God,' yet thou dost name Him after the king," he said. Nebuchadnezzar himself hastened after the messenger to bring back the letter and have it changed. He had advanced scarce three steps when he was restrained by the angel Gabriel, for even the few paces he had walked for the glory of God earned him his great power over Israel. A further step would have extended his ability to inflict harm immeasurably.

For eighteen years daily a heavenly voice resounded in the palace of Nebuchadnezzar, saying: "O thou wicked slave, go and destroy the house of thy Lord, for His children hearken not unto Him." But Nebuchadnezzar was beset with fears lest God prepare a fate for him similar to that of his ancestor Sennacherib. He practiced belomancy and consulted other auguries, to assure himself that he was against Jerusalem would result favorably. When he shook up the arrows, and questioned whether he was to go to Rome or Alexandria, not one arrow sprang up, but when he questioned about Jerusalem, one sprang up. He sowed seeds and set out planets; for Rome or Alexandria nothing came up; for Jerusalem everything sprouted and grew. He lighted candles and lanterns; for Rome or Alexandria they refused to burn, for Jerusalem they shed their light. He floated vessels on the Euphrates; for Rome or Alexandria they did not move, for Jerusalem they swam.

Still the fears of Nebuchadnezzar were not allayed. His determination to attack the Holy City ripened only after God Himself had shown him how He had bound the hands of the archangel Michael, the patron of the Jews, behind his back, in order to render him powerless to bring to his wards. So the campaign against Jerusalem was undertaken.

THE CAPTURE OF JERUSALEM

If the Babylonians thought that the conquest of Jerusalem was an easy task, they were greatly mistaken. For three years God endured the inhabitants with strength to withstand the onslaughts of the enemy, in the hope that the Jews would amend their evil ways and abandon their godless conduct, so that the threatened punishment might be annulled.

Among the many heroes in the beleaguered city that was bidding defiance to the Babylonians, one by the name of Akiba was particularly distinguished. The stones were hurled at the walls of the city from the catapults wielded by the enemy without, he was wont to catch on his feet, and throw them back upon the besiegers. Once it happened that a stone was so cast as to drop, not upon the wall, but in front of it. In his swift race toward it, Akiba was precipitated into the space between the inner and the outer wall. He quickly reassured his friends in the city, that his fall had in no wise harmed him. He was only a little shaken up and weak; as soon as he had his accustomed daily meal, a roasted ox, he would be able to scale the wall and resume the struggle with the Babylonians. But human strength and artifice avail naught against God. A gust of wind arose, and Akiba was thrown from the wall, and he died. Thereupon the Chaldeans made a breach in the wall, and penetrated into the city.

Equally fruitless were the endeavors of Hanamel, the uncle of Jeremiah, to save the city. He conjured the angels up, armed them, and had them occupy the walls. The Chaldeans retreated in terror at the sight of the heavenly host. But God changed the names of the angels, and brought them back to heaven. Hanamel's exorcisms availed naught. When he called the Angel of the Water, for instance, the response would come from the Angel of Fire, who bore the former name of his companion. Then Hanamel resorted to the extreme measure of summoning the Prince of the World, who raised Jerusalem high up in the air. But God thrust the city down again, and the enemy entered unhindered.

Nevertheless, the capture of the city could not have been accomplished if Jeremiah had been present. His deeds were as a firm pillar for the city, and his prayers as a stony wall. Therefore God sent the prophet on an errand out of the city. He was made to go to his native place, Anathoth, to take possession of a field, his by right of inheritance. Jeremiah rejoiced; he took this as a sign that God would be gracious to Judah, else He would not have commanded him to take possession of a piece of land. Scarcely had the prophet left Jerusalem when an angel descended upon the wall of the city and caused a breach to appear, at the same time crying out: "Let the enemy come and enter the house, for the Master of the house is no longer therein. The enemy has leave to despoil it and destroy it. Go ye into the vineyard and snap the vines asunder, for the Watchman hath gone away and abandoned it. But let no man boast and say, he and his have vanquished the city. Nay, a conquered city have ye conquered, a dead people have ye killed."

The enemy rushed in and ascended the Temple mount, and on the spot whereon King Solomon had been in the habit of sitting when he took counsel with the elders, the Chaldeans plotted how to reduce the Temple to ashes. During their sinister deliberations, they beheld four angels, each with a flaming torch in his hand, descending and setting fire to the four corners of the Temple. The high priest, seeing the flames shoot up, cast the keys of the Temple heavenward, saying: "Here are the keys of Thy house; it seems I am an untrustworthy custodian," and, as he turned, he was seized by the enemy and slaughtered in the very place on which he had been wont to offer the daily sacrifice. With him perished his daughter, her blood mingling with her father's. The priests and the Levites threw themselves into the flames with their harps and trumpets, and, to escape the violence feared from the licentious Chaldeans, the virgins who wove the curtains for the sanctuary followed their example. Still more horrible was the carnage caused among the people by Nebuzaradan, spurred on as he was by the sight of the blood of the murdered prophet Zechariah seething on the floor of the Temple. At first the Jews sought to conceal the true story connected with the blood. At length they had to confess, that it was the blood of a prophet who had prophesied the destruction of the Temple, and for his candor had been slain by the people. Nebuzaradan, to appease the prophet, ordered the scholars of the kingdom to be executed first on the bloody spot, then the school children, and at last the young priests, more than a million souls in all. But the blood of the prophet went on seething and reeking, until Nebuzaradan exclaimed: "Zechariah, Zechariah, the good in Israel I have slaughtered. Dost thou desire the destruction of the whole people?" Then the blood ceased to seethe.

Nebuzaradan was startled by the thought, if the Jews, who had a single life upon their conscience, were made to atone so cruelly, what would be his own fate! He left Nebuchadnezzar and became a proselyte.

THE GREAT LAMENT

On his return from Anathoth, Jeremiah saw, at a distance, smoke curling upward from the Temple mount, and his spirit was joyful. He thought the Jews had repented of their sins, and were bringing incense offerings. Once within the city walls, he knew the truth, that the Temple had fallen a prey to the incendiary. Overwhelmed by grief, he cried out: "O Lord, Thou didst entice me, and I permitted myself to be enticed; Thou didst send me forth out of Thy house that Thou mightest destroy it."

God Himself was deeply moved by the destruction of the Temple, which He had abandoned that the enemy might enter and destroy it. Accompanied by the angels, He visited the ruins, and gave vent to His sorrow: "Woe is Me on account of My house. Where are My children, where My priests, where My beloved? But what could I do for you? Did I not warn you? Yet you would not mend your ways." "To-day," God said to Jeremiah, "I am like a man who has an only son. He prepares the marriage canopy for him, and his only beloved dies under it. Thou doest seem to feel but little sympathy with Me and with My children. Go, summon Abraham, Isaac, Jacob, and Moses from their graces. They know how to mourn." "Lord of the world," replied Jeremiah, "I know not where Moses is buried." "Stand on the banks of the Jordan," said God, "and cry: 'Thou son of Amram, son of Amram, arise, see how wolves have devoured thy sheep.'"

Jeremiah repaired to the Double Cave, and spake to the Patriarchs: "Arise, ye are summoned to appear before God." When they asked him the reason of the summons, he feigned ignorance, for he feared to tell them the true reason; they might have cast reproaches upon him that so great a disaster had overtaken Israel in his time. Then Jeremiah journeyed on to the banks of the Jordan, and there he called as he had been bidden: "Thou son of Amram, son of Amram, arise, thou are cited to appear before God." "What has happened this day, that God calls me unto Him?" asked Moses. "I know not," replied Jeremiah again. Moses thereupon went to the angels, and from them he learned that the Temple had been destroyed, and Israel banished from his land. Weeping and mourning, Moses joined the Patriarchs, and together, rending their garments and wringing their hands, they betook themselves to the ruins of the Temple. Here their wailing was augmented by the loud lamentations of the angels: "How desolate are the highways to Jerusalem, the highways destined for travel without end! How deserted are the streets that once were thronged at the seasons of the pilgrimages! O Lord of the world, with Abraham the father of Thy people, who taught the world to know Thee as the ruler of the universe, Thou didst make a covenant, that through him and his descendants the earth should be filled with people, and now Thou hast dissolved Thy covenant with him. O Lord of the world! Thou hast scorned Zion and Jerusalem, once Thy chosen habitation. Thou hast dealt more harshly with Israel than with the generation of Enosh, the first idolaters."

God thereupon said to the angels: "Why do ye array yourselves against Me with your complaints?" "Lord do the world," they replied, "on account of Abraham, Thy beloved, who has come into Thy house wailing and weeping, yet Thou payest no heed unto him." Thereupon God: "Since My beloved ended his earthly career, he has not been in My house. 'What hath My beloved to do in My house'?"

Now Abraham entered into the conversation: "Why, O Lord of the world, hast Thou exiled my children, delivered them into the hands of the nations, who torture them with all tortures, and who have rendered desolate the sanctuary, where I was ready to bring Thee my son Isaac as a sacrifice?" "Thy children have sinned," said God, "they have transgressed the whole Torah, they have offended against every letter of it." Abraham: "Who is there that will testify against Israel, that he has transgressed the Torah?" God: "Let the Torah herself appear and testify." The Torah came, and Abraham addressed her: "O my daughter, dost thou indeed come to testify against Israel, to say that he violated thy commandments? Dost thou feel no shame? Remember the day on which God offered thee to all the peoples, all the nations of the earth, and they all rejected thee with disdain. Then my children came to Sinai, they accepted thee, and they honored thee. And now, on the day of their distress, thou standest up against them?" Hearing this, the Torah stepped aside, and did not testify. "Let the twenty-two letters of the Hebrew alphabet in which Torah is written come and testify against Israel," said God. They appeared without delay, and Alef, the first letter, was about to testify against Israel, when Abraham interrupted it with the words: "Thou chief of all letters, thou comest to testify against Israel in the time of his distress? Be mindful of the day on which God revealed Himself on Mount Sinai, beginning His words with thee: 'Anoki the Lord thy God.' No people, no nation accepted thee, only my children, and now thou comest to testify against them!" Alef stepped aside and was silent. The same happened with the second letter Bet, and with the third, Gimel, and with all the rest all of them retired abashed, and opened not their mouth. Now Abraham turned to God and said: "O Lord of the world! When I was a hundred years old, Thou didst give me a son, and when he was in the flower of his age, thirty-seven years old, Thou didst command me to sacrifice him to Thee, and I, like a monster, without compassion, I bound him upon the altar with mine own hands. Let that plead with Thee, and have Thou pity on my children."

Then Isaac raised his voice and spake: "O Lord of the world, when my father told me, 'God will provide Himself the lamb for a burnt offering, my son,' I did not resist Thy word. Willingly I let myself be tied to the altar, my throat was raised to meet the knife. Let that plead with Thee, and have Thou pity on my children."

Then Jacob raised his voice and spake: "O Lord of the world, for twenty years I dwelt in the house of Laban, and when I left it, I met with Esau, who sought to murder my children, and I risked my life for theirs. And now they are delivered into the hands of their enemies, like sheep led to the shambles, after I coddled them like fledglings breaking forth from their shells, after I suffered anguish for their sake all the days of my life. Let that plead with Thee, and have Thou pity on my children."

And at last Moses raised his voice and spake: "O Lord of the world, was I not a faithful shepherd unto Israel for forty long years? Like a steed I ran ahead of him in the desert, and when the time came for him to enter the Promised Land, Thou didst command: 'Here in the desert shall thy bones drop!' And now that the children of Israel are exiled, Thou hast sent for me to mourn and lament over them. That is what the people mean when they say: The good fortune of the master is none for the slave, but the master's woe is his woe." And turning to Jeremiah, he continued: "Walk before me, I will lead them back; let us see who will venture to raise a hand against them." Jeremiah replied: "The roads cannot be passed, they are blocked with corpses." But Moses was not to be deterred, and the two, Moses following Jeremiah, reached the rivers of Babylon. When the Jews saw Moses, they said: "The son of Amram has ascended from his grave to redeem us from our enemies." At that moment a heavenly voice was heard to cry out: "It is decreed!" And Moses said: "O my children, I cannot redeem you, the decree is unalterable may God redeem you speedily," and he departed from them.

The children of Israel raised their voices in sore lamentations, and the sound of their grief pierced to the very heavens. Meantime Moses returned to the Fathers, and reported to them to what dire suffering the exiled Jews were exposed, and they all broke out into woe-begone plaints. In his bitter grief, Moses exclaimed: "Be cursed, O sun, why was not thy light extinguished in the hour in which the enemy invaded the sanctuary?" The sun replied: "O faithful shepherd, I sware by the life, I could not grow dark. The heavenly powers would not permit it. Sixty fiery scourges they dealt me, and they said, 'Go and let thy light shine forth,'" Another last complaint Moses uttered: "O Lord of the world, Thou hast written it in Thy Torah: 'And whether it be cow or ewe, ye shall not kill it and her young both in one day.' How many mothers have they slaughtered with their children and Thou art silent!"

Then, with the suddenness of a flash, Rachel, our mother, stood before the Holy One, blessed be He: "Lord of the world," she said, "Thou knowest how overwhelming was Jacob's love for me, and when I observed that my father thought to put Leah in my place, I gave Jacob secret signs, that the plan of my father might be set at naught. But then I repented me of what I had done, and to spare my sister mortification, I disclosed the signs to her. More than this, I myself was in the bridal chamber, and when Jacob spake with Leah, I made reply, lest her voice betray her. I, a woman, a creature of flesh and blood, of dust and ashes, was not jealous of my rival. Thou, O God, everlasting King, Thou eternal and merciful Father, why wast Thou jealous of the idols, empty vanities? Why hast Thou driven out my children, slain them with swords, left them at the mercy of their enemies?" Then the compassion of the Supreme God was awakened, and He said: "For thy sake, O Rachel, I will lead the children of Israel back to their land."

JEREMIAH'S JOURNEY TO BABYLON

When Nebuchadnezzar dispatched his general Nebuzaradan to the capture of Jerusalem, he gave him three instructions regarding the mild treatment of Jeremiah: "Take him, and look well to him, and do him no harm; but do unto him even as he shall say unto thee." At the same time he enjoined him to use pitiless cruelty toward the rest of the people. But the prophet desired to share the fate of his suffering brethren, and when he saw a company of youths in the pillory, he put his own head into it. Nebuzaradan would always withdraw him again. Thereafter if Jeremiah saw a company of old men clapped in chains, he would join them and share their ignominy, until Nebuzaradan released him. Finally, Nebuzaradan said to Jeremiah: "Lo, thou art one of three things; either thou are a prophesier of false things, or thou art a despiser of suffering, or thou art a shedder of blood. A prophesier of false things for since many a year hast thou been prophesying the downfall of this city, and now, when thy prophecy has come true, thou sorrowest and mournest. Or a despiser of suffering for I seek to do thee naught harmful, and thou thyself pursuest what is harmful to thee, as thou to say, 'I am indifferent to pain.' Or a shedder of blood for the king has charged me to have a care of thee, and let no harm come upon thee, but as thou insistest upon seeking evil for thyself, it must be that the king may hear of thy misfortune, and put me to death."

At first Jeremiah refused Nebuzaradan's offer to let him remain in Palestine. He joined the march of the captives going to Babylon, along the highways streaming with blood and strewn with corpses. When they arrived at the borders of the Holy Land, they all, prophet and people, broke out into loud wails, and Jeremiah said: "Yes, brethren and countrymen, all this hath befallen you, because ye did not hearken unto the words of my prophecy." Jeremiah journeyed with them until they came to the banks of the Euphrates. Then God spoke to the prophet: "Jeremiah, if thou remainest here, I shall go with them, and if thou goest with them, I shall remain here." Jeremiah replied: "Lord of the world, if I go with them, what doth it avail them? Only if their King, their Creator accompanies them, will it bestead them."

When the captives saw Jeremiah make preparations to return to Palestine, they began to weep and cry: "O Father Jeremiah, wilt thou, too, abandon us?" "I call heaven and earth to witness," said the prophet, "had you wept but once in Zion, ye had not been driven out."

Beset with terrors was the return journey for the prophet. Corpses lay everywhere, and Jeremiah gathered up all the fingers that lay about; he strained them to his heart, fondled them, kissed them, and wrapped them in his mantle, saying sadly: "Did I not tell you, my children, did I not say to you, 'Give glory to the Lord your God, before He cause darkness, and before your feet stumble upon the dark mountains'?"

Dejected, oppressed by his grief, Jeremiah saw the fulfilment of his prophecy against the coquettish maidens of Jerusalem, who had pursued but the pleasures and enjoyments of the world. How often had the prophet admonished them to do penance and lead a God-fearing life! In vain; whenever he threatened them with the destruction of Jerusalem, they said: "Why should we concern ourselves about it?" "A prince will take me unto wife," said one, the other, "A prefect will marry me." And at first it seemed the expectations of Jerusalem's fair daughters would be realized, for the most aristocratic of the victorious Chaldeans were charmed by the beauty of the women of Jerusalem, and offered them their hand and their rank. But God sent disfiguring and repulsive diseases upon the women, and the Babylonians cast them off, threw them violently out of their chariots, and ruthlessly drove them over the prostrate bodies.

TRANSPORTATION OF THE CAPTIVES

Nebuchadnezzar's orders were to hurry the captives along the road to Babylon without stop or stay. He feared the Jews might else find opportunity to supplicate the mercy of God, and He, compassionate as He is, would release them instantly they did penance. Accordingly, there was no pause in the forward march, until the Euphrates was reached. There they were within the borders of the empire of Nebuchadnezzar, and he thought he had nothing more to fear.

Many of the Jews died as soon as they drank of the Euphrates. In their native land they had been accustomed to the water drawn from springs and wells. Mourning over their dead and over the others that had fallen by the way, they sat on the banks of the river, while Nebuchadnezzar and his princes on their vessels celebrated their victory amid song and music. The king noticed that the princes of Judah, though they were in chains, bore no load upon their shoulders, and he called to his servants: "Have you no load for these?" They took the parchment scrolls of the law, tore them in pieces, made sacks of them, and filled them with sand; these they loaded upon the backs of the Jewish princes. At sight of this disgrace, all Israel broke out into loud weeping. The voice of their sorrow pierced the very heavens, and God determined to turn the world once more into chaos, for He told Himself, that after all the world was created but for the sake of Israel. The angels hastened thither, and they spake before God: "O Lord of the world, the universe is Thine. Is it not enough that Thou hast dismembered Thy earthly house, the Temple? Wilt Thou destroy Thy heavenly house, too?" God restraining them said: "Do ye think I am a creature of flesh and blood, and stand in need of consolation? Do I not know beginning and end of all things? Go rather and remove their burdens from the princes of Judah." Aided by God the angels descended, and they carried the loads put upon the Jewish captives until they reached Babylon.

On their way, they passed the city of Bari. The inhabitants thereof were not a little astonished at the cruelty of Nebuchadnezzar, who made the captives march naked. The people of Bari stripped their slaves of their clothes, and presented the slaves to Nebuchadnezzar. When the king expressed his astonishment thereat, they said: "We thought thou wert particularly pleased with naked men." The king at once ordered the Jews to be arrayed in their garments. The reward accorded the Bariites was that God endowed them forever with beauty and irresistible grace.

The compassionate Bariites did not find many imitators. The very opposite quality was displayed by the Ammonites, Moabites, Edomites, and Arabs. Despite their close kinship with Israel, their conduct toward the Jews was dictated by cruelty. The two first-mentioned, the Ammonites and the Moabites, when they heard the prophet foretell the destruction of Jerusalem, hastened without a moment's delay to report it to Nebuchadnezzar, and urge him to attack Jerusalem. The scruples of the Babylonian king, who feared God, and all the reasons he advanced against a combat with Israel, they refuted, and finally they induced him to act as they wished. At the capture of the city, while all the strange nations were seeking booty, the Ammonites and the Moabites threw themselves into the Temple to seize the scroll of the law, because it contained the clause against their entering into the "assembly of the Lord even to the tenth generation." To disgrace the faith of Israel, they plucked the Cherubim from the Holy of Holies and dragged them through the streets of Jerusalem, crying aloud at the same time: "Behold these sacred things that belong to the Israelites, who say ever they have no idols."

The Edomites were still more hostile in the hour of Israel's need. They went to Jerusalem with Nebuchadnezzar, but they kept themselves at a distance from the city, there to await the outcome of the battle between the Jews and the Babylonians. If the Jews had been victorious, they would have pretended they had come to bring them aid. When Nebuchadnezzar's victory became known, they showed their true feelings. Those who escaped the sword of the Babylonians, were hewn down by the hand of the Edomites.

But in fiendish cunning these nations were surpassed by the Ishmaelites. Eighty thousand young priests, each with a golden shield upon his breast, succeeded in making their way through the ranks of Nebuchadnezzar and in reaching the Ishmaelites. They asked for water to drink. The reply of the Ishmaelites was: "First eat, and then you may drink," at the same time handing them salt food. Their thirst was increased, and the Ishmaelites gave them leather bags filled with nothing but air instead of water. When they raised them to their mouths, the air entered their bodies, and they fell dead.

Other Arabic tribes showed their hostility openly; as the Palmyrenes, who put eighty thousand archers at the disposal of Nebuchadnezzar in his war against Israel.

THE SONS OF MOSES

If Nebuchadnezzar thought, that once he had the Jews in the regions of the Euphrates they were in his power forever, he was greatly mistaken. It was on the very banks of the great river that he suffered the loss of a number of his captives. When the first stop was made by the Euphrates, the Jews could no longer contain their grief, and they broke out into tears and bitter lamentations. Nebuchadnezzar bade them be silent, and as though to render obedience to his orders the harder, he called upon the Levites, the minstrels of the Temple to sing the songs of Zion for the entertainment of his guests at the banquet he had arranged. The Levites consulted with one another. "Not enough that the Temple lies in ashes because of our sins, should we add to our transgressions by coaxing music from the strings of our holy harps in honor of these 'dwarfs'?" they said, and they determined to offer resistance. The murderous Babylonians mowed them down in heaps, yet they met death with high courage, for it saved their sacred instruments from the desecration of being used before idols and for the sake of idolaters.

The Levites who survived the carnage the Sons of Moses they were bit their own fingers off, and when they were asked to play, they showed their tyrants mutilated hands, with which it was impossible to manipulate their harps. At the fall of night a cloud descended and enveloped the Sons of Moses and all who belonged to them. They were hidden from their enemies, while their own way was illuminated by a pillar of fire. The cloud and the pillar vanished at break of day, and before the Sons of Moses lay a tract of land bordered by the sea on three sides. For their complete protection God made the river Sambation to flow on the fourth side. This river is full of sand and stones, and on the six working days of the week, they tumble over each other with such vehemence that the crash and the roar are heard far and wide. But on the Sabbath the tumultuous river subsides into quiet. As a guard against trespassers on that day, a column of cloud stretches along the whole length of the river, and none can approach the Sambation within three miles. Hedged in as they are, the Sons of Moses yet communicate with their brethren of the tribes of Naphtali, Gad, and Asher, who dwell near the banks of the Sambation. Carrier pigeons bear letters hither and thither.

In the land of the Sons of Moses there are none but clean animals, and in every respect the inhabitants lead a holy and pure life, worthy of their ancestor Moses. They never use an oath, and, if perchance an oath escapes the lips of one of them, he is at once reminded of the Divine punishment connected with his act his children will die at a tender age.

The Sons of Moses live peaceably and enjoy prosperity as equals through their common Jewish faith. They have need of neither prince nor judge, for they know not strife and litigation. Each works for the welfare of the community, and each takes from the common store only what will satisfy his needs. Their houses are built of equal height, that no one may deem himself above his neighbor, and that that the fresh air may not be hindered from playing freely about all alike. Even at night their doors stand wide open, for they have naught to fear from thieves, nor are wild animals known in their land. They all attain a good old age. The son never dies before the father. When a death occurs, there is rejoicing, because the departed is known to have entered into life everlasting in loyalty to his faith. The birth of a child, on the other hand, calls forth mourning, for who can tell whether the being ushered into the world will be pious and faithful? The dead are buried near the doors of their own houses, in order that their survivors, in all their comings and goings, may be reminded of their own end. Disease is unknown among them, for they never sin, and sickness is sent only to purify from sins.

EBED-MELECH

The Sons of Moses were not the only ones to escape from under the heavy hand of Nebuchadnezzar. Still more miraculous was the deliverance of the pious Ethiopian Ebed-melech from the hands of the Babylonians. He was saved as a reward for rescuing Jeremiah when the prophet's life was jeopardized. On the day before the destruction of the Temple, shortly before the enemy forced his way into the city, the Ethiopian was sent, by the prophet Jeremiah acting under Divine instruction, to a certain place in front of the gates of the city, to dole out refreshments to the poor from a little basket of figs he was to carry with him. Ebed-melech reached the spot, but the heat was so intense that he fell asleep under a tree, and there he slept for sixty-six years. When he woke up, the figs were still fresh and juicy, but all the surroundings had so changed, he could not make out where he was. His confusion increased when he entered the city to seek Jeremiah, and found nothing as it had been. He accosted an old man, and asked him the name of the place. When he was told it was Jerusalem, Ebed-melech cried out in amazement: "Where is Jeremiah, where is Baruch, and where are all the people?" The old man was not a little astonished at these questions. How was it possible that one who had known Jeremiah and Jerusalem should be ignorant of the events that had passed sixty years before? In brief words he told Ebed-melech of the destruction of the Temple and of the captivity of the people, but what he said found no credence with his auditor. Finally Ebed-melech realized that God had performed a great miracle for him, so that he had been spared the sight of Israel's misfortune.

While he was pouring out his heart in gratitude to God, an eagle descended and led him to Baruch, who lived not far from the city. Thereupon Baruch received the command from God to write to Jeremiah that the people should remove the strangers from the midst of them, and then God would lead them back to Jerusalem. The letter written by Baruch and some of the figs that had retained their freshness for sixty-six years were carried to Babylonia by an eagle, who had told Baruch that he had been sent to serve him as a messenger. The eagle set out on his journey. His first halting-place was a dreary waste spot to which he knew Jeremiah and the people would come it was the burial-place of the Jews which Nebuchadnezzar had given the prophet at his solicitation. When the eagle saw Jeremiah and the people approach with a funeral train, he cried out: "I have a message for thee, Jeremiah. Let all the people draw nigh to receive the good tidings." As a sign that his mission was true, the eagle touched the corpse, and it came to life. Amidst tears all the people cried unto Jeremiah: "Save us! What must we do to return to our land?"

The eagle brought Jeremiah's answer to Baruch, and after the prophet had sent the Babylonian women away, he returned to Jerusalem with the people. Those who would not submit to the orders of Jeremiah relative to the heathen women, were not permitted by the prophet to enter the holy city, and as they likewise were not permitted to return to Babylonia, they founded the city of Samaria near Jerusalem.

THE TEMPLE VESSELS

The task laid upon Jeremiah had been twofold. Besides giving him charge over the people in the land of their exile, God had entrusted to him the care of the sanctuary and all it contained. The holy Ark, the altar of incense, and the holy tent were carried by an angel to the mount whence Moses before his death had viewed the land divinely assigned to Israel. There Jeremiah found a spacious place, in which he concealed these sacred utensils. Some of his companions had gone with him to note the way to the cave, but yet they could not find it. When Jeremiah heard of their purpose, he censured them, for it was the wish of God that the place of hiding should remain a secret until the redemption, and then God Himself will make the hidden things visible.

Even the Temple vessels not concealed by Jeremiah were prevented from falling into the hands of the enemy; the gates of the Temple sank into the earth, and other parts and utensils were hidden in a tower at Bagdad by the Levite Shimur and his friends. Among these utensils was the seven-branched candlestick of pure gold, every branch set with twenty-six pearls, and beside the pearls two hundred stones of inestimable worth. Furthermore, the tower at Bagdad was the hiding-place for seventy-seven golden tables, and for the gold with which the walls of the Temple had been clothed within and without. The tables had been taken from Paradise by Solomon, and in brilliance they outshone the sun and the moon, while the gold from the walls excelled in amount and worth all the gold that had existed from the creation of the world until the destruction of the Temple. The jewels, pearls, gold, and silver, and precious gems, which David and Solomon had intended for the Temple were discovered by the scribe Hilkiah, and he delivered them to the angel Shamshiel, who in turn deposited the treasure in Borsippa. The sacred musical instruments were taken charge of and hidden by Baruch and Zedekiah until the advent of the Messiah, who will reveal all treasures. In his time a stream will break forth from under the place of the Holy of Holies, and flow through the lands to the Euphrates, and, as it flows, it will uncover all the treasures buried in the earth.

BARUCH

At the time of the destruction of the Temple, one of the prominent figures was Baruch, the faithful attendant of Jeremiah. God commanded him to leave the city one day before the enemy was to enter it, in order that his presence might not render it impregnable. On the following day, he and all other pious men having abandoned Jerusalem, he saw from a distance how the angels descended, set fire to the city walls, and concealed the sacred vessels of the Temple. At first his mourning over the misfortunes of Jerusalem and the people knew no bounds. But he was in a measure consoled at the end of a seven days' fast, when God made known to him that the day of reckoning would come for the heathen, too. Other Divine visions were vouchsafed him. The whole future of mankind was unrolled before his eyes, especially the history of Israel, and he learned that the coming of the Messiah would put an end to all sorrow and misery, and usher in the reign of peace and joy among men. As for him, he would be removed from the earth, he was told, but not through death, and only in order to be kept safe against the coming of the end of all time.

Thus consoled, Baruch addressed an admonition to the people left in Palestine, and wrote two letters of the same tenor to the exiles, one to the nine tribes and a half, the other to the two tribes and a half. The letter to the nine tribes and a half of the captivity was carried to them by an eagle.

Five years after the great catastrophe, he composed a book in Babylon, which contained penitential prayers and hymns of consolation, exhorting Israel and urging the people to return to God and His law. This book Baruch read to King Jeconiah and the whole people on a day of prayer and penitence. On the same occasion a collection was taken up among the people, and the funds thus secured, together with the silver Temple vessels made by order of Zedekiah after Jeconiah had been carried away captive, were sent to Jerusalem, with the request that the high priest Joakim and the people should apply the money to the sacrificial service and to prayers for the life of King Nebuchadnezzar and his son Belshazzar. Thus they might ensure peace and happiness under Babylonian rule. Above all, they were to supplicate God to turn away His wrath from His people.

Baruch sent his book also to the residents of Jerusalem, and they read it in the Temple on distinguished days, and recited the prayers it contains.

Baruch is one of the few mortals who have been privileged to visit Paradise and know its secrets. An angel of the Lord appeared to him while he was lamenting over the destruction of Jerusalem and took him to the seven heavens, to the place of judgment where the doom of the godless is pronounced, and to the abodes of the blessed.

He was still among the living at the time in which Cyrus permitted the Jews to return to Palestine, but on account of his advanced age he could not avail himself of the permission. So long as he was alive, his disciple Ezra remained with him in Babylonia, for "the study of the law is more important than the building of the Temple." It was only after the death of Baruch that he decided to gather together the exiles who desired to return to the Holy Land and rebuild the Temple in Jerusalem.

THE TOMBS OF BARUCH AND EZEKIEL

The piety of Baruch and the great favor he enjoyed with God were made known to later generations many years after his death, through the marvellous occurrences connected with his tomb. Once a Babylonian prince commanded a Jew, Rabbi Solomon by name, to show him the grave of Ezekiel, concerning which he had heard many remarkable tales. The Jew advised the prince first to enter the tomb of Baruch, which adjoined that of Ezekiel. Having succeeded in this, he might attempt the same with the tomb of Ezekiel, the teacher of Baruch. In the presence of his grandees and his people the prince tried to open the grave of Baruch, but his efforts were fruitless. Whosoever touched it, was at once stricken dead. An old Arab advised the prince to call upon the Jews to gain entrance for him, seeing that Baruch had been a Jew, and his books were still being studied by Jews. The Jews prepared themselves by fasts, prayers, penitence, and almsgiving, and they succeeded in opening the grave without a mishap. Baruch was found lying on marble bier, and the appearance of the corpse was as though he had only then passed away. The prince ordered the bier to be brought to the city, and the body to be entombed there. He thought it was not seemly that Ezekiel and Baruch should rest in the same grave. But the bearers found it impossible to remove the bier more than two thousands ells from the original grave; not even with the help of numerous draught-animals could it be urged a single step further. Following the advice of Rabbi Solomon, the prince resolved to enter the bier on the spot they had reached and also to erect an academy there. These miraculous happenings induced the prince to go to Mecca. There he became convinced of the falseness of Mohammedanism, of which he had hitherto been an adherent, and he converted to Judaism, he and his whole court.

Near the grave of Baruch there grows a species of grass whose leaves are covered with gold dust. As the sheen of the gold is not readily noticeable by day, the people seek out the place at night, mark the very spot on which the grass grows, and return by day and gather it.

Not less famous is the tomb of Ezekiel, at a distance of two thousand ells from Baruch's. It is overarched by a beautiful mausoleum erected by King Jeconiah after Evil-merodach had released him from captivity. The mausoleum existed down to the middle ages, and it bore on its walls the names of the thirty-five thousand Jews who assisted Jeconiah in erecting the monument. It was the scene of many miracles. When great crowds of people journeyed thither to pay reverence to the memory of the prophet, the little low gate in the wall surrounding the grave enlarged in width and height to admit all who desired to enter. Once a prince vowed to give a colt to the grave of the prophet, if but his mare which had been sterile would bear one. When his wish was fulfilled, however, he did not keep his promise. But the filly ran a distance equal to a four days' journey to the tomb, and his owner could not recover it until he deposited his value in silver upon the grace. When people went on long journeys, they were in the habit of carrying their treasures to the grave of the prophet, and beseeching him to let none but the rightful heirs remove them thence. The prophet always granted their petition. Once when an attempt was made to take some books from the grave of Ezekiel, the ravager suddenly became sick and blind. For a time a pillar of fire, visible at a great distance, rose above the grave of the prophet, but it disappeared in consequence of the unseemly conduct of the pilgrims who resorted thither.

Not far from the grave of Ezekiel was the grave of Barozak, who once appeared to a rich Jew in a dream. He spoke: "I am Barozak, one of the princes who were led into captivity with Jeremiah. I am one of the just. If thou wilt erect a handsome mausoleum for me, thou wilt be blessed with progeny." The Jew did as he had been bidden, and he who had been childless, shortly after became a father.

DANIEL

The most distinguished member of the Babylonian Diaspora was Daniel. Though not a prophet, he was surpassed by none in wisdom, piety, and good deeds. His firm adherence to Judaism he displayed from his early youth, when, a page at the royal court, he refused to partake of the bread, wine, and oil of the heathen, even though the enjoyment of them was not prohibited by the law. In general, his prominent position at the court was maintained at the cost of many a hardship, for he and his companions, Hananiah, Mishael, and Azariah, were envied their distinctions by numerous enemies, who sought to compass their ruin.

Once they were accused before King Nebuchadnezzar of leading an unchaste life. The king resolved to order their execution. But Daniel and his friends mutilated certain parts of their bodies, and so demonstrated how unfounded were the charges against them.

As a youth Daniel gave evidence of his wisdom, when he convicted two old sinners of having testified falsely against Susanna, as beautiful as she was good. Misled by the perjured witnesses, the court had condemned Susanna to death. Then Daniel, impelled by a higher power, appeared among the people, proclaimed that wrong had been done, and demanded that the case be re-opened. And so it was. Daniel himself cross-questioned the witnesses one after the other. The same questions were addressed to both, and as the replies did not agree with each other, the false witnesses stood condemned, and they were made to suffer the penalty they would have had the court inflict upon their victim.

Daniel's high position in the state dates from the time when he interpreted Nebuchadnezzar's dream. The king said to the astrologers and magicians: "I know my dream, but I do not want to tell you what it was, else you will invent anything at all, and pretend it is the interpretation of the dream. But if you tell me the dream, then I shall have confidence in your interpretation of it."

After much talk between Nebuchadnezzar and his wise men, they confessed that the king's wish might have been fulfilled, if but the Temple had still existed. The high priest at Jerusalem might have revealed the secret by consulting the Urim and Thummim. At this point the king became wrathful against his wise men, who had advised him to destroy the Temple, though they must have known how useful it might become to the king and the state. He ordered them all to execution. Their life was saved by Daniel, who recited the king's dream, and gave its interpretation. The king was so filled with admiration of Daniel's wisdom that he paid him Divine honors. Daniel, however, refused such extravagant treatment he did not desire to be the object of idolatrous veneration. He left Nebuchadnezzar in order to escape the marks of honor thrust upon him, and repaired to Tiberias, where he build a canal. Besides, he was charged by the king with commissions, to bring fodder for cattle to Babylonia and also swine from Alexandria.

THE THREE MEN IN THE FURNACE

During Daniel's absence Nebuchadnezzar set up an idol, and its worship was exacted from all his subject under penalty of death by fire. The image could not stand on account of the disproportion between its height and its thickness. The whole of the gold and silver captured by the Babylonians in Jerusalem was needed to give it steadiness.

All the nations owning the rule of Nebuchadnezzar, including even Israel, obeyed the royal command to worship the image. Only the three pious companions of Daniel, Hananiah, Mishael, and Azariah, resisted the order. In vain Nebuchadnezzar urged upon them, as an argument in favor if idolatry, that the Jews had been so devoted to heathen practices before the destruction of Jerusalem that they had gone to Babylonia for the purpose of imitating the idols there and bringing the copies they made to Jerusalem. The three saints would not hearken to these seductions of the king, nor when he referred them to such authorities as Moses and Jeremiah, in order to prove to them that they were under obligation to do the royal bidding. They said to him: "Thou art our king in all that concerns service, taxes, poll-money, and tribute, but with respect to thy present command thou art only Nebuchadnezzar. Therein thou and the dog are alike unto us. Bark like a dog, inflate thyself like a water-bottle, and chirp like a cricket."

Now Nebuchadnezzar's wrath transcended all bound, and he ordered the three to be cast into a red hot furnace, so hot that the flames of its fire darted to the height of forty-nine ells beyond the oven, and consumed the heathen standing about it. No less than four nations were thus exterminated. While the three saints were being thrust into the furnace, they addressed a fervent prayer to God, supplicating His grace toward them, and entreating Him to put their adversaries to shame. The angels desired to descend and rescue the three men in the furnace. But God forbade it: "Did the three men act thus for your sakes? Nay, they did it for Me; and I will save them with Mine own hands." God also rejected the good offices of Yurkami, the angel of hail who offered to extinguish the fire in the furnace. The angel Gabriel justly pointed out that such a miracle would not be sufficiently striking to arrest attention. His own proposition was accepted. He, the angel of fire, was deputed to snatch the three men from the red hot furnace. He executed his mission by cooling off the fire inside of the oven, while on the outside the heat continued to increase to such a degree that the heathen standing around the furnace were consumed. The three youths thereupon raised their voices together in a hymn of praise to God, thanking Him for His miraculous help. The Chaldeans observed the three men pacing up and down quietly in the furnace, followed by a fourth the angel Gabriel as by an attendant. Nebuchadnezzar, who hastened thither to see the wonder, was stunned with fright, for he recognized Gabriel to be the angel who in the guise of a column of fire had blasted the army of Sennacherib. Six other miracles happened, all of them driving terror to the heart of the king: the fiery furnace which had been sunk in the ground raised itself into the air; it was broken; the bottom dropped out; the image erected by Nebuchadnezzar fell prostrate; four nations were wasted by fire; and Ezekiel revived the dead in the valley of Dura.

Of the last, Nebuchadnezzar was apprised in a peculiar way. He had a drinking vessel made of the bones of a slain Jew. When he was about to use it, life began to stir in the bones, and a blow was planted in the king's face, while a voice announced: "A friend of this man is at this moment reviving the dead!" Nebuchadnezzar now offered praise to God for the miracles performed, and if an angel had not quickly struck him a blow on his mouth, and forced him into silence, his psalms of praise would have excelled the Psalter of David.

The deliverance of the three pious young men was a brilliant vindication of their ways, but at the same time it caused great mortification to the masses of the Jewish people, who had complied with the order of Nebuchadnezzar to worship his idol. Accordingly, when the three men left the furnace which they did not do until Nebuchadnezzar invited them to leave the heathen struck all the Jews they met in the face, deriding them at the same time: "You who have so marvellous a God pay homage to an idol!" The three men thereupon left Babylonia and went to Palestine, where they joined their friend, the high priest Joshua.

Their readiness to sacrifice their lives for the honor of God had been all the more admirable as they had been advised by the prophet Ezekiel that no miracle would be done for their sakes. When the king's command to bow down before the idol was published, and the three men were appointed to act as the representatives of the people, Hananiah and his companions resorted to Daniel for his advice.

He referred them to the prophet Ezekiel, who counselled flight, citing his teacher Isaiah as his authority. The three men rejected his advice, and declared themselves ready to suffer the death of martyrs. Ezekiel bade them tarry until he inquired of God, whether a miracle would be done for them. The words of God were: "I shall not manifest Myself as their savior. They caused My house to be destroyed, My palace to be burnt, My children to be dispersed among the heathen, and now they appeal for My help. As I live, I will not be found of them."

Instead of discouraging the three men, this answer but infused new spirit and resolution in them, and they declared with more decided emphasis than before, that they were ready to meet death. God consoled the weeping prophet by revealing to him, that He would save the three saintly heroes. He had sought to restrain them from martyrdom only to let their piety and steadfastness appear the brighter.

On account of their piety it became customary to swear by the Name of Him who supports the world on three pillars, the pillars being the saints Hananiah, Mishael, and Azariah. Their deliverance from death by fire worked a great effect upon the disposition of the heathen. They were convinced of the uselessness of their idols, and with their own hands they destroyed them.

EZEKIEL REVIVES THE DEAD

Among the dead whom Ezekiel restored to life at the same time when the three men were redeemed from the fiery furnace were different classes of persons. Some were the Ephraimites that had perished in the attempt to escape from Egypt before Moses led the whole nation out of the land of bondage. Some were the godless among the Jews that had polluted the Temple at Jerusalem with heathen rites, and those still more godless who in life had not believed in the resurrection of the dead. Others of those revived by Ezekiel were the youths among the Jews carried away captive to Babylonia by Nebuchadnezzar whose beauty was so radiant that it darkened the very splendor of the sun. The Babylonian women were seized with a great passion for them, and at the solicitation of their husbands, Nebuchadnezzar ordered a bloody massacre of the handsome youths. But the Babylonian women were not yet cured of their unlawful passion; the beauty of the young Hebrews haunted them until their corpses lay crushed before them, their graceful bodies mutilated. These were the youths recalled to life by the prophet Ezekiel. Lastly, he revived some that had perished only a short time before. When Hananiah, Mishael, and Azariah were saved from death, Nebuchadnezzar thus addressed the other Jews, those who had yielded obedience to his command concerning the worship of the idol: "You know that your God can help and save, nevertheless you paid worship to an idol which is incapable of doing anything. This proves that, as you have destroyed your own land by your wicked deeds, so you are now trying to destroy my land with your iniquity." Forthwith he commanded that they all be executed, sixty thousand in number. Twenty years passed, and Ezekiel was vouchsafed the vision in which God bade him repair to the Valley of Dura, where Nebuchadnezzar had set up his idol, and had massacred the host of the Jews. Here God showed him the dry bones of the slain with the question: "Can I revive these bones?" Ezekiel's answer was evasive, and as a punishment for his little faith, he had to end his days in Babylon, and was not granted even burial in the soil of Palestine. God then dropped the dew of heaven upon the dry bones, and "sinews were upon them, and flesh came up, and skin covered them above." At the same time God sent forth winds to the four corners of the earth, which unlocked the treasure houses of souls, and brought its own soul to each body. All came to life except one man, who, as God explained to the prophet, was excluded from the resurrection because he was a usurer.

In spite of the marvellous miracle performed from them, the men thus restored to life wept, because they feared they would have no share at the end of time in the resurrection of the whole of Israel. But the prophet assured them, in the name of God, that their portion in all that had been promised Israel should in no wise be diminished.

NEBUCHADNEZZAR A BEAST

Nebuchadnezzar, the ruler of the whole world, to whom even the wild animals paid obedience, his pet was a lion with a snake coiled about its neck, did not escape punishment for his sins. He was chastised as none before him. He whom fear of God had at first held back from a war against Jerusalem, and who had to be dragged forcibly, as he sat on his horse, to the Holy of Holies by the archangel Michael, he later became so arrogant that he thought himself a god, and cherished the plan of enveloping himself in a cloud, so that he might live apart from men. A heavenly voice resounded: "O thou wicked man, son of a wicked man, and descendant of Nimrod the wicked, who incited the world to rebel against God! Behold, the days of the years of a man are threescore years and ten, or perhaps by reason of strength fourscore years. It takes five hundred years to traverse the distance of the earth from the first heaven, and as long a time to penetrate from the bottom to the top of the first heaven, and not less are the distances from one of the seven heavens to the next. How, then, canst thou speak of ascending like unto the Most High 'above the heights of the clouds'?" For this transgression of deeming himself more than a man, he was punished by being made to live for some time as a beast among beasts, treated by them as though he were one of them. For forty days he led this life. As far down as his navel he had the appearance of an ox, and the lower part of his body resembled that of a lion. Like an ox he ate grass, and like a lion he attacked a curious crowd, but Daniel spent his time in prayer, entreating that the seven years of this brutish life allotted to Nebuchadnezzar might be reduced to seven months. His prayer was granted. At the end of forty days reason returned to the king, the next forty days he passed in weeping bitterly over his sins, and in the interval that remained to complete the seven months he again lived the life of a beast.

HIRAM

Hiram, the king of Tyre, was a contemporary of Nebuchadnezzar, and in many respects resembled him. He, too, esteemed himself a god, and sought to make men believe in his divinity by the artificial heavens he fashioned for himself. In the sea he erected four iron pillars, on which he build up seven heavens, each five hundred ells larger than the one below. The first was a plate of glass of five hundred square ells, and the second a plate of iron of a thousand square ells. The third, of lead, and separated from the second by canals, contained huge round boulders, which produced the sound of thunder on the iron. The fourth heaven was of brass, the fifth of copper, the sixth of silver, and the seventh of gold, all separated from each other by canals. In the seventh, thirty-five hundred ells in extent, he had diamonds and pearls, which he manipulated so as to produce the effect of flashes and sheets of lightening, while the stones below imitated the growling of the thunder.

As Hiram was thus floating above the earth, in his vain imagination deeming himself superior to the rest of men, he suddenly perceived the prophet Ezekiel next to himself. He had been waved thither by a wind. Frightened and amazed, Hiram asked the prophet how he had risen to his heights. The answer was: "God brought me here, and He bade me ask thee why thou art so proud, thou born of woman?" The king of Tyre replied defiantly: "I am not one born of woman; I live forever, and as God resides on the sea, so my abode is on the sea, and as He inhabits seven heavens, so do I. See how many kings I have survived! Twenty-one of the House of David, and as many of the Kingdom of the Ten Tribes, and no less than fifty prophets and ten high priests have I buried." Thereupon God said: "I will destroy My house, that henceforth Hiram may have no reason for self-glorification, because all his pride comes only from the circumstance that he furnished the cedar-trees for the building of the Temple." The end of this proud king was that he was conquered by Nebuchadnezzar, deprived of this throne, and made to suffer a cruel death. Though the Babylonian king was the step-son of Hiram, he had no mercy with him. Daily he cut off a bit of the flesh of his body, and forced the Tyrian king to eat it, until the finally perished. Hiram's palace was swallowed by the earth, and in the bowels of the earth it will remain until it shall emerge in the future world as the habitation of the pious.

THE FALSE PROPHETS

Not only among the heathen, but also among the Jews there were very sinful people in those days. The most notorious Jewish sinners were the two false prophets Ahab and Zedekiah. Ahab came to the daughter of Nebuchadnezzar and said: "Yield thyself to Zedekiah," telling her this in the form of a Divine message. The same was done by Zedekiah, who only varied the message by substituting the name of Ahab. The princess could not accept such messages as Divine, and she told her father what had occurred. Though Nebuchadnezzar was so addicted to immoral practices that he was in the habit of making his captive kings drunk, and then satisfying his unnatural lusts upon them, and a miracle had to interpose to shield the pious of Judah against this disgrace, yet he well knew that the God of the Jews hates immorality. He therefore questioned Hananiah, Mishael, and Azariah about it, and they emphatically denied the possibility that such a message could have come from God. The prophets of lies refused to recall their statements, and Nebuchadnezzar decided to subject them to the same fiery test as he had decreed for the three pious companions of Daniel. To be fair toward them, the king permitted them to choose a third fellow-sufferer, some pious man to share their lot. Seeing no escape, Ahab and Zedekiah asked for Joshua, later the high priest, as their companion in the furnace, in the hope that his distinguished merits would suffice to save all three of them. They were mistaken. Joshua emerged unhurt, only his garments were seared, but the false prophets were consumed. Joshua explained the singeing of his garments by the fact that he was directly exposed to the full fury of the flames. But the truth was that he had to expiate the sins of his sons, who had contracted marriages unworthy of their dignity and descent. Therefore their father escaped death only after the fire had burnt his garments.

DANIEL'S PIETY

No greater contrast to Hiram and the false prophets Ahab and Zedekiah can be imagined than is presented by the character of the pious Daniel. When Nebuchadnezzar offered him Divine honors, he refused what Hiram sought to obtain by every means in his power. The Babylonian king felt so ardent an admiration for Daniel that he sent him from the country when the time arrived to worship the idol he had erected in Dura, for he knew very well that Daniel would prefer death in the flames to disregard of the commands of God, and he could not well have cast the man into the fire to whom he had paid Divine homage. Moreover, it was the wish of God that Daniel should not pass through the fiery ordeal at the same time as his three friends, in order that their deliverance might not be ascribed to him.

In spite of all this, Nebuchadnezzar endeavored to persuade Daniel by gentle means to worship an idol. He had the golden diadem of the high priest inserted in the mouth of an idol, and by reason of the wondrous power that resides in the Holy Name inscribed on the diadem, the idol gained the ability to speak, and it said the words: "I am thy God." Thus were many seduced to worship the image. But Daniel could not be misled so easily. He secured permission from the king to kiss the idol. Laying his mouth upon the idol's, he adjured the diadem in the following words:

"I am but flesh and blood, yet at the same time a messenger of God. I therefore admonish thee, take heed that the Name of the Holy One, blessed be He, may not be desecrated, and I order thee to follow me." So it happened. When the heathen came with music and song to give honor to the idol, it emitted no sound, but a storm broke loose and overturned it.

On still another occasion Nebuchadnezzar tried to persuade Daniel to worship an idol, this time a dragon that devoured all who approached it, and therefore was adored as a god by the Babylonians. Daniel had straw mixed with nails fed to him, and the dragon ate and perished almost immediately.

All this did not prevent Daniel from keeping the welfare of the king in mind continually. Hence it was that when Nebuchadnezzar was engaged in setting his house in order, he desired to mention 'Daniel in his will as one of his heirs. But the Jew refused with the words: "Far be it from me to leave the inheritance of my fathers for that of the uncircumcised."

Nebuchadnezzar died after having reigned forty years, as long as King David. The death of the tyrant brought hope and joy to many a heart, for his severity had been such that during his lifetime none dared laugh, and when he descended to Sheol, its inhabitants trembled, fearing he had come to reign over them, too. However, a heavenly voice called to him: "Go down, and be thou laid down with the uncircumcised."

The interment of this great king was anything but what one might have expected, and for this reason: During the seven years spent by Nebuchadnezzar among the beast, his son Evil-merodach ruled in his stead. Nebuchadnezzar reappeared after his period of penance, and incarcerated his son for life. When the death of Nebuchadnezzar actually did occur, Evil-merodach refused to accept the homage the nobles brought him as the new king, because he feared that his father was not dead, but had only disappeared as once before, and would return again. To convince him of the groundlessness of his apprehension, the corpse of Nebuchadnezzar, badly mutilated by his enemies, was dragged through the streets.

Shortly afterward occurred the death of Zedekiah, the dethroned king of Judah. His burial took place amid great demonstrations of sympathy and mourning. The elegy over him ran thus: "Alas that King Zedekiah had to die, he who quaffed the lees which all the generations before him accumulated."

Zedekiah reached a good old age, for though it was in his reign that the destruction of Jerusalem took place, yet it was the guilt of the nation, not of the king, that had brought about the catastrophe.

XI. THE RETURN OF THE CAPTIVITY

BELSHAZZAR'S FEAST

WHEN God resolved to take revenge upon Babylon for all the sufferings it had inflicted on Israel, He chose Darius and Cyrus as the agents of vengeance. Cyrus, the king of Persia, and his father-in-law Darius, the king of Media, together went up against Belshazzar, the ruler of the Chaldeans. The war lasted a considerable time, and fortune favored first one side, then the other, until finally the Chaldeans won a decisive victory. To celebrate the event, Belshazzar arranged a great banquet, which was served from the vessels taken out of the Temple at Jerusalem by his father. While the king and his guests were feasting, the angel sent by God put the "Mene, Mene, Tekel, Upharsin" on the wall, Aramaic words in Hebrew characters, written with red ink. The angel was seen by none but the king. His grandees and the princes of the realm who were present at the orgy perceived nothing. The king himself did not see the form of the angel, only his awesome fingers as they traced the words were visible to him.

The interpretation given to the enigmatical words by Daniel put an end to the merry-making of the feasters. They scattered in dread and fear, leaving none behind except the king and his attendants. In the same night the king was murdered by an old servant, who knew Daniel from the time of Nebuchadnezzar, and doubted not that his sinister prophecy would be fulfilled. With the head of King Belshazzar he betook himself to Darius and Cyrus, and told them how his master had desecrated the sacred vessels, told them of the wonderful writing on the wall, and of the way it had been interpreted by Daniel. The two kings were moved by his recital to vow solemnly that they would permit the Jews to return to Palestine, and would grant them the use of the Temple vessels.

They resumed the war against Babylonia with more energy, and God vouchsafed them victory. They conquered the whole of Belshazzar's realm, and took possession of the city of Babylon, whose inhabitants, young and old, were made to suffer death. The subjugated lands were divided between Cyrus and Darius, the latter receiving Babylon and Media, the former Chaldea, Persia, and Assyria.

But this is not the whole story of the fall of Babylon. The wicked king Belshazzar arranged the banquet at which the holy vessels were desecrated in the fifth year of his reign, because he thought it wholly certain then that all danger was past of the realization of Jeremiah's prophecy, foretelling the return of the Jews to Palestine at the end of seventy years of Babylonian rule over them. Nebuchadnezzar had governed twenty-five years, and Evil-merodach twenty-three, leaving five years in the reign of Belshazzar for the fulfilment of the appointed time. Not enough that the king scoffed at God by using the Temple vessels, he needs must have the pastry for the banquet, which was given on the second day of the Passover festival, made of wheaten flour finer than that used on this day for the `Omer in the Temple.

Punishment followed hard upon the heels of the atrocity. Cyrus and Darius served as door-keepers of the royal palace on the evening of the banquet. They had received orders from Belshazzar to admit none, though he should say he was the king himself. Belshazzar was forced to leave his apartments for a short time, and he went out unnoticed by the two door-keepers. On his return, when he asked to be admitted, they felled him dead, even while he was asseverating that he was the king.

DANIEL UNDER THE PERSIAN KINGS

Daniel left Belshazzar and fled to Shushtar, where he was kindly received by Cyrus, who promised him to have the Temple vessels taken back to Jerusalem, provided Daniel would pray to God to grant him success in his war with the king of Mosul. God gave Daniel's prayer a favorable hearing, and Cyrus was true to his promise.

Daniel now received the Divine charge to urge Cyrus to rebuild the Temple. To this end he was to introduce Ezra and Zerubbabel to the king. Ezra then went from place to place and called upon the people to return to Palestine. Sad to say, only a tribe and a half obeyed his summons. Indeed, the majority of the people were so wroth against Ezra that they sought to slay him. He escaped the peril to his life only by a Divine miracle.

Daniel, too, was exposed to much suffering at this time. King Cyrus cast him into a den of lions, because he refused to bow down before the idol of the king. For seven days Daniel lay among the wild beasts, and not a hair of his head was touched. When the king at the end of the week found Daniel alive, he could not but acknowledge the sovereign grandeur of God. Cyrus released Daniel, and instead had his calumniators thrown to the lions. In an instant they were rent in pieces.

In general Cyrus fell far short of coming up to the expectations set in him for piety and justice. Though he granted permission to the Jews to rebuild the Temple, they were to use no material but wood, so that it might easily be destroyed if the Jews should take it into their head to rebel against him. Even in point of morals, the Persian king was not above reproach.

Another time Cyrus pressingly urged Daniel to pay homage to the idol Bel. As proof of the divinity of the idol the king advanced the fact that it ate the dishes set before it, a report spread by the priests of Bel, who entered the Temple of the idol at night, through subterranean passages, themselves ate up the dishes, and then attributed their disappearance to the appetite of the god. But Daniel was too shrewd to be misled by a fabricated story. He had the ashes strewn upon the floor of the Temple, and the foot-prints visible the next morning convinced the king of the deceit practiced by the priests.

Pleasant relations did not continue to subsist forever between Cyrus and Darius. A war broke out between them, in which Cyrus lost life and lands. Fearing Darius, Daniel fled to Persia. But an angel of God appeared to him with the message: "Fear not the king, not unto him will I surrender thee." Shortly afterward he received a letter from Darius reading as follows: "Come to me, Daniel! Fear naught, I shall be even kinder to thee than Cyrus was." Accordingly Daniel returned to Shushtar, and was received with great consideration by Darius.

One day the king chanced to remember the sacred garments brought by Nebuchadnezzar out of the Temple at Jerusalem to Babylon. They had vanished, and no trace of them could be discovered. The king suspected Daniel of having had something to do with their disappearance. It booted little that he protested his innocence, he was cast into prison. God sent an angel who was to blind Darius, telling him at the same time that he was deprived of the light of his eyes because he was keeping the pious Daniel in durance, and sight would be restored to him only if Daniel interceded for him. The king at once released Daniel, and the two together journeyed to Jerusalem to pray on the holy place for the restoration of the king. An angel appeared to Daniel, and announced to him that his prayer had been heard. The king had but to wash his eyes, and vision would return to them. So it happened. Darius gave thanks to God, and in his gratitude assigned the tithe of his grain to the priests and the Levites. Besides, he testified his appreciation to Daniel by loading him down with gifts, and both returned to Shushtar. The recovery of the king convinced many of his subjects of the omnipotence of God, and they converted to Judaism.

Following the advice of Daniel, Darius appointed a triumvirate to take charge of the administration of his realm, and Daniel was made the chief of the council of three. His high dignity he was second to none but the king himself exposed him to envy and hostility on all sides. His enemies plotted his ruin. With cunning they induced the king to sign an order attaching the penalty of death to prayers addressed to any god or any man other than Darius. Though the order did not require Daniel to commit a sin, he preferred to give his life for the honor of the one God rather than omit his devotions to Him. When his jealous enemies surprised him during his prayers, he did not interrupt himself. He was dragged before the king, who refused to give credence to the charge against Daniel. Meanwhile the hour for the afternoon prayer arrived, and in the presence of the king and his princes Daniel began to perform his devotions. This naturally rendered unavailing all efforts made by the king to save his friend from death. Daniel was cast into a pit full of lions. The entrance to the pit was closed up with a rock, which had all of its own accord rolled from Palestine to protect him against any harm contemplated by his enemies. The ferocious beasts welcomed the pious Daniel like dogs fawning upon their master on his return home, licking his hands and wagging their tails.

While this was passing in Babylon, an angel appeared to the prophet Habakkuk in Judea. He ordered the prophet to bring Daniel the food he was about to carry to his laborers in the field. Astonished, Habakkuk asked the angel how he could carry it to so great a distance, whereupon he was seized by his hair, and in a moment set down before Daniel. They dined together, and then the angel transported Habakkuk back to his place in Palestine. Early in the morning Darius went to the pit of the lions to discover the fate of Daniel. The king called his name, but he received no answer, because Daniel was reciting the Shema at that moment, after having spent the night in giving praise and adoration to God. Seeing that he was still alive, the king summoned the enemies of Daniel to the pit. It was their opinion that the lions had not been hungry, and therefore Daniel was still unhurt. The king commanded them to put the beasts to the test with their own persons. The result was that the hundred and twenty-two enemies of Daniel, together with their wives and children numbering two hundred and forty-four persons, were torn in shreds by fourteen hundred and sixty-four lions.

The miraculous escape of Daniel brought him more distinguished consideration and greater honors than before. The king published the wonders done by God in all parts of his land, and called upon the people to betake themselves to Jerusalem and help in the erection of the Temple.

Daniel entreated the king to relieve him of the duties of his position, for the performance of which he no longer felt himself fit, on account of his advanced age. The king consented on condition that Daniel designate a successor worthy of him. His choice fell upon Zerubbabel. Loaded with rich presents and amid public demonstrations designed to honor him, Daniel retired from public life. He settled in the city of Shushan, where he abode until his end. Though he was no prophet, God vouchsafed to him a knowledge of the "end of time" not granted his friends, the prophets Haggai, Zechariah, and Malachi, but even he, in the fulness of his years, lost all memory of the revelation with which he had been favored.

THE GRAVE OF DANIEL

Daniel was buried in Shushan, on account of which a sore quarrel was enkindled among the inhabitants of the city. Shushan is divided in two parts by a river. The side containing the grave of Daniel was occupied by the wealthy inhabitants, and the poor citizens lived on the other side of the river. The latter maintained that they, too, would be rich if the grave of Daniel were in their quarter. The frequent disputes and conflicts were finally adjusted by a compromise; one year the bier of Daniel reposed on one side of the river, the next year on the other. When the Persian king Sanjar came to Shushan, he put a stop to the practice of dragging the bier hither and thither. He resorted to another device for guarding the peace of the city. He had the bier suspended from chains precisely in the middle of the bridge spanning the river. In the same spot he erected a house of prayer for all confessions, and out of respect to Daniel he prohibited fishing in the river for a distance of a mile on either side of the memorial building. The sacredness of the spot appeared when the godless tried to pass by. They were drowned, while the pious remained unscathed. Furthermore, the fish that swam near it had heads glittering like gold.

Beside the house of Daniel lay a stone, under which he had concealed the holy Temple vessels. Once an attempt was made to roll the stone from its place, but whoever ventured to touch it, fell dead. The same fate overtook all who later tried to make excavations near the spot; a storm broke out and mowed them down.

ZERUBBABEL

The successor to Daniel in the service of the king, Zerubbabel, enjoyed equally as much royal consideration and affection. He occupied a higher position than all the other servants and officials, and he and two others constituted the body-guard of the king. Once when the king lay wrapped in deep slumber, his guards resolved to write down what each of them considered the mightiest thing in the world, and he who wrote the sagest saying should be given rich presents and rewards by the king. What they wrote they laid under the pillow on which the head of the king rested, that he might not delay to make a decision after he awoke. The first one wrote: "Wine is the mightiest thing there is"; the second wrote: "The king is the mightiest on earth," and the third, Zerubbabel, wrote: "Women are the mightiest in the world, but truth prevails over all else." When the king awoke, and he perused the document, he summoned the grandees of his realm and the three youths as well. Each of the three was called upon to justify his saying. In eloquent words the first described the potency of wine. When it takes possession of the senses of a man, he forgets grief and sorrow. Still more beautiful and convincing were the words of the second speaker, when his turn came to establish the truth of his saying, that the king was the mightiest on earth. Finally Zerubbabel depicted in glowing words the power of woman, who rules even over kings. "But," he continued, "truth is supreme over all; the whole earth asks for truth, the heavens sing the praises of truth, all creation quakes and trembles before truth, naught of wrong can be found in truth. Unto truth belongeth the might, the dominion, the power, and the glory of all times. Blessed be the God of truth." When Zerubbabel ceased from speaking, the assembly broke out into the words: "Great is truth, it is mightier than all else!" The king was so charmed with the wisdom of Zerubbabel that he said to him: "Ask for aught thou wishest, it shall be granted thee." Zerubbabel required nothing for himself, he only sought permission of the king to restore Jerusalem, rebuild the sanctuary, and return the holy Temple vessels to the place whence they had been carried off. Not only did Darius grant what Zerubbabel wished for, not only did he give him letters of safe-conduct, but he also conferred numerous privileges upon the Jews who accompanied Zerubbabel to Palestine, and he sent abundant presents to the Temple and its officers.

As unto his predecessor Daniel, so unto Zerubbabel, God vouchsafed a knowledge of the secrets of the future. Especially the archangel Metatron dealt kindly with him. Besides revealing to him the time at which the Messiah would appear, he brought about an interview between the Messiah and Zerubbabel.

In reality, Zerubbabel was none other than Nehemiah, who was given this second name because he was born in Babylon. Richly endowed as Zerubbabel-Nehemiah was with admirable qualities, he yet did not lack faults. He was excessively self-complacent, and he did not hesitate to fasten a stigma publicly upon his predecessors in the office of governor in the land of Judah, among whom was so excellent a man as Daniel. To punish him for these transgressions, the Book of Ezra does not bear the name of its real author Nehemiah.

When Darius felt his end approach, he appointed his son-in-law Cyrus, who had hitherto reigned only over Persia, to be the ruler over his kingdom as well. His wish was honored by the princes of Media and Persia. After Darius had departed this life, Cyrus was proclaimed king.

In the very first year of his reign, Cyrus summoned the most distinguished of the Jews to appear before him, and he gave them permission to return to Palestine and rebuild the Temple at Jerusalem. More than this, he pledged himself to contribute to the Temple service in proportion to his means, and pay honor to the God who had invested him with strength to subdue the Chaldeans. These actions of Cyrus partly flowed from his own pious inclinations, and partly were due to his desire to accomplish the dying behests of Darius, who had admonished him to give the Jews the opportunity of rebuilding the Temple.

When the first sacrifice was to be brought by the company of Jews who returned to Jerusalem under the leadership of Ezra, and set about restoring the Temple, they missed the celestial fire which had dropped from heaven on the altar in the time of Moses, and had not been extinguished so long as the Temple stood. They turned in supplication to God to be instructed by Him. The celestial fire had been hidden by Jeremiah at the time of the destruction of the Holy City, and the law did not permit them to bring "strange fire" upon the altar of God. An old man suddenly remembered the spot in which Jeremiah had buried the holy fire, and he led the elders thither. They rolled away the stone covering the spot, and from under it appeared a spring flowing not with water, but with a sort of oil. Ezra ordered this fluid to be sprinkled upon the altar, and forthwith an all-consuming flame shot up. The priests themselves scattered in fright. But after the Temple and its vessels were purified by the flame, it confined itself to the altar never more to leave it, for the priest guarded it so that it might not be extinguished.

Among the band of returned exiles were the prophets Haggai, Zechariah, and Malachi. Each one of them had a place of the greatest importance to fill in the rebuilding of the Temple. By the first the people were shown the plan of the altar, which was larger than the one that had stood in Solomon's Temple. The second informed them of the exact location of the altar, and the third taught them that the sacrifices might be brought on the holy place even before the completion of the Temple. On the authority of one of the prophets, the Jews, on their return from Babylonia, gave up their original Hebrew characters, and re-wrote the Torah in the "Assyrian" characters still in use at this day.

While the Temple work was in progress, the builders found the skull of Araunah, the owner of the Temple site in the time of David. The priests, unlearned as they were, could not decide to what extent the corpse lying there had defiled the holy place. It was for this that Haggai poured out his reproaches upon them.

EZRA

The complete resettlement of Palestine took place under the direction of Ezra, or, as the Scriptures sometimes call him, Malachi. He had not been present at the earlier attempts to restore the sanctuary, because he could not leave his old teacher Baruch, who was too advanced in years to venture upon the difficult journey to the Holy Land.

In spite of Ezra's persuasive efforts, it was but a comparatively small portion of the people that joined the procession winding its way westward to Palestine. For this reason the prophetical spirit did not show itself during the existence of the Second Temple. Haggai, Zechariah, and Malachi were the last representatives of prophecy. Nothing was more surprising than the apathy of the Levites. They manifested no desire to return to Palestine. Their punishment was the loss of the tithes, which were later given to the priest, though the Levites had the first claim upon them.

In restoring the Jewish state in Palestine, Ezra cherished two hopes, to preserve the purity of the Jewish race, and to spread the study of the Torah until it should become the common property of the people at large. To help on his first purpose, he inveighed against marriages between the Jews and the nations round about. He himself had carefully worked out his own pedigree before he consented to leave Babylonia, and in order to perpetuate the purity of the families and groups remaining in the East, he took all the "unfit" with him to Palestine.

In the realization of his second hope, the spread of the Torah, Ezra was so zealous and efficient that it was justly said of him: "If Moses had not anticipated him, Ezra would have received the Torah." In a sense he was, indeed, a second Moses. The Torah had fallen into neglect and oblivion in his day, and he restored and re-established it in the minds of his people. It is due to him chiefly that it was divided up into portions, to be read annually, Sabbath after Sabbath, in the synagogues, and he it was, likewise, who originated the idea of re-writing the Pentateuch in "Assyrian" characters. To further his purpose still more, he ordered additional schools for children to be established everywhere, though the old ones sufficed to satisfy the demand. He thought the rivalry between the old and the new institutions would redound to the benefit of the pupils.

Ezra is the originator of institutions known as "the ten regulations of Ezra." They are the following: 1. Readings from the Torah on Sabbath afternoons. 2. Readings from the Torah on Mondays and Thursdays. 3. Sessions of the court on Mondays and Thursdays. 4. To do laundry work on Thursdays, not Fridays. 5. To eat garlic on Friday on account of its salutary action. 6. To bake bread early in the morning that it may be ready for the poor whenever they ask for some. 7. Women are to cover the lower parts of their bodies with a garment called Sinar. 8. Before taking a ritual bath, the hair is to be combed. 9. The ritual bath prescribed for the unclean is to cover the case of one who desires to offer prayer or study the law. 10. Permission to peddlers to sell cosmetics to women in the towns.

Ezra was not only a great teacher of his people and their wise leader, he was also their advocate with the celestials, to whom his relation was of a peculiarly intimate character. Once he addressed a prayer to God, in which he complained of the misfortune of Israel and the prosperity of the heathen nations. Thereupon the angel Uriel appeared to him, and instructed him how that evil has its appointed time in which to run its course, as the dead have their appointed time to sojourn in the nether world. Ezra could not rest satisfied with this explanation, and in response to his further question, seven prophetic visions were vouchsafed him, and interpreted by the angel for him. They typified the whole course of history up to his day, and disclosed the future to his eyes. In the seventh vision he heard a voice from a thornbush, like Moses aforetimes, and it admonished him to guard in his heart the secrets revealed to him. The same voice had given Moses a similar injunction: "These words shalt thou publish, those shalt thou keep secret." Then his early translation from earth was announced to him. He besought God to let the holy spirit descend upon him before he died, so that he might record all that had happened since the creation of the world as it was set down in the Torah, and guide men upon the path that leads to God.

Hereupon God bade him take the five experienced scribes, Sarga, Dabria, Seleucia, Ethan, and Aziel, with him into retirement, and dictate to them for forty days. After one day spent with these writers in isolation, remote from the city and from men, a voice admonished him: "Ezra, open thy mouth, and drink whereof I give thee to drink." He opened his mouth, and a chalice was handed to him, filled to the brim with a liquid that flowed like water, but in color resembled fire. His mouth opened to drink, and for forty days it was not closed. During all that time, the five scribes put down, "in signs they did not understand," they were the newly adopted Hebrew characters, all that Ezra dictated to them, and it made ninety-four books. At the end of the forty days' period, God spoke to Ezra thus: "The twenty-four books of the Holy Scriptures thou shalt publish, for the worthy and the unworthy alike to read; but the last seventy books thou shalt withhold from the populace, for the perusal of the wise of thy people." On account of his literary activity, he is called "the Scribe of the science of the Supreme Being unto all eternity."

Having finished his task, Ezra was removed from this mundane world, and he entered the life everlasting. But his death did not occur in the Holy Land. It overtook him at Khuzistan, in Persia, on his journey to King Artachshashta.

At Raccia, in Mesopotamia, there stood, as late as the twelfth century, the synagogue founded by Ezra when he was journeying from Babylonia to Palestine.

At his grave, over which columns of fire are often seen to hover at night, a miracle once happened. A shepherd fell asleep by the side of it. Ezra appeared to him and bade him tell the Jews that they were to transport his bier to another spot. If the master of the new place refused assent, he was to be warned to yield permission, else all the inhabitants of his place would perish. At first the master refused to allow the necessary excavations to be made. Only after a large number of the non-Jewish inhabitants of the place had been stricken down suddenly, he consented to have the corpse transported thither. As soon as the grave was opened, the plague ceased.

Shortly before the death of Ezra, the city of Babylon was totally destroyed by the Persians. There remained but a portion of the wall which was impregnable by human strength. All the prophecies hurled against the city by the prophets were accomplished. To this day there is a spot on its site which no animal can pass unless some of the earth of the place is strewn upon it.

THE MEN OF THE GREAT ASSEMBLY

At the same time with Ezra, or, to speak more accurately, under his direction, the Great Assembly carried on its beneficent activities, which laid the foundations of Rabbinical Judaism, and constituted the binding link between the Jewish Prophet and the Jewish Sage. The great men who belonged to this august assembly once succeeded, through the efficacy of their prayers, in laying hands upon the seducers unto sin, and confining them, to prevent them from doing more mischief. Thus they banished from the world "the desire unto idolatry." They tried to do the same to "the desire unto lustfulness." This evil adversary warned them against making away with him, for the world would cease to exist without him. For three days they kept him a prisoner, but then they had to dismiss him and let him go free. They found that not even an egg was to be had, for sexual appetite had vanished from the world. However, he did not escape altogether unscathed. They plastered up his eyes, and from that time on he gave up inflaming the passions of men against their blood relations.

Among the decrees and ordinances of the Great Assembly, the most prominent is the fixation of the prayer of the Eighteen Benedictions. The several benedictions composing this prayer date back to remote ancient times. The Patriarchs were their authors, and the work of the Great Assembly was to put them together in the order in which we now have them. We know how each of the benedictions originated: 1. When Abraham was saved from the furnace angels spoke: "Blessed art Thou, O Lord, the Shield of Abraham," which is the essence of the first of the Eighteen. 2. When Isaac lay stunned by fright on Mount Moriah, God sent His dew to revive him, whereupon the angels spoke: "Blessed art Thou, O Lord, who quickenest the dead." 3. When Jacob arrived at the gates of heaven and proclaimed the holiness of God, the angels spoke: "Blessed art Thou, O Lord, Thou holy God." 4. When Pharaoh was about to make Joseph the ruler over Egypt, and it appeared that he was unacquainted with the seventy tongues which an Egyptian sovereign must know, the angel Gabriel came and taught him those languages, whereupon the angels spoke: "Blessed art Thou, O Lord, who graciously bestowest knowledge." 5. When Reuben committed the trespass against his father, sentence of death was pronounced upon him in the heavens. But when he repented, he was permitted to continue to live, and the angels spoke: "Blessed art Thou, O Lord, who hast delight in repentance." 6. When Judah had committed a trespass against Tamar, and confessing his guilt obtained forgiveness, the angels spoke: "Blessed art Thou, O Lord, who pardonest greatly." 7. When Israel was sore oppressed by Mizraim, and God proclaimed his redemption, the angels spoke: "Blessed art Thou, O Lord, who redeemest Israel." 8. When the angel Raphael came to Abraham to soothe the pain of his circumcision, the angels spoke: "Blessed art Thou, O Lord, who healest the sick." 9. When Israel's sowing in the land of the Philistines bore an abundant harvest, the angels spoke: "Blessed art Thou, O Lord, who blessest the years." 10. When Jacob was reunited with Joseph and Simon in Egypt, the angels spoke: "Blessed art Thou, O Lord, who gatherest the dispersed of Thy people Israel." 11. When the Torah was revealed and God communicated the code of laws to Moses, the angels spoke: "Blessed art Thou, O Lord, who lovest righteousness and justice." 12. When the Egyptians were drowned in the Red Sea, the angels spoke: "Blessed art Thou, O Lord, who shatterest the enemy and humiliatest the presumptuous." 13. When Joseph laid his hands on the eyes of his father Jacob, the angels spoke: "Blessed art Thou, O Lord, who are the stay and the support of the pious." 14. When Solomon built the Temple, the angels spoke: "Blessed art Thou, O Lord, who buildest Jerusalem." 15. When the children of Israel singing hymns of praise unto God passed through the Red Sea, the angels spoke: "Blessed art Thou, O Lord, who causest the hour of salvation to sprout forth." 16. When God lent a gracious ear to the prayer of the suffering Israelites in Egypt, the angels spoke: "Blessed art Thou, O Lord, who hearest our prayer." 17. When the Shekinah descended between the Cherubim in the Tabernacle, the angels spoke: "Blessed art Thou, O Lord, who wilt restore Thy Divine Presence to Jerusalem." 18. When Solomon dedicated his Temple, the angels spoke: "Blessed art Thou, O Lord, whose Name is worthy of praise." 19. When Israel entered the Holy Land, the angels spoke: "Blessed art Thou, O Lord, who establishest peace."

XII. ESTHER

THE FEAST FOR THE GRANDEES

THE Book of Esther is the last of the Scriptural writings. The subsequent history of Israel and all his suffering we know only through oral tradition. For this reason the heroine of the last canonical book was named Esther, that is, Venus, the morning-star, which sheds its light after all the other stars have ceased to shine, and while the sun still delays to rise. Thus the deeds of Queen Esther cast a ray of light forward into Israel's history at its darkest.

The Jews at the time of Ahaseurus were like the dove about to enter her nest wherein a snake lies coiled. Yet she cannot withdraw, because a falcon bides without to swoop down upon her. In Shushan the Jews were in the clutches of Haman, and in other lands they were at the mercy of many murderous enemies to their race, ready to do the bidding of Haman to destroy and to slay them, and cause them to perish.

But the rescue of the Jews from the hand of their adversaries is only a part of this wonderful chapter in the history of Israel. No less important is the exalted station to which they rose in the realm of Ahasuerus after the fall of Haman, especially the power and dignity to which Esther herself attained. On this account the magnificent feast prepared by Ahasuerus for his subjects belongs to the history of Esther.

The splendor of his feast is the gauge whereby to measure the wealth and power she later enjoyed.

Ahasuerus was not the king of Persia by right of birth. He owed his position to his vast wealth, with which he purchased dominion over the whole world.

He had various reasons for giving a gorgeous feast. The third year of his reign was the seventieth since the beginning of Nebuchadnezzar's rule, and Ahasuerus thought it quite certain that the time had passed for the fulfilment of the prophecy of Jeremiah foretelling the return of Israel to the Holy Land. The Temple was still in ruins, and Ahasuerus was convinced that the Jewish kingdom would never again be restored. Needless to say, it was not Jeremiah who erred. Not with the accession of King Nebuchadnezzar had the prophet's term of years begun, but with the destruction of Jerusalem. Reckoned in this way, the seventy years of desolation were at an end exactly at the time when Darius, the son of Ahasuerus, permitted the rebuilding of the Temple.

Beside this mistaken cause for a celebration, there were reasons personal to Ahasuerus why he desired to give expression to joy. A short time before, he had crushed a rebellion against himself, and this victory he wanted to celebrate with pomp and ceremony. The first part of the celebration was given over to the hundred and twenty-seven rulers of the hundred and twenty-seven provinces of his empire. His purpose was to win the devotion of those of them with whom otherwise he did not come in direct contact. But can it be said with certainty that this was a good policy? If he had not first made sure of the loyalty of his capital, was it not dangerous to have these rulers near him in case of an insurrection?

For six whole months he celebrated the feast for the grandees the nobles and the high officials, the latter of whom, according to the constitution, were all required to be Medians under the Persian king Ahasuerus, as they would have had to be Persians under a Median king.

This was the program of the feast: In the first month Ahasuerus showed his treasures to his guests; in the second, the delegates of the king's royal vassals saw them; in the third the presents were exposed to view; in the fourth the guests were invited to admire his literary possessions, among them the sacred scroll; in the fifth his pearl and diamond-studded ornaments of gold were put on exhibition; and in the sixth he displayed the treasures which had been given him as tribute. All this vast wealth, however, appertained to the crown, it was not his personal property. When Nebuchadnezzar felt his end draw nigh, he resolved to sink his immense treasures in the Euphrates rather than let them ascend to his son Evil-merodach, so great was his miserliness. But, again, when Cyrus gave the Jews permission to build the Temple, his divinely appointed reward was that he discovered the spot in the river at which the treasures were sunk, and he was permitted to take possession of them. These were the treasures of which Ahasuerus availed himself to glorify his feast. So prodigious were they that during the six months of the feast he unlocked six treasure-chambers daily to display their contents to his guests.

When Ahasuerus boasted of his wealth, which he had no right to do, as his treasures had come from the Temple, God said: "Verily, has the creature of flesh and blood any possessions of his own? I alone possess treasures, for 'the silver is mind, and the gold is mine.'"

Among the treasures displayed were the Temple vessels, which Ahasuerus had desecrated in his drinking bouts. When the noble Jews who had been invited to the capital saw these, they began to weep, and they refused to take further part in the festivities. Thereupon the king commanded that a separate place be assigned to the Jews, so that their eyes might be spared the painful sight.

This was not the only incident that aroused poignant memories in them, for Ahasuerus arrayed himself in the robes of state once belonging to the high priests at Jerusalem, and this, too, made the Jews smart uncomfortably. The Persian king had wanted to mount the throne of Solomon besides, but herein he was thwarted, because its ingenious construction was an enigma to him. Egyptian artificers tried to fashion a throne after the model of Solomon's, but in vain. After two years' work they managed to produce a weak imitation of it, and upon this Ahasuerus sat during his splendid feast.

THE FESTIVITIES IN SHUSHAN

At the expiration of the hundred and eighty days allotted to the feast for the nobles, Ahasuerus arranged a great celebration for the residents of Shushan, the capital city of Elam. From the creation of the world until after the deluge the unwritten law had been in force, that the first-born son of the patriarchs was to be the ruler of the world. Thus, Seth was the successor to Adam, and he was followed in turn by Enosh, and so the succession went on, from first-born son to first-born son, down to Noah and his oldest son Shem. Now, the first-born son of Shem was Elam, and, according to custom, he should have been given the universal dominion which was his heritage. Shem, being a prophet, knew that Abraham and his posterity, the Israelites, would not spring from the family of Elam, but from that of Arpachshad. Therefore he named Arpachshad as his successor, and through him rulership descended to Abraham, and so to Isaac, Jacob, and Judah, and to David and his posterity, down to the last Judean king Zedekiah, who was deprived of his sovereignty by Nebuchadnezzar.

Then it was that God spake thus: "So long as the government rested in the hands of My children, I was prepared to exercise patience. The misdeeds of the one were made good by the other. If one of them was wicked, the other was pious. But now that the dominions has been wrested from My children, it shall at least revert to its original possessors. Elam was the first-born son of Shem, and his seed shall be given the rule." So it happened that Shushan, the capital city of Elam, became the seat of government.

That there were any celebrations in Shushan was due to Haman, who even in those early days was devising intrigues against the Jews. He appeared before Ahasuerus, and said: "O king, this people is a peculiar people. May it please thee to destroy it." Ahasuerus replied: "I fear the God of this people; He is very mighty, and I bear in mind what befell Pharaoh for his wicked treatment of the Israelites." "Their God," said Haman, "hates an unchaste life. Do thou, therefore, prepare feasts for them, and order them to take part in the merry-makings. Have them eat and drink and act as their heart desireth, so that their God may become wrathful against them."

When Mordecai heard of the feasts that were planned, he advised the Jews not to join in them. All the prominent men of his people and many of the lower classes took his advice to heart. They fled from Shushan, to avoid being compelled to take part in the festivities. The rest remained in the city and yielded to force; they participated in the celebrations, and even permitted themselves to eat of food prepared by the heathen, though the king had taken care not to offend the religious conscience of the Jews in such details. He had been so punctilious that there was no need for them to drink wine touched by the hand of an idolater, let alone eat forbidden food. The arrangements for the feast were entirely in the charge of Haman and Mordecai, so that neither Jew nor Gentile might absent himself for religious reasons.

It was the aim of the king to let every guest follow the inclination of his heart. When Ahasuerus issued the order, that the officers of his house were to "do according to every man's pleasure," God became wroth with him. "Thou villain," He said, "canst thou do every man's pleasure? Suppose two men love the same woman, can both marry her? Two vessels sail forth together from a port, the one desires a south wind, the other a north wind. Canst thou produce a wind to satisfy the two? On the morrow Haman and Mordecai will appear before thee. Wilt thou be able to side with both?"

The scene of the festivities was in the royal gardens. The upper branches of the high trees were made to interlace with each other, so as to form vaulted arches, and the smaller trees with aromatic foliage were taken up out of the ground, and placed in artfully constructed tents. From tree to tree stretched curtains of byssus, white and sapphire blue, and vivid green and royal purple, fastened to their supports by ropes depending from round silver beams, these in turn resting on pillars of red, green, yellow, white, and glittering blue marble. The couches were made of delicate draperies, their frames stood on silver feet, and the rods attached to them were of gold. The floor was tiled with crystal and marble, outlined with precious stones, whose brilliance illuminated the scene far and wide.

The wine and the other beverages were drunk only from golden vessels, yet Ahasuerus was so rich that no drinking cup was used more than a single time. But magnificent as these utensils of his were, when the holy vessels of the Temple were brought in, the golden splendor of the others was dimmed; it turned dull as lead. The wine was in each case older than its drinker. To prevent intoxication from unaccustomed drinks, every guest was served with the wine indigenous to his native place. In general, Ahasuerus followed the Jewish rather than the Persian manner. It was a banquet rather than a drinking bout. In Persia a custom prevailed that every participant in a banquet of wine had to drain a huge beaker far exceeding the drinking capacity of any human being, and do it he must, though he lost reason and life. The office butler accordingly was very lucrative, because the guests at such wassails were in the habit of bribing him to purchase the liberty of drinking as little as they pleased or dared. This Persian habit of compelling excess in drinking was ignored at Ahasuerus's banquet; every guest did as he chose.

The royal bounty did not show itself in food and drink alone. The king's guests could also indulge in the pleasures of the dance if they were so minded. Dancers were provided, who charmed the company with their artistic figures displayed upon the purple-covered floor. That the enjoyment of the participants might in no wise be marred, as by separation from their families, all were permitted to bring their households with them, and merchants were released from the taxes imposed upon them.

So sure was Ahasuerus of his success as a host that he dared say to his Jewish guests: "Will your God be able to match this banquet in the future world?" Whereunto the Jews replied: "The banquet God will prepare for the righteous in the world to come is that of which it is written, 'No eye hath seen it but God's; He will accomplish it for them that wait upon Him.' If God were to offer us a banquet like unto thine, O king, we should say, Such as this we ate at the table of Ahasuerus."

VASTHI'S BANQUET

The banquet given by Queen Vashti to the women differed but slightly from Ahasuerus's. She sought to emulate her husband's example even in the point of exhibiting treasures. Six store-chambers she displayed daily to the women she had bidden as guests; aye, she did not even shrink from arraying herself in the high-priestly garments. The meats and dishes, as at Ahasuerus's table, were Palestinian, only instead of wine, liqueurs were served, and sweets.

As the weak sex is subject to sudden attacks of indisposition, the banquet was given in the halls of the palace, so that the guests might at need withdraw to the adjoining chambers. The gorgeously ornamented apartments of the palace, besides, were more attractive to the feminine taste than the natural beauties of the royal gardens, "for a woman would rather reside in beautiful chambers and possess beautiful clothes than eat fatted calves." Nothing interested the women more than to become acquainted with the arrangement of the interior of the palace, "for women are curious to know all things." Vashti gratified their desire. She showed them all there was to be seen, describing every place as she came to it: This is the dining-hall, this the wine-room, this the bed-chamber.

Vashti, too, was actuated by a political motive when she determined to give her banquet. By inviting the wives of hostages in case the men rose in insurrection against the king. For Vashti knew the ways of statecraft. She not only was the wife of a king, but also the daughter of a king, of Belshazzar. The night of Belshazzar's murder in his own palace, Vashti, alarmed by the confusion that ensued, and not knowing of the death of her father, fled to the apartments in which he was in the habit of sitting. The Median Darius had already ascended the throne of Belshazzar, and so it happened that Vashti, instead of finding the hoped-for refuge with her father, ran straight into the hands of his successor. But he had compassion with her, and gave her to his son Ahasuerus for wife.

THE FATE OF VASHTI

Though Ahasuerus had taken every precaution to prevent intemperate indulgence in wine, his banquet revealed the essential difference between Jewish and pagan festivities. When Jews are gathered about a festal board, they discuss a Halakah, or a Haggadah, or, at the least, a simple verse from the Scriptures. Ahasuerus and his boon companions rounded out the banquet with prurient talk. The Persians lauded the charms of the women of their people, while the Medians admitted none superior to the Median women. Then "the fool" Ahasuerus up and spake: "My wife is neither a Persian nor a Median, but a Chaldean, yet she excels all in beauty. Would you convince yourselves of the truth of my words?" "Yes," shouted the company, who were deep in their cups, "but that we may properly judge of her natural charms, let her appear before us unadorned, yes, without any apparel whatsoever," and Ahasuerus agreed to the shameless condition.

The thing was from God, that so insensate a demand should be made of Vashti by the king. A whole week Mordecai had spent in fasting and praying, supplicating God to mete out punishment to Ahasuerus for his desecration of the Temple utensils. On the seventh day of the week, on the Sabbath, when Mordecai after his long fast took food, because fasting is forbidden on the Sabbath day, God heard his prayer and the prayer of the Sanhedrin. He sent down seven Angels of Confusion to put an end to Ahasuerus's pleasure. They were named: Mehuman, Confusion; Biztha, Destruction of the House; Harbonah, Annihilation; Bigtha and Abagtha, the Pressers of the Winepress, for God had resolved to crush the court of Ahasuerus as one presses the juice from grapes in a press; Zetha, Observer of Immorality;

and Carcas, Knocker.

There was a particular reason why this interruption of the feast took place on the Sabbath. Vashti was in the habit of forcing Jewish maidens to spin and weave on the Sabbath day, and to add to her cruelty, she would deprive them of all their clothes. It was on the Sabbath, therefore, that her punishment overtook her, and for the same reason it was put into the king's heart to have her appear in public stripped of all clothing.

Vashti recoiled from the king's revolting order. But it must not be supposed that she shrank from carrying it out because it offended her moral sense. She was not a whit better than her husband. She fairly revelled in the opportunity his command gave her to indulge in carnal pleasures once again, for it was exactly a week since she had been delivered of a child. But God sent the angel Gabriel to her to disfigure her countenance. Suddenly signs of leprosy appeared on her forehead, and the marks of other diseases on her person. In this state it was impossible for her to show herself to the king. She made a virtue of necessity, and worded her refusal to appear before him arrogantly: "Say to Ahasuerus: 'O thou fool and madman! Hast thou lost thy reason by too much drinking? I am Vashti, the daughter of Belshazzar, who was a son of Nebuchadnezzar, the Nebuchadnezzar who scoffed at kings and unto whom princes were a derision, and even thou wouldst not have been deemed worthy to run before my father's chariot as a courier. Had he lived, I should never have been given unto thee for wife. Not even those who suffered the death penalty during the reign of my forefather Nebuchadnezzar were stripped bare of their clothing, and thou demandest that I appear naked in public! Why, it is for thine own sake that I refuse to heed they order. Either the people will decide that I do not come up to thy description of me, and will proclaim thee a liar, or, bewitched by my beauty, they will kill thee in order to gain possession of me, saying, Shall this fool be the master of so much beauty?'"

The first lady of the Persian aristocracy encouraged Vashti to adhere to her resolution. "Better," her adviser said, when Ahasuerus's second summons was delivered to Vashti, together with his threat to kill her unless she obeyed, "better the king should kill thee and annihilate thy beauty, than that thy person should be admired by other eyes than thy husband's, and thus thy name be disgraced, and the name of thy ancestors."

When Vashti refused to obey the repeated command to appear before the king and the hundred and twenty-seven crowned princes of the realm, Ahasuerus turned to the Jewish sages, and requested them to pass sentence upon his queen. Their thoughts ran in this wise: If we condemn the queen to death, we shall suffer for it as soon as Ahasuerus becomes sober, and hears it was at our advice that she was executed. But if we admonish him unto clemency now, while he is intoxicated, he will accuse us of not paying due deference to the majesty of the king. They therefore resolved upon neutrality. "Since the destruction of the Temple," they said to the king, "since we have not dwelt in our land, we have lost the power to give sage advice, particularly in matters of life and death. Better seek counsel with the wise men of Ammon and Moab, who have ever dwelt at ease in their land, like wine that hath settled on its lees, and hath not been emptied from vessel to vessel.

Thereupon Ahasuerus put his charge against Vashti before the seven princes of Persia, Carshena, Shethar, Admatha, Tarshish, Meres, Marsena, and Memucan, who came from Africa, India, Edom, Tarsus, Mursa, Resen, and Jerusalem, respectively. The names of these seven officials, each representing his country, were indicative of their office. Carshena had the care of the animals, Shethar of the wine, Admatha of the land, Tarshish of the palace, Meres of the poultry, Marsena of the bakery, and Memucan provided for the needs of all in the palace, his wife acting as housekeeper.

This Memucan, a native of Jerusalem, was none other than Daniel, called Memucan, "the appointed one," because he was designated by God to perform miracles and bring about the death of Vashti.

When the king applied for advice to these seven nobles, Memucan was the first to speak up, though in rank he was inferior to the other six, as appears from the place his name occupies in the list. However, it is customary, as well among Persians as among Jews, in passing death sentence, to begin taking the vote with the youngest of the judges on the bench, to prevent the juniors and the less prominent from being overawed by the opinion of the more influential.

It was Memucan's advice to the king to make an example of Vashti, so that in future no woman should dare refuse obedience to her husband. Daniel-Memucan had had unpleasant experiences in his conjugal life. He had married a wealthy Persian lady, who insisted upon speaking to him in her own language exclusively.

Besides, personal antipathy existed between Daniel and Vashti. He had in a measure been the cause of her refusal to appear before the king and his princes. Vashti hated Daniel, because it was he who had prophesied his death to her father, and the extinction of his dynasty. She could not endure his sight, wherefore she would not show herself to the court in his presence. Also, it was Daniel who, by pronouncing the Name of God, had caused the beauty of Vashti to vanish, and her face to be marred. In consequence of all this, Daniel advised, not only that Vashti should be cast off, but that she should be made harmless forever by the hangman's hand. His advice was endorsed by his colleagues, and approved by the king. That the king might not delay execution of the death sentence, and Daniel himself thus incur danger to his own life, he made Ahasuerus swear the most solemn oath known to the Persians, that it would be carried out forthwith. At the same time a royal edict was promulgated, making it the duty of wives to obey their husbands. With special reference to Daniel's domestic difficulties, it was specified that the wife must speak the language of her lord and master.

The execution of Vashti brought most disastrous consequences in its train. His whole empire, which is tantamount to saying the whole world, rose against Ahasuerus. The widespread rebellion was put down only after his marriage with Esther, but not before it had inflicted upon him the loss of one hundred and twenty-seven provinces, the half of his kingdom. Such was his punishment for refusing permission to rebuild the Temple. It was only after the fall of Haman, when Mordecai had been made the chancellor of the empire, that Ahasuerus succeeded in reducing the revolted provinces to submission.

The death of Vashti was not undeserved punishment, for it had been she who had prevented the king from giving his consent to the rebuilding of the Temple. "Wilt thou rebuild the Temple," said she, reproachfully, "which my ancestors destroyed?"

THE FOLLIES OF AHASUERUS

Ahasuerus is the prototype of the unstable, foolish ruler. He sacrificed his wife Vashti to his friend Haman-Memucan, and later on again his friend Haman to his wife Esther. Folly possessed him, too, when he arranged extravagant festivities for guests from afar, before he had won, by means of kindly treatment, the friendship of his surroundings, of the inhabitants of his capital. Ridiculous is the word that describes his edict bidding wives obey their husbands. Every one who read it exclaimed: "To be sure, a man is master in his own house!" However, the silly decree served its purpose. It revealed his true character to the subjects of Ahasuerus, and thenceforward they attached little importance to his edicts. This was the reason why the decree of annihilation directed against the Jews failed of the effect expected by Haman and Ahasuerus. The people regarded it as but another of the king's foolish pranks, and therefore were ready to acquiesce in the revocation of the edict when it came.

The king's true character appeared when he grew sober after the episode with Vashti. Learning that he had had her executed, he burst out furiously against his seven counsellors, and in turn ordered them to death.

Foolish, too, is the only word to describe the manner in which he set about discovering the most beautiful woman in his dominion. King David on a similar occasion wisely sent out messengers who were to bring to him the most beautiful maiden in the land, and there was none who was not eager to enjoy the honor of giving a daughter of his to the king. Ahasuerus's method was to have his servants gather together a multitude of beautiful maidens and women from all parts, and among them he proposed to make choice. The result of this system was that the women concealed themselves to avoid being taken into the harem of the king, when it was not certain that they would be found worthy of becoming his queen.

With his stupidity Ahasuerus combined wantonness. He ordered force to be used in taking the maidens from their parents and the wives from their husbands, and then he confined them in his harem. On the other hand, the moral sense of the heathen was so degraded that many maidens displayed their charms to public view, so that they might be sure to attract the admiring attention of the royal emissaries.

As for Esther, for four years Mordecai kept her concealed in a chamber, so that the king's scouts could not discover her. But her beauty had long been known to fame, and when they returned to Shushan, they had to confess to the king, that the most superbly beautiful woman in the land eluded their search. Thereupon Ahasuerus issued a decree ordaining the death penalty for the woman who should secrete herself before his emissaries. There was nothing left for Mordecai to do but fetch Esther from her hiding-place, and immediately she was espied and carried to the palace of the king.

MORDECAI

The descent of Mordecai and of his niece Esther is disposed of in a few words in the Scripture. But he could trace it all the way back to the Patriarch Jacob, from whom he was forty-five degrees removed. Beside the father of Mordecai, the only ancestor of his who is mentioned by name is Shimei, and he is mentioned for a specific reason. This Shimei is none other then the notorious son of Gera, the rebel who had so scoffed and mocked at David fleeing before Absalom that he would have been killed by Abishai, if David had not generously interfered in his favor. David's prophetic eye discerned in Shimei the ancestor of Israel's savior in the time of Ahasuerus. For this reason he dealt leniently with him, and on his death-bed he bade his son Solomon reserve vengeance until Shimei should have reached old age and could beget no more children. Thus Mordecai deserves both appellations, the Benjamite and the Judean, for he owed his existence not only to his actual Benjamite forebears on his father's side, but also to the Judean David, who kept his ancestor Shimei alive.

Shimei's distinction as the ancestor of Israel's redeemer was due to the merits of his wife. When Jonathan and Ahimaaz, David's spies in his war against his son, fled before the myrmidons of Absalom, they found the gate of Shimei's house open. Entering, they concealed themselves in the well. That they escaped detection was due to the ruse of Shimei's pious wife. She quickly transformed the well into a lady's chamber. When Absalom's men came and looked about, they desisted from searching the place, because they reasoned, that men as saintly as Jonathan and Ahimaaz would not have taken refuge in the private apartment of a woman. God determined, that for having rescued two pious men He would reward her with two pious descendants, who should in turn avert the ruin of Israel.

On his mother's side, Mordecai was, in very deed, a member of the tribe of Judah. In any event, he was a son of Judah in the true sense of the word; he publicly acknowledged himself a Jew, and he refused to touch of the forbidden food which Ahasuerus set before his guest at his banquet.

His other appellatives likewise point to his piety and his excellencies. His name Mordecai, for instance, consists of Mor, meaning "myrrh," and Decai, "pure," for he was as refined and noble as pure myrrh. Again, he is called Ben Jair, because he "illumined the eyes of Israel"; and Ben Kish, because when he knocked at the gates of the Divine mercy, they were opened unto him, which is likewise the origin of his name Ben Shimei, for he was heard by God when he offered up prayer. Still another of Mordecai's epithets was Bilshan, "master of languages." Being a member of the great Sanhedrin he understood all the seventy languages spoken in the world. More than that, he knew the language of the deaf mutes. It once happened that no new grain could be obtained at Passover time. A deaf mute came and pointed with one hand to the roof and with the other to the cottage. Mordecai understood that these signs meant a locality by the name of Gagot-Zerifim, Cottage-Roofs, and, lo, new grain was found there for the 'Omer offering. On another occasion a deaf mute pointed with one hand to his eye and with the other to the staple of the bolt on the door. Mordecai understood that he meant a place called En-Soker, "dry well," for eye and spring are the same word, En, in Aramaic, and Sikra also has a double meaning, staple and exhaustion.

Mordecai belonged to the highest aristocracy of Jerusalem, he was of royal blood, and he was deported to Babylonian together with King Jeconiah, by Nebuchadnezzar, who at that time exiled only the great of the land. Later he returned to Palestine, but remained only for a time. He preferred to live in the Diaspora, and watch over the education of Esther. When Cyrus and Darius captured Babylon, Mordecai, Daniel, and the Jewish community of the conquered city accompanied King Cyrus to Shushan, where Mordecai established his academy.

ESTHER'S BEAUTY AND PIETY

The birth of Esther caused the death of her mother. Her father had died a little while before, so she was entirely orphaned. Mordecai and his wife interested themselves in the poor babe. His wife became her nurse, and he himself did not hesitate, when there was need for it, to do services for the child that are usually performed only by women.

Both her names, Esther as well as Hadassah, are descriptive of her virtues. Hadassah, or Myrtle, she is called, because her good deeds spread her fame abroad, as the sweet fragrance of the myrtle pervades the air in which it grows. In general, the myrtle is symbolic of the pious, because, as the myrtle is ever green, summer and winter alike, so the saints never suffer dishonor, either in this world or in the world to come. In another way Esther resembled the myrtle, which, in spite of its pleasant scent, has a bitter taste. Esther was pleasant to the Jews, but bitterness itself to Haman and all who belonged to him.

The name Esther is equally significant. In Hebrew it means "she who conceals," a fitting name for the niece of Mordecai, the woman who well knew how to guard a secret, and long hid her descent and faith from the king and the court. She herself had been kept concealed for years in the house of her uncle, withdrawn from the searching eyes of the king's spies. Above all she was the hidden light that suddenly shone upon Israel in his rayless darkness.

In build, Esther was neither tall nor short, she was exactly of average height, another reason for calling her Myrtle, a plant which likewise is neither large nor small. In point of fact, Esther was not a beauty in the real sense of the word. The beholder was bewitched by her grace and her charm, and that in spite of her somewhat sallow, myrtle-like complexion. More than this, her enchanting grace was not the grace of youth, for she was seventy-five years old when she came to court, and captivated the hearts of all who saw her, from king to eunuch. This was in fulfilment of the prophecy which God made to Abraham when he was leaving the home of his father: "Thou art leaving the house of thy father at the age of seventy-five. As thou livest, the deliverer of thy children in Media also shall be seventy-five years old."

Another historical event pointed forward to Esther's achievement. When the Jews, after the destruction of Jerusalem, broke out into the wail, "We are orphans and fatherless," God said: "in very sooth, the redeemer whom I shall send unto you in Media shall also be an orphan fatherless and motherless."

Ahasuerus put Esther between two groups of beauties, Median beauties to right of her, and Persian beauties to left of her. Yet Esther's comeliness outshone them all. Not even Joseph could vie with the Jewish queen in grace. Grace was suspended above him, but Esther was fairly laden down with it. Whoever saw her, pronounced her the ideal of beauty of his nation. The general exclamation was: "This one is worthy of being queen." In vain Ahasuerus had sought a wife for four years, in vain fathers had spent time and money bringing their daughters to him, in the hope that one or the other would appeal to his fancy. None among the maidens, none among the women, pleased Ahasuerus. But scarcely had he set eyes upon Esther when he thrilled with the feeling, that he had at last found what he had long yearned for.

All these years the portrait of Vashti had hung in his chamber. He had not forgotten his rejected queen. But once he beheld Esther, Vashti's picture was replaced by hers. Maiden grace and womanly charm were in her united.

The change in her worldly position wrought no change in Esther's ways and manners. As she retained her beauty until old age, so the queen remained as pure in mind and soul as ever the simple maiden had been. All the other women who entered the gates of the royal palace made exaggerated demands, Esther's demeanor continued modest and unassuming. The others insisted that the seven girl pages assigned to them should have certain peculiar qualities, as, that they should not differ, each from her mistress, in complexion and height. Esther uttered no wish whatsoever.

But her unpretending ways were far from pleasing to Hegai, chief of the eunuchs of the harem. He feared lest the king discover that Esther did nothing to preserve her beauty, and would put the blame for it upon him, an accusation that might bring him to the gallows. To avoid such a fate, he loaded Esther down with resplendent jewels, distinguishing her beyond all the other women gathered in the palace, as Joseph, by means of costly gifts lavished upon him, had singled out her ancestor Benjamin from among his brethren.

Hegai paid particular attention to what Esther ate. For her he brought dishes from the royal table, which, however, she refused obstinately to ouch. Only such things passed her lips as were permitted to Jews. She lived entirely on vegetable food, as Hananiah, Mishael, and Azariah had aforetimes done at the court of Nebuchadnezzar. The forbidden tidbits she passed over to the non-Jewish servants. Her personal attendants were seven Jewish maidens as consistently pious as herself, whose devotion to the ritual law Esther could depend upon.

Otherwise Esther was cut off from all intercourse with Jews, and she was in danger of forgetting when the Sabbath bath came around. She therefore adopted the device of giving her seven attendants peculiar names, to keep her in mind of the passage of time. The first one was called Hulta, "Workaday," and she was in attendance upon Esther on Sundays. On Mondays, she was served by Rok`ita, to remind her of Rek`ia, "the Firmament," which was created on the second day of the world. Tuesday's maid was called Genunita, "Garden," the third day of creation having produced the world of plants. On Wednesday, she was reminded by Nehorita's name, "the Luminous," that it was the day on which God had made the great luminaries, to shed their light in the sky; on Thursday by Ruhshita, "Movement," for on the fifth day the first animated beings were created; on Friday, the day on which the beasts came into being, by Hurfita, "little Ewelamb"; and on the Sabbath her bidding was done by Rego`ita, "Rest." Thus she was sure to remember the Sabbath day week after week.

Mordecai's daily visits to the gate of the palace had a similar purpose. Thus Esther was afforded the opportunity of obtaining instruction from him on all ritual doubts that might assail her. This lively interest displayed by Mordecai in Esther's physical and spiritual welfare is not wholly attributable to an uncle's and guardian's solicitude in behalf of an orphaned niece. A much closer bond, the bond between husband and wife, united them, for when Esther had grown to maidenhood, Mordecai had espoused her. Naturally, Esther would have been ready to defend her conjugal honor with her life. She would gladly have suffered death at the hands of the king's bailiffs rather than yield herself to a man not her husband. Luckily, there was no need for this sacrifice, for her marriage with Ahasuerus was but a feigned union. God has sent down a female spirit in the guise of Esther to take her place with the king. Esther herself never lived with Ahasuerus as his wife.

At the advice of her uncle, Esther kept her descent and her faith a secret.

Mordecai's injunction was dictated by several motives. First of all it was his modesty that suggested secrecy. He thought the king, if he heard from Esther that she had been raised by him, might offer to install him in some high office. In point of fact, Mordecai was right in his conjecture; Ahasuerus had pledged himself to make lords, princes, and kings of Esther's friends and kinspeople, if she would but name them.

Another reason for keeping Esther's Jewish affiliations a secret was Mordecai's apprehension, that the fate of Vashti overtake Esther, too. If such were in store for her, he desired at least to guard against the Jews' becoming her fellowsufferers. Besides, Mordecai knew only too well the inimical feelings entertained by the heathen toward the Jews, ever since their exile from the Holy Land, and he feared that the Jew-haters, to gratify their hostility against the Jews, might bring about the ruin of Esther and her house.

Mindful of the perils to which Esther was exposed, Mordecai allowed no day to pass without assuring himself of her well-being. His compensation therefore came from God: "Thou makest the well-being of a single soul they intimate concern. As thou livest, the well-being and good of thy whole nation Israel shall be entrusted to thee as thy task." And to reward him for his modesty, God said: "Thou withdrawest thyself from greatness; as thou livest, I will honor thee more than all men on earth."

Vain were the efforts made by Ahasuerus to draw her secret from Esther. He arranged great festivities for the purpose, but she guarded it well. She had an answer ready for his most insistent questions: "I know neither my people nor my family, for I lost my parents in my earliest infancy." But as the king desired greatly to show himself gracious to the nation to which the queen belonged, he released all the peoples under his dominion from the payment of taxes and imposts. In this way, he thought, her nation was bound to be benefited.

When the king saw that kindness and generosity left her untouched, he sought to wrest the secret from her by threats. Once when she parried his inquiries in the customary way, saying, "I am an orphan, and God, the Father of the fatherless, in His mercy, has brought me up," he retorted: I shall gather virgins together the second time." His purpose was to provoke the jealousy of Esther, "for a woman is jealous of nothing so much as a rival."

When Mordecai noticed that women were being brought to court anew, he was overcome with anxiety for his niece. Thinking that the fate of Vashti might have befallen her, he was impelled to make inquires about her.

As for Esther herself, she was but following the example of her race. She could keep silent in all modesty, as Rachel, the mother of Benjamin, had kept a modest silence when her father gave her sister Leah to Jacob for wife instead of herself, and as Saul the Benjamite was modestly reserved when, questioned by his uncle, he told about the finding of his she-asses, but nothing about his elevation to the kingship. Rachel and Saul were recompensed for their self-abnegation by being given a descendant like Esther.

THE CONSPIRACY

Once the following conversation took place between Ahasuerus and Esther. The king asked Esther: "Whose daughter art thou?"

Esther: "And whose son art thou?"

Ahasuerus: "I am a king, and the son of a king."

Esther: "And I am a queen, the daughter of kings, a descendant of the royal family of Saul. If thou art, indeed, a real prince, how couldst thou put Vashti to death?"

Ahasuerus: "It was not to gratify my own wish, but at the advice of the great princes of Persia and Media."

Esther: "Thy predecessors took no advice from ordinary intelligences; they were guided by prophetical counsel. Arioch brought Daniel to Nebuchadnezzar, king of Babylon, and Belshazzar, too, summoned Daniel before him."

Ahasuerus: "Is there aught left of those toothsome morsels? Are there still prophets abroad?

Esther: "Seek and thou wilt find."

The result was that Mordecai was given the position at court once occupied by the chamberlains Bigthan and Teresh. Indignant that a place once filled by senators should be given to a barbarian, the ousted officials resolved to be revenged upon the king and take his life. Their purpose was to administer poison, which seemed easy of accomplishment, as they were the royal butlers, and could find many occasions to drop poison into a cup of water before handing it to the king. The plan successfully carried out would have satisfied their vengeful feelings, not only as to the king, but as to Mordecai as well. It would have made it appear that the death of Ahasuerus was attributable to the circumstance, that he had entrusted his person to the care of the Jew, as his life had been secure under Bigthan and Teresh. They discussed their plans in the presence of Mordecai, acting upon the unwarranted assumption, that he would not understand the language they spoke, the Tarsian, their native tongue. They were ignorant of the fact, that Mordecai was a member of the Sanhedrin, and as such knew all the seventy languages of the world. Thus their own tongue betrayed them to ruin.

However, Mordecai had no need to make use of his great knowledge of languages; he obtained his information about the plot of the two chamberlains through prophetical channels. Accordingly, he appeared one night in the palace. By a miracle the guards at the gates had not seen him, and he could enter unrestrained. Thus he overheard the conversation between the two conspirators.

Mordecai had more than a single reason for preventing the death of Ahasuerus. In the first place, he desired to secure the king's friendship for the Jews, and more especially his permission for the rebuilding of the Temple. Then he feared, if the king were murdered immediately after his rise to a high place in the state, the heathen would assign as the cause of the disaster his connection with the Jews his marriage with Esther and the appointment of Mordecai to office.

Esther's confidence in Mordecai's piety was so great that she unhesitatingly gave credence to the message she received from him concerning the mischievous plot hatched against the king. She believed that God would execute the wishes of Mordecai. Albeit Bigthan and Teresh had no plans of the sort attributed to them by her uncle, they would conceive then now in order to make Mordecai's words true. That Esther's confidence was justified appeared at once. The conspirators got wind of their betrayal to the king, and in good time they removed the poison they had already placed in Ahasuerus's cup. But that the lie might not be given to Mordecai, God caused poison to appear where none had been, and the conspirators were convicted of their crime. The king had the water analyzed which he was given to drink, and it was made manifest that it contained poison. Other evidence besides existed against the two plotters. It was established that both had at the same time busied themselves about the person of the king, though the regulations of the palace assigned definite hours of service to the one different from those assigned to the other. This made it clear that they intended to perpetrate a dark deed in common.

The two conspirators sought to escape the legitimate punishment for their dastardly deed by ending their own life. But their intention was frustrated, and they were nailed to the cross.

HAMAN THE JEW-BAITER

The conspiracy of Bigthan and Teresh determined the king never again to have two chamberlains guard his person. Henceforward he would entrust his safety to a single individual, and he appointed Haman to the place. This was an act of ingratitude toward Mordecai, who, as the king's savior, had the most cogent claims upon the post. But Haman possessed one important advantage, he was the owner of great wealth. With the exception of Korah he was the richest man that had ever lived, for he had appropriated to himself the treasures of the Judean kings and of the Temple.

Ahasuerus had an additional reason for distinguishing Haman. He was well aware of Mordecai's ardent desire to see the Temple restored, and he instinctively felt he could not deny the wish of the man who had snatched him from untimely death. Yet he was not prepared to grant it. To escape from the dilemma he endeavored to make Haman act as a counterpoise against Mordecai, that "what the one built up, the other might pull down."

Ahasuerus had long been acquainted with Haman's feeling against the Jews. When the quarrel about the rebuilding of the Temple broke out between the Jews and their heathen adversaries, and the sons of Haman denounced the Jews before Ahasuerus, the two parties at odds agreed to send each a representative to the king, to advocate his case. Mordecai was appointed the Jewish delegate, and no more rabid Jew-hater could be found than Haman, to plead the cause of the antagonists of the Temple builders.

As for his character, that, too, King Ahasuerus had had occasion to see in its true light, because Haman is but another name for Memucan, the prince who is chargeable in the last resort with the death of Vashti. At the time of the king's wrath against the queen, Memucan was still lowest in the rank among the seven princes of Persia, yet, arrogant as he was, he was the first to speak up when the king put his question about the punishment due to Vashti an illustration of the popular adage: "The common man rushes to the front." Haman's hostility toward Vashti dated from her banquet, to which the queen had failed to bid his wife as guest. Moreover, she had once insulted him by striking him a blow in the face. Besides, Haman calculated, if only Vashti's repudiation could be brought about, he might succeed in marrying his own daughter to the king. He was not the only disappointed man at court. In part the conspiracy of Bigthan and Teresh was a measure of revenge against Ahasuerus for having made choice of Esther instead of a kinswoman of theirs.

Esther once married to the king, however, Haman made the best of a bad bargain. He tried by every means in his power to win the friendship of the queen. Whether she was Jewess or heathen, he desired to claim kinship with her as a Jewess through the fraternal bond between Esau and Jacob, as a heathen easily enough, "for all the heathen area akin to one another."

MORDECAI'S PRIDE

When Ahasuerus raised Haman to his high office, he at the same time issued the order, that all who saw him were to prostrate themselves before him and pay him Divine honors. To make it manifest that the homage due to him had an idolatrous character, Haman had the image of an idol fastened to his clothes, so that whoever bowed down before him, worshipped an idol at the same time. Mordecai alone of all at court refused to obey the royal order. The highest officials, even the most exalted judges, showed Haman the reverence bidden by the king. The Jews themselves entreated Mordecai not to call forth the fury of Haman, and cause the ruin of Israel thereby. Mordecai, however, remained steadfast; no persuasions could move him to pay to a mortal the tribute due to Divinity.

Also the servants of the king who sat at the gate of the royal palace said to Mordecai: "Wherein art thou better than we, that we should pay reverence to Haman and prostrate ourselves, and thou doest naught of all commanded us in the matter?" Mordecai answered, saying "O ye fools without understanding! Hear ye my words and make meet reply thereunto. Who is man that he should act proudly and arrogantly man born of woman and few in days? At his birth there is weeping and travailing, in his youth pain and groans, all his days are 'full of trouble,' and in the end he returns unto dust. Before such an one I should prostrate myself? I bend the knee before God alone, the only living One in heaven, He who is the fire consuming all other fires; who holds the earth in His arms; who stretches out the heavens in His might; who darkens the sun when it pleases Him, and illumines the darkness; who commanded the sand to set bounds unto the seas; who made the waters of the sea salt, and caused its waves to spread an aroma as of wine; who chained the sea as with manacles, and held it fast in the depths of the abyss that it might not overflow the land; it rages, yet it cannot pass its limits. With His word He created the firmament, which He stretched out like a cloud in the air; He cast it over the world like a dark vault, like a tent it is spread over the earth. In His strength He upholds all there is above and below. The sun, the moon, and the Pleiades run before Him, the stars and the planets are not idle for a single moment; they rest not, they speed before Him as His messengers, going to the right and to the left, to do the will of Him who created them. To Him praise is due, before Him we must prostrate ourselves."

The court officials spake and said: "Yet we know well that thy ancestor Jacob prostrated himself before Haman's ancestor Esau!"

Whereunto Mordecai made reply: "I am a descendant of Benjamin, who was not yet born when his father Jacob and his brothers cast themselves upon the earth before Esau. My ancestor never showed such honor to a mortal. Therefore was Benjamin's allotment of land in Palestine privileged to contain the Temple. The spot whereon Israel and all the peoples of the earth prostrated themselves before God belonged to him who had never prostrated himself before mortal man. Therefore I will not bend my knee before this sinner Haman, nor cast myself to earth before him."

Haman at first tried to propitiate Mordecai by a show of modesty. As though he had not noticed the behavior of Mordecai, he approached him, and saluted him with the words: "Peace be with thee, my lord!" But Mordecai bluntly replied: "There is no peace, saith my God, to the wicked."

The hatred of Mordecai cherished by Haman was due to more than the hereditary enmity between the descendants of Saul and Agag. Not even Mordecai's public refusal to pay the homage due to Haman suffices to explain its virulence. Mordecai was aware of a certain incident in the past of Haman. If he had divulged it, the betrayal would have been most painful to the latter. This accounts for the intensity of his feeling.

It once happened that a city in India rebelled against Ahasuerus. In great haste troops were dispatched thither under the command of Mordecai and Haman. It was estimated that the campaign would require three years, and all preparations were made accordingly. By the end of the first year Haman had squandered the provisions laid in to supply the part of the army commanded by him, for the whole term of the campaign. Greatly embarrassed, he requested Mordecai to give him aid. Mordecai, however, refused him succor; they both had been granted the same amount of provisions for an equal number of men. Haman then offered to borrow from Mordecai and pay him interest. This, too, Mordecai refused to do, and for two reasons. If Mordecai had supplied Haman's men with provisions, his own would have to suffer, and as for interest, the law prohibits it, saying "Unto thy brother thou shalt not lend upon usury," and Jacob and Esau, the respective ancestors of Mordecai and Haman, had been brothers.

When starvation stared them in the face, the troops commanded by Haman threatened him with death unless he gave them their rations. Haman again resorted to Mordecai, and promised to pay him as much as ten per cent interest. The Jewish general continued to refuse the offer. But he professed himself willing to help him out of his embarrassment on one condition, that Haman sell himself to Mordecai as his slave. Driven into a corner, he acquiesced, and the contract was written upon Mordecai's knee-cap, because there was no paper to be found in the camp.

The bill of sale ran thus: "I, Haman, the son of Hammedatha of the family of Agag, was sent out by King Ahasuerus to make war upon an Indian city, with an army of sixty thousand soldiers, furnished with the necessary provisions. Precisely the same commission was given by the king to Mordecai, the son of Shimei of the tribe of Benjamin. But I squandered the provisions entrusted to me by the king, so that I had no rations to give to my troops. I desired to borrow from Mordecai on interest, but, having regard to the fact that Jacob and Esau were brothers, he refused to lend me upon usury, and I was forced to sell myself as slave to him. If, now, I should at any time decline to serve him as a slave, or deny that I am his slave, or if my children and children's children unto the end of all time should refuse to do him service, if only a single day of the week; or if I should act inimically toward him on account of this contract, as Esau did toward Jacob after selling him his birthright; in all these cases, a beam of wood is to be plucked out of the house of the recalcitrant, and he is to be hanged upon it. I, Haman, the son of Hammedatha of the family of Agag, being under no restraint, do hereby consent with my own will, and bind myself to be slave in perpetuity to Mordecai, in accordance with the contents of this document."

Later, when Haman attained to high rank in the state, Mordecai, whenever he met him, was in the habit of stretching out his knee toward him, so that he might see the bill of sale. This so enraged him against Mordecai and against the Jews that he resolved to extirpate the Jewish people.

CASTING THE LOTS

Haman's hatred, first directed against Mordecai alone, grew apace until it included Mordecai's colleagues, all the scholars, whom he sought to destroy, and not satisfied with even this, he plotted the annihilation of the whole of Mordecai's people, the Jews.

Before beginning to lay out his plans, he desired to determine the most favorable moment for his undertaking, which he did by casting lots.

First of all he wanted to decide on the day of the week. The scribe Shimshai began to cast lots. Sunday appeared inappropriate, being the day on which God created heaven and earth, whose continuance depends on Israel's existence. Were it not for God's covenant with Israel, there would be neither day nor night, neither heaven nor earth. Monday showed itself equally unpropitious for Haman's devices, for it was the day on which God effected the separation between the celestial and the terrestrial waters, symbolic of the separation between Israel and the heathen. Tuesday, the day on which the vegetable world was created, refused to give its aid in bringing about the ruin of Israel, who worships God with branches of palm trees. Wednesday, too, protested against the annihilation of Israel, saying: "On me the celestial luminaries were created, and like unto them Israel is appointed to illumine the whole world. First destroy me, and then Thou mayest destroy Israel." Thursday said: "O Lord, on me the birds were created, which are used for sin offerings. When Israel shall be no more, who will bring offerings? First destroy me, and then Thou mayest destroy Israel." Friday was unfavorable to Haman's lots, because it was the day of the creation of man, and the Lord God said to Israel, "Ye are men." Least of all was the Sabbath day inclined to make itself subservient to Haman's wicked plans. It said: "The Sabbath is a sign between Israel and God. First destroy me, and then Thou mayest destroy Israel!"

Baffled, Haman gave up all idea of settling upon a favorable day of the week. He applied himself to the task of searching out the suitable month for his sinister undertaking. As it appeared to him, Adar was the only one of the twelve owning naught that might be interpreted in favor of the Jews. The rest of them seemed to be enlisted on their side. In Nisan Israel was redeemed from Egypt; in Iyar Amlek was overcome; In Siwan the Ethiopian Zerah was smitten in the war with Asa; in Tammuz the Amorite kings were subjugated; in Ab the Jews won a victory over Arad, the Canaanite; in Tishri the Jewish kingdom was firmly established by the dedication of Solomon's Temple, while in Heshwan the building of the Temple at Jerusalem was completed; Kislew and Tebet were the months during which Sihon and Og were conquered by the Israelites, and in Shebat occurred the sanguinary campaign of the eleven tribes against the godless children of Benjamin. Not alone was Adar a month without favorable significance in Jewish history, but actually a month of misfortune, the month in which Moses died. What Haman did not know was, that Adar was the month in which occurred also the birth of Moses.

Then Haman investigated the twelve signs of the zodiac in relation to Israel, and again it appeared that Adar was the most unfavorable month for the Jews. The first constellation, the Ram, said to Haman, "'Israel is a scattered sheep,' and how canst thou expect a father to offer his son for slaughter?"

The Bull said: "Israel's ancestor was 'the firstling bullock.'"

The Twins: "As we are twins, so Tamar bore twins to Judah."

The Crab: "As I am called Saratan, the scratcher, so it is said of Israel, 'All that oppress him, he shall scratch sorely.'"

The Lion: "God is called the lion, and is it likely the lion will permit the fox to bite his children?"

The Virgin: "As I am a virgin, so Israel is compared unto a virgin."

The Balance: "Israel obeys the law against unjust balances in the Torah, and must therefore be protected by the Balance."

The Scorpion: "Israel is like unto me, for he, too, is called scorpion."

The Archer: "The sons of Judah are masters of the bow, and the bows of mighty men directed against them will be broken."

The Goat: "It was a goat that brought blessing unto Jacob, the ancestor of Israel, and it stands to reason that the blessing of the ancestor cannot cause misfortune to the descendant."

The Water-bearer: "His dominion is likened unto a bucket, and therefore the Water-bearer cannot but bring him good."

The Fishes were the only constellation which, at least according to Haman's interpretation, made unfavorable prognostications as to the fate of the Jews. It said that the Jews would be swallowed like fishes. God however spake: "O thou villain! Fishes are sometimes swallowed, but sometimes they swallow, and thou shalt be swallowed by the swallowers." And when Haman began to cast lots, God said: "O thou villain, son of a villain! What thy lots have shown thee is thine own lot, that thou wilt be hanged."

THE DENUNCIATION OF THE JEWS

His resolve to ruin the Jews taken, Haman appeared before Ahasuerus with his accusation against them. "There is a certain people," he said, "the Jews, scattered abroad and dispersed among the peoples in all the provinces of the kingdom. They are proud and presumptuous. In Tebet, in the depth of winter, they bathe in warm water, and they sit in cold water in summer. Their religion is diverse from the religion of every other people, and their laws from the laws of every other land. To our laws they pay no heed, our religion finds no favor with them, and the decrees of the king they do not execute. When their eye falls upon us, they spit out before us, and they consider us as unclean vessels. When we levy them for the king's service, they either jump upon the wall, and hide within the chambers, or they break through the walls and escape. If we hasten to arrest them, they turn upon us, glare at us with their eyes, grind their teeth, stamp their feet, and so intimidate us that we cannot hold them fast. They do not give us their daughters unto wives, nor do they take our daughters unto wives. If one of them has to do the king's service, he idles all the day long. If they want to buy aught of us, they say, 'This is a day for doing business.' But if we want to buy aught of them, they say, 'We may do no business to-day,' and thus we can buy nothing from them on their market-days.

"Their time they pass in this wise: The first hour of the day, they say, they need for reciting the Shema; the second for praying; the third for eating; the fourth for saying grace, to give thanks to God for the food and drink He has granted them; the fifth hour they devote to their business affairs; in the sixth they already feel the need of rest; in the seventh their wives call for them, saying, 'come home, ye weary ones, who are so exhausted by the king's service!'

"The seventh day they celebrate as their Sabbath; they go to the synagogues on that day, read out of their books, translate pieces from their Prophets, curse our king, and execrate our government, saying: 'This is the day whereon the great God rested; so may He grant us rest from the heathen.'

"The women pollute the waters with their ritual baths, which they take after the seven days of their defilement. On the eighth day after the birth of sons, they circumcise them mercilessly, saying, 'This shall distinguish us from all other nations.' At the end of thirty days, and sometimes twenty-nine, they celebrate the beginning of the month. In the month of Nisan they observe eight days of Passover, beginning the celebration by kindling a fire of brushwood to burn up the leaven. They put all the leaven in their homes out of sight before they use the unleavened bread, saying, 'This is the day whereon our fathers were redeemed from Egypt.' Such is the festival they call Pesah. They go to their synagogues, read out of their books, and translate from the writings of the Prophets, saying: 'As the leaven has been removed out of our houses, so may this wicked dominion be removed from over us.'

"Again, in Siwan, they celebrate two days, on which they go to their synagogues, recite the Shema, and offer up prayers, read out of the Torah, and translate from the books of their Prophets, curse our king, and execrate our government. This is the holiday which they call Azarta, the closing festival. They ascend to the roofs of their synagogues, and throw down apples, which are picked up by those below, with the words, 'As these apples are gathered up, so may we be gathered together from our dispersion among the heathen.' They say they observe this festival, because on these days the Torah was revealed to their ancestors on Mount Sinai.

"On the first of Tishri they celebrate the New Year again they go to their synagogues, read out of their books, translate pieces from the writings of their Prophets, curse our king, execrate our government, and blow the trumpets, saying: 'On this Day of Memorial may we be remembered unto good, and our enemies unto evil.'

"On the ninth day of the same month they slaughter cattle, geese, and poultry, they eat and drink and indulge in dainties, they and their wives, their sons and their daughters. But the tenth day of the same month they call the Great Fast, and all of them fast, they together with their wives, their sons, and their daughters, yea, they even torture their little children without mercy, forcing them to abstain from food. They say: 'On this day our sins are pardoned, and are added to the sum of the sins committed by our enemies.' They go to their synagogues, read from their books, translate from the writings of their Prophets, curse our king, and execrate our government, saying: 'May this empire be wiped off from the face of the earth like unto our sins.' They supplicate and pray that the king may die, and his rule be made to cease.

"On the fifteenth of the same month they celebrate the Feast of Tabernacles. They cover the roofs of their houses with foliage, they resort to our parks, where they cut down palm branches for their festal wreaths, pluck the fruit of the Etrog, and cause havoc among the willows of the brook, by breaking down the hedges in their quest after Hosha'not, saying: 'As does the king in the triumphal procession, so do we.' Then they repair to their synagogues to pray, and read out of their books, and make circuits with their Hosha'not, all the while jumping and skipping like goats, so that there is no telling whether they curse us or bless us. This is Sukkot, as they call it, and while it lasts, they do none of the king's service, for, they maintain, all work is forbidden them on these days.

"In this way they waste the whole year with tomfoolery and fiddle-faddle, only in order to avoid doing the king's service. At the expiration of every period of fifty years they have a jubilee year, and every seventh year is a year of release, during which the land lies fallow, for they neither sow nor reap therein, and sell us neither fruits nor other products of the field, so that those of us who live among them die of hunger. At the end of every period of twelve months, they observe the New Year, at the end of every thirty days the New Moon, and every seventh day is the Sabbath, the day on which, as they say, the Lord of the world rested."

After Haman had finished his arraignment of the Jews, God said: "Thou didst well enumerate the holidays of the Jews, yet thou didst omit the two Purim and Shushan-Purim which the Jews will celebrate to commemorate thy fall."

Clever though Haman's charge was, the vindication of the Jews was no whit less clever. For they found a defender in the archangel Michael. While Haman was delivering his indictment, he spoke thus to God: "O Lord of the world! Thou knowest well that the Jews are not accused of idolatry, nor of immoral conduct, nor of shedding blood; they are accused only of observing Thy Torah." God pacified him: "As thou livest, I have not abandoned them, I will not abandon them."

Haman's denunciations of the Jewish people found a ready echo in the heart of the king. He replied: "I, too, desire the annihilation of the Jews, but I fear their God, for He is mighty beyond compare, and He loves His people with a great love. Whoever rises up against them, He crushes under their feet. Just think of Pharaoh! Should his example not be a warning to us? He ruled the whole world, yet, because he oppressed the Jews, he was visited with frightful plagues. God delivered them from the Egyptians, and cleft the sea for them, a miracle never done for any other nation, and when Pharaoh pursued them with an army of six hundred thousand warriors, he and his host together were drowned in the sea. Thy ancestor Amalek, O Haman, attacked them with four hundred thousand heroes, and all of them God delivered into the hands of Joshua, who slew them. Sisera had forty thousand generals under him, each one commander of a hundred thousand men, yet they all were annihilated. The God of the Jews ordered the stars to consume the warriors of Sisera, and then He caused the great general to fall into the power of a woman, to become a by-word and a reproach forever. Many and valorous rulers have risen up against them, they all were cast down by their God and crushed unto their everlasting disgrace. Now, then, can we venture aught against them?"

Haman, however, persisted. Day after day he urged the king to consent to his plan. Ahasuerus thereupon called together a council of the wise men of all nations and tongues. To them he submitted the question, whether the Jews ought not to be destroyed, seeing they differed from all other peoples. The sage councillors inquired: "Who is it that desires to induce thee to take so fatal a step? If the Jewish nation is destroyed, the world itself will cease to be, for the world exists only for the sake of the Torah studied by Israel. Yea, the very sun and moon shed their light only for the sake of Israel, and were it not for him, there were neither day nor night, and neither dew nor rain would moisten the earth. More than this, all other nations beside Israel are designated as 'strangers' by God, but Israel He called in His love 'a people near to Him,' and His 'children.' If men do not suffer their children and kinsmen to be attacked with impunity, how much less will God sit by quiet when Israel is assailed God the Ruler over all things, over the powers in heaven above and on earth beneath, over the spirits and the souls God with whom it lies to exalt and to degrade, to slay and to revive."

Haman was ready with a reply to these words of the wise: "The God who drowned Pharaoh in the sea, and who did all the wonders and signs ye have recounted, that God is now in His dotage, He can neither see nor protect. For did not Nebuchadnezzar destroy His house, burn His palace, and scatter His people to all corners of the earth, and He was not able to do one thing against it? If He had had power and strength, would he not have displayed them? This is the best proof that He was waxed old and feeble."

When the heathen sages heard these arguments advance by Haman, they agreed to his plan, and put their signature to an edict decreeing the persecution of the Jews.

THE DECREE OF ANNIHILATION

This is the text of the decree which Haman issued to the heads of all the nations regarding the annihilation of the Jews: "This herein is written by me, the great officer of the king, his second in rank, the first among the grandees, and one of the seven princes, and the most distinguished among the nobles of the realm. I, in agreement with the rulers of the provinces, the princes of the king, the chiefs and the lords, the Eastern kings and the satraps, all being of the same language, write you at the order of King Ahasuerus this writing sealed with his signet, so that it may not be sent back, concerning the great eagle Israel. The great eagle had stretched out his pinions over the whole world; neither bird nor beast could withstand him. But there came the great lion Nebuchadnezzar, and dealt the great eagle a stinging blow. His pinions snapped, his feathers were plucked out, and his feet were hacked off. The whole world has enjoyed rest, cheer, and tranquillity since the moment the eagle was chased from his eyrie until this day. Now we notice that he is using all efforts to secure wings. He is permitting his feathers to grow, with the intention of covering us and the whole world, as he did unto our forefathers. At the instance of King Ahasuerus, all the magnates of the king of Media and Persia are assembled, and we are writing you our joint advice, as follows: 'Set snares for the eagle, and capture him before he renews his strength, and soars back to his eyrie.' We advise you to tear out his plumage, break his wings, give his flesh to the fowl of heaven, split the eggs lying in his nest, and crush his young, so that his memorial may vanish from the world. Our counsel is not like unto Pharaoh's; he sought to destroy only the men of Israel; to the women he did no harm. It is not like unto the plan of Esau, who wanted to slay his brother Jacob and keep his children as slaves. It is not like unto the tactics of Amalek, who pursued Israel and smote the hindmost and feeble, but left the strong unscathed. It is not like unto the policy of Nebuchadnezzar, who carried them away into exile, and settled them near his own throne. And it is not like unto the way of Sennacherib, who assigned a land unto the Jews as fair as their own had been. We, recognizing clearly what the situation is, have resolved to slay the Jews, annihilate them, young and old, so that their name and their memorial may be no more, and their posterity may be cut off forever."

The edict issued by Ahasuerus against the Jews ran thus: "To all the peoples, nations, and races: Peace be with you! This is to acquaint you that one came to us who is not of our nation and of our land, an Amalekite, the son of great ancestors, and his name is Haman. He made a trifling request of me, saying: 'Among us there dwells a people, the most despicable of all, who are a stumbling-block in every time. They are exceeding presumptuous, and they know our weakness and our shortcomings. They curse the king in these words, which are constantly in their mouths: "God is the King of the world forever and ever: He will make the heathen to perish out of His land: He will execute vengeance and punishments upon the peoples." From the beginning of all time they have been ungrateful, as witness their behavior toward Pharaoh. With kindness he received them, their wives, and their children, at the time of a famine. He gave up to them the best of his land. He provided them with food and all they needed. Then Pharaoh desired to build a palace, and he requested the Jews to do it for him. They began the work grudgingly, amid murmurings, and it is not completed unto this day. In the midst of it, they approached Pharaoh with these words: "We wish to offer sacrifices to our God in a place that is a three days' journey from here, and we petition thee to lend us silver and gold vessels, and clothes, and apparel." So much did they borrow, that each one bore ninety ass-loads off with him, and Egypt was emptied out. When, the three days having elapsed, they did not return, Pharaoh pursued them in order to recover the stolen treasures. What did the Jews? They had among them a man by the name of Moses, the son of Amram, an arch-wizard, who had been bred in the house of Pharaoh. When they reached the sea, this man raised his staff, and cleft the waters, and led the Jews through them dryshod, while Pharaoh and his host were drowned.

"'Their God helps them as long as they observe His law, so that none can prevail against them. Balaam, the only prophet we heathens ever had, they slew with the sword, as they did unto Sihon and Og, the powerful kings of Canaan, whose land they took after killing them. Likewise they brought ruin upon Amalek, the great and glorious ruler they, and Saul their king, and Samuel their prophet. Later they had an unmerciful king, David by name, who smote the Philistines, the Ammonites, and the Moabites, and not one of them could discomfit him. Solomon, the son of this king, being wise and sagacious, built them a house of worship in Jerusalem, that they might not scatter to all parts of the world. But after they had been guilty of many crimes against their God, He delivered them into the hand of King Nebuchadnezzar, who deported them to Babylonia.

"'To this day they are among us, and though they are under our hand, we are of none account in their eyes. Their religion and their laws are different from the religion and he laws of all the other nations. Their sons do not marry with our daughters, our gods they do not worship, they have no regard for our honor, and they refuse to bend the knee before us. Calling themselves freemen, they will not do our service, and our commands they heed not.'

"Therefore the grandees, the princes, and the satraps have been assembled before us, we have taken counsel together, and we have resolved an irrevocable resolution, according to the laws of the Medes and Persians, to extirpate the Jews from among the inhabitants of the earth. We have sent the edict to the hundred and twenty-seven provinces of my empire, to slay them, their sons, their wives, and their little children, on the thirteenth day of the month of Adar none is to escape.

As they did to our forefathers, and desired to do unto us, so shall be done unto them, and their possessions are to be given over to the spoilers. Thus shall ye do, that ye may find grace before me. This is the writing of the letter which I send to you, Ahasuerus king of Media and Persia."

The price Haman offered the king for the Jews was ten thousand hundredweights of silver. He took the number of the Jews at their exodus from Egypt, six hundred thousand, as the basis of his calculation, and offered a half-shekel for every soul of them, the sum each Israelite had to pay yearly for the maintenance of the sanctuary. Though the sum was so vast that Haman could not find coin enough to pay it, but promised to deliver it in the form of silver bars, Ahasuerus refused the ransom. When Haman made the offer, he said: "Let us cast lots. If thou drawest Israel and I draw money, then the sale stands as a valid transaction. If the reverse, it is not valid." Because of the sins of the Jews, the sale was confirmed by the lots. But Haman was not too greatly pleased with his own success. He disliked to give up so large a sum of money. Observing his ill humor, Ahasuerus said: "Keep the money; I do not care either to make or to lose money on account of the Jews."

For the Jews it was fortunate that the king did not accept money for them, else his subjects would not have obeyed his second edict, the one favorable to the Jews. They would have been able to advance the argument, that the king, by accepting a sum of money for them, had resigned his rights over the Jews in favor of Haman, who, therefore, could deal with them as he pleased.

The agreement between Ahasuerus and Haman was concluded at a carouse, by way of punishment for the crime of the sons of Jacob, who had unmercifully sold their brother Joseph into slavery to the Ishmaelites while eating and drinking.

The joy of this Jew-hating couple for Ahasuerus hated the Jews with no less fierce a hatred than Haman did was shared by none. The capital city of Shushan was in mourning and sorely perplexed. Scarcely had the edict of annihilation been promulgated against the Jews, when all sorts of misfortunes began to happen in the city. Women who were hanging up their wash to dry on the roofs of the houses dropped dead; men who went to draw water fell into the wells, and lost their lives. While Ahasuerus and Haman were making merry in the palace, the city was thrown into consternation and mourning.

SATAN INDICTS THE JEWS

The position of the Jews after the royal edict became known beggars description. If a Jew ventured abroad on the street to make a purchase, he was almost throttled by the Persians, who taunted him with these words: "Never mind, tomorrow will soon be here, and then I shall kill thee, and take thy money away from thee." If a Jew offered to sell himself as a slave, he was rejected; not even the sacrifice of his liberty could protect him against the loss of his life.

Mordecai, however, did not despair; he trusted in the Divine help. On his way from the court, after Haman and his ilk had informed him with malicious joy of the king's pleasure concerning the Jews, he met Jewish children coming from school. He asked the first child what verse from the Scriptures he had studied in school that day, and the reply was: "Be not afraid of sudden fear, neither of the desolation of the wicked when it cometh." The verse committed to memory by the second was: "Let them take counsel together, but it shall be brought to naught; let them speak the word, but it shall not stand; for God is with us." And the verse which the third had learnt was: "And even to old age I am He, and even to hoar hairs I will carry you: I have made and will bear; yea, I will carry and will deliver."

When Mordecai heard these verses, he broke out into jubilation, astonishing Haman not a little. Mordecai told him, "I rejoice at the good tidings announced to me by the school children." Haman thereupon fell into such a rage that he exclaimed: "In sooth, they shall be the first to feel the weight of my hand."

What gave Mordecai the greatest concern, was the certainty that the danger had been invited by the Jews themselves, through their sinful conduct in connection with the banquets given by Ahasuerus. Eighteen thousand five hundred Jews had taken part in them; they had eaten and drunk, intoxicated themselves and committed immoralities, as Haman had foreseen, the very reason, indeed, he had advised the king to hold the banquets.

Thereupon Satan had indicted the Jews. The accusations which he produced against them were of such a nature that God at once ordered writing materials to be brought to Him for the decree of annihilation, and it was written and sealed.

When the Torah heard that Satan's designs against the Jews had succeeded, she broke out into bitter weeping before God, and her lamentations awakened the angels, who likewise began to wail, saying: "If Israel is to be destroyed, of what avail is the whole world?"

The sun and the moon heard the lamentations of the angels, and they donned their mourning garb and also wept bitterly and wailed, saying: "Is Israel to be destroyed, Israel who wanders from town to town, and from land to land, only for the sake of the study of the Torah; who suffers grievously under the hand of the heathen, only because he observes the Torah and the sign of the covenant?"

In great haste the prophet Elijah ran to the Patriarchs and to the other prophets, and to the saints in Israel, and addressed these words to them: "O ye fathers of the world! Angels, and the sun and the moon, and heaven and earth, and all the celestial hosts are weeping bitterly. The whole world is seized with throes as of a woman in travail, by reason of your children, who have forfeited their life on account of their sins, and ye sit quiet and tranquil." Thereupon Moses said to Elijah: "Knowest thou any saints in the present generation of Israel?" Elijah named Mordecai, and Moses sent the prophet to him, with the charge that he, the "saint of the living generation," should unite his prayers with the prayers of the saints among the dead, and perhaps the doom might be averted from Israel. But Elijah hesitated. "O faithful shepherd," he said, "the edict of annihilation issued by God is written and sealed." Moses, however, did not desist; he urged the Patriarchs: "If the edict is sealed with wax, your prayers will be heard; if with blood, then all is vain."

Elijah hastened to Mordecai, who, when first he heard what God had resolved upon, tore his garments and was possessed by a great fear, though before he had confidently hoped that help would come form God. He gathered together all the school children, and had them fast, so that their hunger should drive them to moan and groan. Then it was that Israel spoke to God: "O Lord of the world! When the heathen rage against me, they do not desire my silver and gold, they desire only that I should be exterminated from off the face of the earth. Such was the design of Nebuchadnezzar when he wanted to compel Israel to worship the idol. Had it not been for Hananiah, Mishael, and Azariah, I had disappeared from the world. Now it is Haman who desires to uproot the whole vine."

Then Mordecai addressed all the people thus: "O people of Israel, that art so dear and precious in the sight of thy Heavenly Father! Knowest thou not what has happened? Hast thou not heard that the king and Haman have resolved to remove us off the face of the earth, to destroy us from beneath the sun? We have no king on whom we can depend, and no prophet to intercede for us with prayers. There is no place whither we can flee, no land wherein we can find safety. We are like sheep without a shepherd, like a ship upon the sea without a pilot. We are like an orphan born after the death of his father, and death robs him of his mother, too, when he has scarce begun to draw nourishment from her breast."

After this address a great prayer-meeting was called outside of Shushan. The Ark containing the scroll of the law, covered with sackcloth and strewn with ashes, was brought thither. The scroll was unrolled, and the following verses read from it: "When thou art in tribulation, and all these things are come upon thee, in the latter days thou shalt return to the Lord thy God, and hearken unto His voice, for the Lord thy God is a merciful God: He will not fail thee, neither destroy thee, nor forget the covenant of they fathers which He swore unto them."

Thereunto Mordecai added words of admonition: "O people of Israel, thou art dear and precious to thy Father in heaven, let us follow the example of the inhabitants of Nineveh, doing as they did when the prophet Jonah came to them to announce the destruction of the city. The king arose from his throne, laid his crown from him, covered himself with sackcloth, and sat in ashes, and he made proclamation, and published through Nineveh by the decree of the king and his nobles, saying, 'Let neither man nor beast, herd nor flock, taste anything; let them not feed, nor drink water, but let them be covered with sackcloth, both man and beast, and let them cry mightily unto God; yea, let them turn every one from his evil way, and from the violence that is in their hands.' Then God repented Him of the evil He had designed to bring upon them, and He did it not. Now, then, let us follow their example, let us hold a fast, mayhap God will have mercy upon us."

Furthermore spake Mordecai: "O Lord of the world! Didst Thou not swear unto our fathers to make us as many as the stars in the heavens? And now we are as sheep in the shambles. What has become of Thine oath?" He cried aloud, though he knew God hears the softest whisper, for he said: "O Father of Israel, what hast Thou done unto me? One single cry of anguish uttered by Esau Thou didst repay with the blessing of his father Isaac, 'By thy sword shalt thou live,' and now we ourselves are abandoned to the mercy of the sword." What Mordecai was not aware of, was that he, the descendant of Jacob, was brought unto weeping and wailing by Haman, the descendant of Esau, as a punishment, because Jacob himself had brought Esau unto weeping and wailing.

THE DREAM OF MORDECAI FULFILLED

Esther, who knew naught of what was happening at court, was greatly alarmed when her attendants told her that Mordecai had appeared in the precincts of the palace clothed in sackcloth and ashes. She was so overcome by fright that she was deprived of the joys of motherhood to which she had been looking forward with happy expectancy. She sent clothes to Mordecai, who, however, refused to lay aside his garb of mourning until God permitted miracles to come to pass for Israel, wherein he followed the example of such great men in Israel as Jacob, David, and Ahab, and of the Gentile inhabitants of Nineveh at the time of Jonah. By no means would he array himself in court attire so long as his people was exposed to sure suffering. The queen sent for Daniel, called also Hathach in the Scriptures, and charged him to learn from Mordecai wherefore he was mourning.

To escape all danger from spying ears, Hathach and Mordecai had their conversation in the open, like Jacob when he consulted with his wives Leah and Rachel about leaving their father Laban. By Hathach Mordecai sent word to the queen, that Haman was an Amalekite, who like his ancestor sought to destroy Israel. He requested her to appear before the king and plead for the Jews, reminding her at the same time of a dream he had once had and told her about.

Once, when Mordecai had spent a long time weeping and lamenting over the misery of the Jews in the Dispersion, and prayed fervently to God to redeem Israel and rebuild the Temple, he fell asleep, and in his sleep a dream visited him. He dreamed he was transported to a desert place he had never seen before. Many nations lived there jumbled together, only one small and despised nation kept apart at a short distance. Suddenly a snake shot up from the midst of the nations, rising higher and higher, and growing stronger and larger in proportion as it rose. It darted in the direction of the spot in which they tiny nation stood, and tried to project itself upon it. Impenetrable clouds and darkness enveloped the little nation, and when the snake was on the point of seizing it, a hurricane arose from the four corners of the world, covering the snake as clothes cover a man, and blew it to bits. The fragments scattered hither and thither like chaff before the wind, until not a speck of the monster was to be found anywhere. Then the cloud and the darkness vanished from above the little nation, the splendor of the sun again enveloped it.

This dream Mordecai recorded in a book, and when the storm began to rage against the Jews, he thought of it, and demanded that Esther go to the king as the advocate of her people. At first she did not feel inclined to accede to the wishes of Mordecai. By her messenger she recalled to his mind, that he himself had insisted upon her keeping her Jewish descent a secret. Besides, she had always tried to refrain from appearing before the king at her own initiative, in order that she might not be instrumental in bringing down sin upon her soul, for she well remembered Mordecai's teaching, that "a Jewish woman, captive among the heathen, who of her own accord goes to them, loses her portion in the Jewish nation." She had been rejoicing that her petitions had been granted, and the king had not come nigh unto her this last month. Was she now voluntarily to present herself before him? Furthermore, she had her messenger inform Mordecai, that Haman had introduced a new palace regulation. Any one who appeared before the king without having been summoned by Haman, would suffer the death penalty. Therefore, she could not, if she would, go to the king to advocate the cause of the Jews.

Esther urged her uncle to refrain from incensing Haman and furnishing him with a pretext for wreaking the hatred of Esau to Jacob upon Mordecai and his nation. Mordecai, however, was firmly convinced that Esther was destined by God to save Israel. How could her miraculous history be explained otherwise? At the very moment Esther was taken to court, he had thought: "Is it conceivable that God would force so pious a woman to wed with a heathen, were it not that she is appointed to save Israel from menacing dangers?"

Firm as Mordecai was in his determination to make Esther take a hand in affairs, he yet did not find it a simple matter to communicate with her. For Hathach was killed by Haman as soon as it was discovered that he was acting as mediator between Mordecai and Esther. There was none to replace him, unto God dispatched the archangels Michael and Gabriel to carry messages from one to the other and back again.

Mordecai sent word to her, if she let the opportunity to help Israel slip by, she would have to give account for the omission before the heavenly court. To Israel in distress, however, help would come from other quarters. Never had God forsaken His people in time of need. Moreover, he admonished her, that, as the descendant of Saul, it was her duty to make reparation for her ancestor's sin in not having put Agag to death. Had he done as he was bidden, the Jews would not now have to fear the machinations of Haman, the offspring of Agag. He bade her supplicate her Heavenly Father to deal with the present enemies of Israel as He had dealt with his enemies in former ages. To give her encouragement, Mordecai continued: "Is Haman so surpassing great that his plan against the Jews must succeed? Dost though mean to say that he is superior to his own ancestor Amalek, whom God crushed when he precipitated himself upon Israel? Is he mightier than the thirty-one kings who fought against Israel and whom Joshua slew 'with the word of God'? Is he stronger than Sisera, who went out against Israel with nine hundred iron chariots, and yet met his death at the hands of a mere woman, the punishment for having withdrawn the use of the water-springs from the Israelites and prevented their wives from taking the prescribed ritual baths and thus from fulfilling their conjugal duty? Is he more powerful than Goliath, who reviled the warriors of Israel, and was slain by David? Or is he more invincible than the sons of Orpah, who waged wars with Israel, and were killed by David and his men? Therefore, do not refrain thy mouth from prayer, and thy lips from supplication, for on account of the merits of our fathers, Israel has ever and ever been snatched out of the jaws of death. He who has at all times done wonders for Israel, will deliver the enemy into our hands now, for us to do with him as seemeth best to us."

What he endeavored to impress upon Esther particularly, was that God would bring help to Israel without her intermediation, but it was to her interest to use the opportunity, for which alone she had reached her exalted place, to make up for the transgressions committed by her house, Saul and his descendants.

Yielding at last to the arguments of Mordecai, Esther was prepared to risk life in this world, in order to secure life in the world to come. She made only one request of her uncle. He was to have the Jews spend three days in prayer and fasting in her behalf, that she might find favor in the eyes of the king. At first Mordecai was opposed to the proclamation of a fast, because it was Passover time, and the law prohibits fasting on the holidays. But he finally assented to Esther's reasoning:

"Of what avail are the holidays, if there is no Israel to celebrate them, and without Israel, there would not be even a Torah. Therefore it is advisable to transgress on law, that God may have mercy upon us."

THE PRAYER OF ESTHER

Accordingly Mordecai made arrangements for a fast and a prayer-meeting. On the very day of the festival, he had himself ferried across the water to the other side of Shushan, where all the Jews of the city could observe the fast together. It was important that the Jewish residents of Shushan beyond all other Jews should do penance and seek pardon from God, because they had committed the sin of partaking of Ahasuerus's banquet. Twelve thousand priests marched in the procession, trumpets in their right hands, and the holy scrolls of the law in their left, weeping and mourning, and exclaiming against God: "Here is the Torah Thou gavest us. Thy beloved people is about to be destroyed. When that comes to pass, who will be left to read the Torah and make mention of Thy name? The sun and the moon will refuse to shed their light abroad, for they were created only for the sake of Israel." Then they fell upon their faces, and said: "Answer us, our Father, answer us, our King." The whole people joined in their cry, and the celestials wept with them, and the Fathers came forth from their graves.

After a three days' fast, Esther arose from the earth and dust, and made preparations to betake herself to the king. She arrayed herself in a silken garment, embroidered with gold from Ophir and spangled with diamonds and pearls sent her from Africa; a golden crown was on her head, and on her feet shoes of gold.

After she had completed her attire, she pronounced the following prayer: "Thou art the great God, the God of Abraham, Isaac, and Jacob, and the God of my father Benjamin. Not because I consider myself without blemish, do I dare appear before the foolish king, but that the people of Israel may not be cut off from the world. Is it not for the sake of Israel alone that the whole world was created, and if Israel should cease to exist, who will come and exclaim 'Holy, holy, holy' thrice daily before Thee? As Thou didst save Hananiah, Mishael, and Azariah out of the burning furnace, and Daniel out of the den of lions, so save me out of the hand of this foolish king, and make me to appear charming and graceful in his eyes. I entreat Thee to give ear to my prayer in this time of exile and banishment from our land. By reason of our sins the threatening words of the Holy Scriptures are accomplished upon us: 'Ye shall sell yourselves unto your enemies for bondmen and for bondwomen, and no man shall buy you.' The decree to kill us has been issued. We are delivered up unto the sword for destruction, root and branch. The children of Abraham covered themselves with sackcloth and ashes, but though the elders sinned, what wrongs have the children committed, and though the children committed wrongs, what have the sucklings done? The nobles of Jerusalem came forth from their graves, for their children were given up to the sword.

"How quickly have the days of our joy flown by! The wicked Haman has surrendered us to our enemies for slaughter.

"I will recount before Thee the deeds of Thy friends, and with Abraham will I begin. Thou didst try him with all temptations, yet didst Thou find him faithful. O that Thou wouldst support his beloved children for his sake, and aid them, so that Thou wouldst bear them as an unbreakable seal upon Thy right hand. Call Haman to account for the wrong he would do us, and be revenged upon the son of Hammedatha. Demand requital of Haman and not of Thy people, for he sought to annihilate us all at one stroke, he, the enemy and afflicter of Thy people, whom he endeavors to hem in on all sides.

"With an eternal bond Thou didst bind us unto Thee. O that Thou wouldst uphold us for the sake of Isaac, who was bound. Haman offered the king ten thousand talents of silver for us. Raise Thou our voice, and answer us, and bring us forth out of the narrow place into enlargement. Thou who breakest the mightiest, crush Haman, so that he may never again rise from his fall. I am ready to appear before the king, to entreat grace for my inheritance. Send Thou an angel of compassion with me on mine errand, and let grace and favor be my companions. May the righteousness of Abraham go before me, the binding of Isaac raise me, the charm of Jacob be put into my mouth, and the grace of Joseph upon my tongue. Happy the man who putteth his trust in God; he is not confounded. He will lend me His right hand and His left hand, with which He created the whole world. Ye, all ye of Israel, pray for me as I pray in your behalf. For whatsoever a man may ask of God in the time of his distress, is granted unto him. Let us look upon the deeds of our fathers and do like unto them, and He will answer our supplications. The left hand of Abraham held Isaac by the throat, and his right hand grasped the knife. He willingly did Thy bidding, nor did he delay to execute Thy command. Heaven opened its windows to give space to the angels, who cried bitterly, and said: 'Woe to the world, if this thing should come to pass!' I also call upon Thee! O answer me, for Thou givest ear unto all who are afflicted and oppressed. Thou art called the Merciful and the Gracious; Thou art slow to anger and great in lovingkindness and truth. Hear our voice and answer us, and lead us out of distress into enlargement. For three days have I fasted in accordance with the number of days Abraham journey to bind his son upon the altar before Thee. Thou didst make a covenant with him, and didst promise him: 'Whenever thy children shall be in distress, I will remember the binding of Isaac favorably unto them, and deliver them out of their troubles.' Again, I fasted three days corresponding to the three classes Israel, priests, Levites, and Israelites, who stood at the foot of Sinai, and said: 'All the Lord hath spoken will we do, and be obedient.'"

Esther concluded her prayer and said: "O God, Lord of hosts! Thou that searchest the heart and the reins, in this hour do Thou remember the merits of Abraham, Isaac, and Jacob, that my petition to Thee may not be turned aside, nor my request be left unfulfilled.'

ESTHER INTERCEDES

After finishing her prayer, Esther betook herself to the king, accompanied by three attendants, one walking to the right of her, the second on the other side, and the third bearing her train, heavy with the precious stones with which it was studded. Her chief adornment was the holy spirit that was poured out over her. But scarcely did she enter the chamber containing the idols, when the holy spirit departed from her, and she cried out in great distress: "Eli, Eli, lamah azabtani! Shall I be chastised for acts that I do against my will, and only in obedience to the promptings of sore need? Why should my fate be different from that of the Mother? When Pharaoh only attempted to approach Sarah, plagues came upon him and his house, but I have been compelled for years to live with this heathen, and Thou dost not deliver me out of his hand. O Lord of the world! Have I not paid scrupulous heed to the three commands Thou didst specially ordain for women?"

To reach the king, Esther had to pass through seven apartments, each measuring ten ells in length. The first three she traversed unhindered; they were too far off for the king to observe her progress through them. But barely had she crossed the threshold of the fourth chamber, when Ahasuerus caught sight of her, and, overcome by rage, he exclaimed: "O for the departed, their like is not found again on earth! How I urged and entreated Vashti to appear before me, but she refused, and I had her killed therefor. This Esther come hither without invitation, like unto a public prostitute."

In consternation and despair Esther stood rooted to the centre of the fourth chamber. Having once allowed her to pass through the doors under their charge, the guards of the first four rooms had forfeited their authority over her; and to the guards in the other three rooms, she had not yet given cause for interfering with her. Yet the courtiers were so confident that Esther was about to suffer the death penalty, that the sons of Haman were already busy dividing her jewels among themselves, and casting lots for her royal purple. Esther herself was keenly aware of her dangerous position. In her need, she besought God: "Eli, Eli, lamah azabtani," and prayed to Him the words which have found their place in the Psalter composed by King David. Because she put her confidence in God, He answered her petition, and sent her three angels to help her: the one enveloped her countenance with "the threads of grace," the second raised her head, and the third drew out the sceptre of Ahasuerus until it touched her. The king turned his head round, to avoid seeing Esther, but the angels forced him to look her way, and be conquered by her seductive charm.

By reason of her long fast, Esther was so weak that she was unable to extend her hand toward the sceptre of the king. The archangel Michael had to draw her near it. Ahasuerus then said: "I see, thou must have a most important request to prefer, else thou hadst not risked thy life deliberately. I am ready to give it thee, even to the half of the kingdom. There is but one petition I cannot grant, and that is the restoration of the Temple. I gave my oath to Geshem the Arabian, Sanballat the Horonite, and Tobiah the Ammonite, not to allow it to be rebuilt, from fear of the Jews, lest they rise up against me."

For the moment, Esther refrained from uttering her petition. All she asked was, that the king and Haman would come to a banquet she proposed to give. She had good reasons for this peculiar course of conduct. She desired to disarm Haman's suspicions regarding her Jewish descent, and to lead her fellow-Jews to fix their hope upon God and not upon her. At the same time, it was her plan to arouse jealousy of Haman in both the king and the princes. She was quite ready to sacrifice her own life, if her stratagems would but involve the life of Haman, too. At the banquet she therefore favored Haman in such manner that Ahasuerus could not but be jealous. She moved her chair close to Haman's, and when Ahasuerus handed her his wine-cup, to let her drink of it first, she passed it on to his minister.

After the banquet, the king repeated his question, and again made the asseveration, that he would fulfill all her wishes at whatever cost, barring only the restoration of the Temple. Esther, however, was not yet ready; she preferred to wait another day before taking up the conflict with Haman. She had before her eyes the example of Moses, who also craved a day's preparation before going out against Amalek, the ancestor of Haman.

Deceived by the attention and distinction accorded him by Esther, Haman felt secure in his position, priding himself not only on the love of the king, but also on the respect of the queen. He felt himself to be the most privileged being in all the wide realm governed by Ahasuerus.

Filled with arrogant self-sufficiency, he passed by Mordecai, who not only refused to give him the honors decreed in his behalf, but, besides, pointed to his knee, inscribed with the bill of sale whereby Haman had become the slave of Mordecai. Doubly and triply enraged, he resolved to make an example of the Jew. But he was not satisfied with inflicting death by a simple kick.

On reaching his home he was disappointed not to find his wife Zeresh, the daughter of the Persian satrap Tattenai. As always when Haman was at court, she had gone to her paramours. He sent for her and his three hundred and sixty-five advisers, and with them he took counsel as to what was to be done to Mordecai. Pointing to a representation of his treasure chamber, which he wore on his bosom, he said: "And all this is worthless in my sight when I look upon Mordecai, the Jew. What I eat and drink loses its savor, if I but think of him."

Among his advisers and sons, of whom there were two hundred and eight, none was so clever as Zeresh his wife. She spoke thus: "If the man thou tellest of is a Jew, thou wilt not be able to do aught to him except by sagacity. If thou castest him into the fire, it will have no effect upon him, for Hananiah, Mishael, and Azariah escaped from the burning furnace unhurt; Joseph went free from prison; Manasseh prayed to God, and He heard him, and saved him from the iron furnace; to drive him out in the wilderness is useless, thou knowest the desert did no evil to the Israelites that passed through it; putting out his eyes avails naught, for Samson blind did more mischief than ever Samson seeing. Therefore hang him, for no Jew has ever escaped death by hanging."

Haman was well pleased with the words of his wife. She fetched artificers in wood and iron, the former to erect the cross, the latter to make the nails. Their children danced around in high glee while Zeresh played upon the cithern, and Haman in his pleasurable excitement said: "To the wood workers I shall give abundant pay, and the iron workers I shall invite to a banquet."

When the cross was finished, Haman himself tested it, to see that all was in working order. A heavenly voice was heard: "It is good for Haman the villain, and for the son of Hammedatha it is fitting."

THE DISTURBED NIGHT

The night during which Haman erected the cross for Mordecai was the first night of Passover, the very night in which miracles without number had ever been done for the Fathers and for Israel. But this time the night of joy was changed into a night of mourning and a night of fears. Wherever there were Jews, they passed the night in weeping and lamenting. The greatest terrors it held for Mordecai, because his own people accused him of having provoked their misfortunes by his haughty behavior toward Haman.

Excitement and consternation reigned in heaven as well as on earth. When Haman had satisfied himself that the cross intended for his enemy was properly constructed, he repaired to the Bet ha-Midrash, where he found Mordecai and all the Jewish school children, twenty-two thousand in number, in tears and sorrow. He ordered them to be put in chains, saying: "First I shall kill off these, and then I shall hang Mordecai." The mothers hastened thither with bread and water, and coaxed their children to take something before they had to encounter death. The children, however, laid their hands upon their books, and said: "As our teacher

Mordecai liveth, we will neither eat nor drink, but we will perish exhausted with fasting." They rolled up their sacred scrolls, and handed them to their teachers with the words: "For our devotion to the study of the Torah, we had hoped to be rewarded with long life, according to the promised held out in the Holy Scriptures. As we are not worthy thereof, remove the books!" The out-cries of the children and of the teachers in the Bet ha-Midrash, and the weeping of the mothers without, united with the supplications of the Fathers, reached unto heaven in the third hour of the night, and God said: "I hear the voice of tender lambs and sheep!" Moses arose and addressed God thus: "Thou knowest well that the voices are not of lambs and sheep, but of the young of Israel, who for three days have been fasting and languishing in fetters, only to be slaughtered on the morrow to the delight of the arch-enemy."

Then God felt compassion with Israel, for the sake of his innocent little ones. He broke the seal with which the heavenly decree of annihilation had been fastened, and the decree itself he tore in pieces. From this moment on Ahasuerus became restless, and sleep was made to flee his eyes, for the purpose that the redemption of Israel might be brought to pass. God sent down Michael, the leader of the hosts of Israel, who was to keep sleep from the king, and the archangel Gabriel descended, and threw the king out of his bed on the floor, no less than three hundred and sixty-five times, continually whispering in his ear: "O thou ingrate, reward him who deserves to be rewarded."

To account for his sleeplessness, Ahasuerus thought he might have been poisoned, and he was about to order the execution of those charged with the preparation of his food. But they succeeded in convincing him of their innocence, by calling to his attention that Esther and Haman had shared his evening meal with him, yet they felt no unpleasant effects. Then suspicions against his wife and his friend began to arise in his mind. He accused them inwardly of having conspired together to put him out of the way. He sought to banish this thought with the reflection, that if a conspiracy had existed against him, his friends would have warned him of it. But the reflection brought others in its train: Did he have any friends? Was it not possible that by leaving valuable services unrewarded, he had forfeited the friendly feelings toward him? He therefore commanded that the chronicles of the kings of Persia be read to him. He would compare his own acts with what his predecessors had done, and try to find out whether he might count upon friends.

What was read to him, did not restore his tranquility of mind, for he saw a poor man before him none other than the angel Michael who called to him continually: "Haman wants to kill thee, and become king in thy stead. Let this serve thee as proof that I am telling thee the truth: Early in the morning he will appear before thee and request permission of thee to kill him who saved thy life. And when thou inquirest of him what honor should be done to him whom the king delighteth to honor, he will ask to be given the apparel, the crown, and the horse of the king as signs of distinction."

Ahasuerus's excitement was soothed only when the passage in the chronicles was reached describing the loyalty of Mordecai. Had the wishes of the reader been consulted, Ahasuerus had never heard this entry, for it was a son of Haman who was filling the office of reader, and he was desirous of passing the incident over in silence. But a miracle occurred the words were heard though they were not uttered!

The names of Mordecai and Israel had a quieting influence upon the king, and he dropped asleep. He dreamed that Haman, sword in hand, was approaching him with evil intent, and when, early in the morning, Haman suddenly, without being announced, entered the antechamber and awakened the king, Ahasuerus was persuaded of the truth of his dream. The king was still further set against Haman by the reply he gave to the question, how honor was to be shown to the man whom the king delighteth to honor. Believing himself to be the object of the king's goodwill, he advised Ahasuerus to have his favorite arrayed in the king's coronation garments, and the crown royal put upon his head. Before him one of the grandees of the kingdom was to run, doing herald's service, proclaiming that whosoever did not prostrate himself and bow down before him whom the king delighteth to honor, would have his head cut off, and his house given over to pillage.

Haman was quick to notice that he had made a mistake, for he saw the king's countenance change color at the mention of the word crown. He therefore took good care not to refer to it again. In spite of this precaution, Ahasuerus saw in the words of Haman a striking verification of his vision, and he was confident that Haman cherished designs against his life and his throne.

THE FALL OF HAMAN

Haman was soon to find out that he had gone far afield in supposing himself to be the man whom the king delighted to honor. The king's command ran: "Hasten to the royal treasure chambers; fetch thence a cover of find purple, a raiment of delicate silk, furnished forth with golden bells and pomegranates and bestrewn with diamonds and pearls, and the large golden crown which was brought me from Macedonia upon the day I ascended the throne. Furthermore, fetch thence the sword and the coat of mail sent me from Ethiopia, and the two veils embroidered with pearls which were Africa's gift. Then repair to the royal stables, and lead forth the black horse whereon I sat at my coronation. With all these insignia of honor, seek out Mordecai!"

Haman: "Which Mordecai?"

Ahasuerus: "Mordecai the Jew."

Haman: "There be many Jews named Mordecai."

Ahasuerus: "The Jew Mordecai who sits at the king's gate."

Haman: "There be many royal gates; I know not which thou meanest."

Ahasuerus: "The gate that leads from the harem to the palace."

Haman: "This man is my enemy and the enemy of my house. Rather would I give him ten thousand talents of silver than do him this honor."

Ahasuerus: "Ten thousand talents of silver shall be given him, and he shall be made lord over thy house, but these honors must thou show unto him."

Haman: "I have ten sons. I would rather have them run before his horse than do him this honor."

Ahasuerus: "Thou, thy sons, and thy wife shall be slaves to Mordecai, but these honors must thou show unto him."

Haman: "O my lord and king, Mordecai is a common man. Appoint him to be ruler over a city, or, if thou wilt, even over a district, rather than I should do him this honor."

Ahasuerus: "I will appoint him ruler over cities and districts. All the kings on land and on water shall pay him obedience, but these honors must thou show unto him."

Haman: "Rather have coins struck bearing thy name together with his, instead of mine as hitherto, than I should do him this honor."

Ahasuerus: "The man who saved the life of the king deserves to have his name put on the coin of the realm. Nevertheless, these honors must thou show unto him."

Haman: "Edicts and writings have been issued to all parts of the kingdom, commanding that the nation to which Mordecai belongs shall be destroyed. Recall them rather than I should do him this honor."

Ahasuerus: "The edicts and writings shall be recalled, yet these honors must thou show unto Mordecai."

Seeing that all petitions and entreaties were ineffectual, and Ahasuerus insisted upon the execution of his order, Haman went to the royal treasure chambers, walking with his head bowed like a mourner's, his ears hanging down, his eyes dim, his mouth screwed up, his heart hardened, his bowels cut in pieces, his loins weakened, and his knees knocking against each other. He gathered together the royal insignia, and took them to Mordecai, accompanied on his way by Harbonah and Abzur, who, at the order of the king, were to take heed whether Haman carried out his wishes to the letter.

When Mordecai saw his enemy approach, he thought his last moment had come. He urged his pupils to flee, that they might not "burn themselves with his coals." But they refused, saying: "In life as in death we desire to be with thee." The few moments left him, as he thought, Mordecai spent in devotion. With words of prayer on his lips he desired to pass away. Haman, therefore, had to address himself to the pupils of Mordecai: "What was the last subject taught you by your teacher Mordecai?" They told him they had been discussing the law of the `Omer, the sacrifice brought on that very day so long as the Temple had stood. At his request, they described some of the details of the ceremony in the Temple connected with the offering. He exclaimed: "Happy are you that your ten farthings, with which you bought the wheat for the `Omer, produced a better effect than my ten thousand talents of silver, which I offered unto the king for the destruction of the Jews."

Meantime Mordecai had finished his prayer. Haman stepped up to him, and said: "Arise, thou pious son of Abraham, Isaac, and Jacob. Thy sackcloth and ashes availed more than my ten thousand talents of silver, which I promised unto the king.

They were not accepted, but thy prayers were accepted by thy Father in heaven."

Mordecai, not yet disabused of the notion that Haman had come to take him to the cross, requested the grace of a few minutes for his last meal. Only Haman's repeated protests assured him. When Haman set about arraying him with the royal apparel, Mordecai refused to put it on until he had bathed, and had dressed his hair. Royal apparel agreed but ill with his condition after three days of sackcloth and ashes. As luck would have it, Esther had issued the command that the bathkeepers and barbers were not to ply their trades on that day, and there was nothing for Haman to do but perform the menial services Mordecai required. Haman tried to play upon the feelings of Mordecai. Fetching a deep sigh, he said: "The greatest in the king's realm is now acting as bathkeeper and barber!" Mordecai, however, did not permit himself to be imposed upon. He knew Haman's origin too well to be deceived; he remembered his father, who had been bathkeeper and barber in a village.

Haman's humiliation was not yet complete. Mordecai, exhausted by his three days' fast, was too weak to mount his horse unaided. Haman had to serve him as footstool, and Mordecai took the opportunity to give him a kick. Haman reminded him of the Scriptural verse: "Rejoice not when thine enemy falleth, and let not thine heart be glad when he is overthrown." Mordecai, however, refused to apply it to himself, for he was chastising, not a personal enemy, but the enemy of his people, and of such it is said in the Scriptures: "And thou shalt tread upon the high places of thine enemies."

Finally, Haman caused Mordecai to ride through the streets of the city, and proclaimed before him: "Thus shall it be done unto the man whom the king delighteth to honor." In front of them marched twenty-seven thousand youths detailed for this service from the court. In their right hands they bore golden cups, and golden beakers in their left hands, and they, too, proclaimed: "Thus shall be done unto the man whom the king delighteth to honor." The procession furthermore was swelled by the presence of Jews. They, however, made a proclamation of different tenor. "Thus shall be done," they cried out, "unto the man whose honor is desired by the King that hath created heaven and earth."

As he rode along, Mordecai gave praise to God: "I will extol Thee, O Lord; for Thou hast raised me up, and hast not made my foes to rejoice over me. O Lord my God, I cried unto Thee, and Thou hast healed me. O Lord, Thou hast brought up my soul from Sheol; Thou hast kept me alive, that I should not go down to the pit." Whereupon his pupils joined in with: "Sing praise unto the Lord, O ye saints of His, and give thanks to His holy name. For His anger is but for a moment; in His favor is life; weeping may tarry for the night, but joy cometh in the morning." Haman added the verse thereto: "As for me, I said in my prosperity, I shall never be moved. Thou, Lord, of Thy favor hadst made my mountain to stand strong. Thou didst hide Thy face; I was troubled." Queen Esther continued: "I cried to Thee, O Lord; and unto the Lord I made supplication. What profit is there in my blood, when I go down to the pit? Shall the dust praise Thee? Shall it declare Thy truth?" and the whole concourse of Jews present cried out: "Thou hast turned for me my mourning into dancing; Thou hast loosed my sackcloth, and girded me with gladness, to the end that my glory may sing praise to Thee, and not be silent. O Lord my God, I will give thanks unto Thee forever."

When this procession passed the house of Haman, his daughter was looking out of the window. She took the man on the horse to be her father, and the leader of it, Mordecai. Raising a vessel filled with offal, she emptied it out over the leader her own father. Scarce had the vessel left her hand, when she realized the truth, and she threw herself from the window, and lay crushed to death on the street below.

In spite of the sudden change in his fortunes, Mordecai ended the eventful day as he had begun it, in prayer and fasting. No sooner was the procession over than he put off the royal robes, and, again covering himself with sackcloth, he prayed until night fell.

Haman was plunged in mourning, partly on account of the deep disgrace to which he had been subjected, partly on account of the death of his daughter. Neither his wife nor his friends could advise him how to mend his sad fortunes. They could hold out only sorry consolation to him: "If this Mordecai is of the seed of the saints, thou wilt not be able to prevail against him. Thou wilt surely encounter the same fate as the kings in their battle with Abraham, and Abimelech in his quarrel with Isaac. As Jacob was victorious over the angel with whom he wrestled, and Moses and Aaron caused the drowning of Pharaoh and his host, so Mordecai will overcome thee in the end."

While they were yet talking, the king's chamberlains came, and hastily carried Haman off to the banquet Esther had prepared, to prevent him and his influential sons from plotting against the king. Ahasuerus repeated his promise, to give Esther whatever she desired, always expecting the restoration of the Temple. This time, casting her eyes heavenward, Esther replied: "If I have found favor in thy sight, O Supreme King, and if it please Thee, O King of the world, let my life be given me, and let my people be rescued out of the hands of its enemy." Ahasuerus, thinking these words were addressed to him, asked in irritation: "Who is he, and where is he, this presumptuous conspirator, who thought to do thus?" These were the first words the king had ever spoken to Esther herself. Hitherto he had always communicated with her through an interpreter. He had not been quite satisfied she was worthy enough to be addressed by the king. Now made cognizant of the fact that she was a Jewess, and of royal descent besides, he spoke to her directly, without the intervention of others.

Esther stretched forth her hand to indicate the man who had sought to take her life, as he had actually taken Vashti's, but in the excitement of the moment, she pointed to the king. Fortunately the king did not observe her error, because an angel guided her hand instantaneously in the direction of Haman, whom her words described: "This is the adversary and the enemy, he who desired to murder thee in thy sleeping-chamber during the night just passed; he who this very day desired to array himself in the royal apparel, ride upon thy horse, and wear they golden crown upon his head, to rise up against thee and deprive thee of thy sovereignty. But God set his undertaking at naught, and the honors he sought for himself, fell to the share of my uncle Mordecai, who this oppressor and enemy thought to hang."

The anger of the king already burnt so fiercely that he hinted to Esther, that whether Haman was the adversary she had in mind or not, she was to designate him as such. To infuriate him still more, God sent ten angels in the guise of Haman's ten sons, to fell down the trees in the royal park. When Ahasuerus turned his eyes toward the interior of the park, he saw the ruthless destruction of which they were guilty. In his rage he went out into the garden. This was the instant utilized by Haman to implore grace for himself from Esther. Gabriel intervened, and threw Haman upon the couch in a posture as though he were about to do violence to the queen. At that moment Ahasuerus reappeared. Enraged beyond description by what he saw, he cried out: "Haman attempts the honor of the queen in my very presence! Come, then, ye peoples, nations, and races, and pronounce judgment over him!"

When Harbonah, originally a friend of Haman and an adversary of Mordecai, heard the king's angry exclamation, he said to him: "Nor is this the only crime committed by Haman against thee, for he was an accomplice of the conspirators Bigthan and Teresh, and his enmity to Mordecai dates back to the time when Mordecai uncovered their foul plots. Out of revenge therefor, he has erected a cross for him." Harbonah's words illustrate the saying: "Once the ox has been cast to the ground, slaughtering knives can readily be found." Knowing that Haman had fallen from his high estate, Harbonah was intent upon winning the friendship of Mordecai. Harbonah was altogether right, for Ahasuerus at once ordered Haman to be hanged. Mordecai was charged with the execution of the king's order, and Haman's tears and entreaties did not in the least move him. He insisted upon hanging him like the commonest of criminals, instead of executing him with the sword, the mode of punishment applied to men of rank guilty of serious misdemeanors.

The cross which Haman, at the advice of his wife Zeresh and of his friends, had erected for Mordecai, was now used for himself. It was made of wood from a thorn-bush. God called all the trees together and inquired which one would permit the cross for Haman to be made of it. The fig-tree said: "I am ready to serve, for I am symbolic of Israel, and, also, my fruits were brought to the Temple as firstfruits." The vine said: "I am ready to serve, for I am symbolic of Israel and, also, my wine is brought to the altar." The apple-tree said: "I am ready to serve, for I am symbolic of Israel." The nut-tree said: "I am ready to serve, for I am symbolic of Israel." The Etrog tree said: "I should have the privilege, for with my fruit Israel praises God on Sukkot." The willow of the brook said: "I desire to serve, for I am symbolic of Israel." The cedar-tree said: "I desire to serve, for I am symbolic of Israel." The palm-tree said: "I desire to serve, for I am symbolic of Israel." Finally the thorn-bush came and said: "I am fitted to do this service, for the ungodly are like pricking thorns." The offer of the thorn-bush was accepted, after God gave a blessing to each of the other trees for its willingness to serve.

A sufficiently long beam cut from a thorn-bush could be found only in the house of Haman, which had to be demolished in order to obtain it. The cross was tall enough for Haman and his ten sons to be hanged upon it. It was planted three cubits deep in the ground, each of the victims required three cubits space in length, one cubit space was left vacant between the feet of the one above and the head of the one below, and the youngest son, Vaizatha, had his feet four cubits from the ground as he hung.

Haman and his ten sons remained suspended a long time, to the vexation of those who considered it a violation of the Biblical prohibition in Deuteronomy, not to leave a human body hanging upon a tree overnight. Esther pointed to a precedent, the descendants of Saul, whom the Gibeonites left hanging half a year, whereby the name of God was sanctified, for whenever the pilgrims beheld them, they told the heathen, that the men had been hanged because their father Saul had laid hand on the Gibeonites. "How much more, then," continued Esther, "are we justified in permitting Haman and his family to hang, they who desired to destroy the house of Israel?"

Beside these ten sons, who had been governors in various provinces, Haman had twenty others, ten of whom died, and the other ten of whom were reduced to beggary. The vast fortune of which Haman died possessed was divided in three parts. The first part was given to Mordecai and Esther, the second to the students of the Torah, and the third was applied to the restoration of the Temple. Mordecai thus became a wealthy man. He was also set up as king of the Jews. As such he had coins struck, which bore the figure of Esther on the obverse, and his own figure on the reverse. However, in the measure in which Mordecai gained in worldly power and consideration, he lost spiritually, because the business connected with his high political station left him no time for the study of the Torah. Previously he had ranked sixth among the eminent scholars of Israel, he now dropped to the seventh place among them. Ahasuerus, on the other hand, was the gainer by the change. As soon as Mordecai entered upon the office of grand chancellor, he succeeded in subjecting to his sway the provinces that had revolted on account of Vashti's execution.

THE EDICT OF THE KING

The edict issued against the Jews was revoked by Ahasuerus in the following terms:

"King Ahasuerus sends this letter to all the inhabitants of water and earth, to all the rulers of districts, and to generals of the army, who dwell in every country; may your peace be great! I write this to you to inform you, that although I rule over many nations, over the inhabitants of land and sea, yet I am not proud of my power, but will rather walk in lowliness and meekness of spirit all my days, in order to provide for you great peace. Unto all who dwell under my dominion, unto all who seek to carry on business on land or on sea, unto all who desire to export goods from one nation to the other, from one people to the other unto them all, I am the same, from one end of the earth to the other, and none may seek to cause excitement on land or on sea, or enmities between one nation and another, between one people and another. I write this, because in spite of our sincerity and honesty with which we love all the nations, revere all the rulers, and do good to all the potentates, there are nevertheless people who were near to the king, and into whose hand the government was entrusted, who by their intrigues and falsehoods misled the king, and wrote letters which are not right before heaven, which are evil before men, and harmful for the empire. This was the petition they requested from the king: that righteous men should be killed, and most innocent blood be shed, of those who have not done any evil, nor were guilty of death such righteous people as Esther, celebrated for all virtues, and Mordecai, wise in every branch of wisdom, there is no blemish to be found in them nor in their nation. I thought that I was requested concerning another nation, and did not know it was concerning the Jews, who were called the Children of the Lord of All, who created heaven and earth, and who led them and their fathers through great and mighty empires. And now as he, Haman, the son of Hammedatha, from Judea, a descendant of Amalek, who came to us and enjoyed much kindness, praise, and dignity from us, whom we made great, and called 'father of the king,' and seated him at the right of the king, did not know how to appreciate the dignity, and how to conduct the affairs of state, but harbored thoughts to kill the king and take away his kingdom, therefore we ordered the son of Hammedatha to be hanged, and all that he desired we have brought upon his head; and the Creator of heaven and earth brought his machinations upon his head."

As a memorial of the wonderful deliverance from the hands of Haman, the Jews of Shushan celebrated the day their arch-enemy had appointed for their extermination, and their example was followed by the Jews of the other cities of the Persian empire, and by those of other countries. Yet the sages, when besought by Esther, refused at first to make it a festival for all times, lest the hatred of the heathen be excited against the Jews. They yielded only after Esther had pointed out to them that the events on which the holiday was based, were perpetuated in the annals of the kings of Persia and Media, and thus the outside world would not be able to misinterpret the joy of the Jews.

Esther addressed another petition to the sages. She begged that the book containing her history should be incorporated in the Holy Scriptures. Because they shrank from adding anything to the triple Canon, consisting of the Torah, the Prophets, and the Hagiographa, they again refused, and again they had to yield to Esther's argument. She quoted the words from Exodus, "Write this for a memorial in a book," spoken by Moses to Joshua, after the battle of Rephidim with the Amalekites. They saw that it was the will of God to immortalize the warfare waged with the Amalekite Haman. Nor is the Book of Esther an ordinary history. Without aid of the holy spirit, it could not have been composed, and therefore its canonization resolved upon "below" was endorsed "above." And as the Book of Esther became an integral and indestructible part of the Holy Scriptures, so the Feast of Purim will be celebrated forever, now and in the future world, and Esther herself by her pious deeds acquired a good name both in this world and in the world to come.

www.bookjungle.com *email: sales@bookjungle.com fax: 630-214-0564 mail: Book Jungle PO Box 2226 Champaign, IL 61825*

The Codes Of Hammurabi And Moses
W. W. Davies

QTY

The discovery of the Hammurabi Code is one of the greatest achievements of archaeology, and is of paramount interest, not only to the student of the Bible, but also to all those interested in ancient history...

Religion   **ISBN:** *1-59462-338-4*   *Pages:*132
MSRP $12.95

The Theory of Moral Sentiments
Adam Smith

QTY

This work from 1749. contains original theories of conscience amd moral judgment and it is the foundation for systemof morals.

Philosophy   **ISBN:** *1-59462-777-0*   *Pages:*536
MSRP $19.95

Jessica's First Prayer
Hesba Stretton

QTY

In a screened and secluded corner of one of the many railway-bridges which span the streets of London there could be seen a few years ago, from five o'clock every morning until half past eight, a tidily set-out coffee-stall, consisting of a trestle and board, upon which stood two large tin cans, with a small fire of charcoal burning under each so as to keep the coffee boiling during the early hours of the morning when the work-people were thronging into the city on their way to their daily toil...

Childrens   **ISBN:** *1-59462-373-2*   *Pages:*84
MSRP $9.95

My Life and Work
Henry Ford

QTY

Henry Ford revolutionized the world with his implementation of mass production for the Model T automobile. Gain valuable business insight into his life and work with his own auto-biography... "We have only started on our development of our country we have not as yet, with all our talk of wonderful progress, done more than scratch the surface. The progress has been wonderful enough but..."

Biographies/   **ISBN:** *1-59462-198-5*   *Pages:*300
MSRP $21.95

www.bookjungle.com email: sales@bookjungle.com fax: 630-214-0564 mail: Book Jungle PO Box 2226 Champaign, IL 61825

The Art of Cross-Examination
Francis Wellman

QTY

I presume it is the experience of every author, after his first book is published upon an important subject, to be almost overwhelmed with a wealth of ideas and illustrations which could readily have been included in his book, and which to his own mind, at least, seem to make a second edition inevitable. Such certainly was the case with me; and when the first edition had reached its sixth impression in five months, I rejoiced to learn that it seemed to my publishers that the book had met with a sufficiently favorable reception to justify a second and considerably enlarged edition. ..

Reference   ISBN: *1-59462-647-2*   Pages:412 MSRP *$19.95*

On the Duty of Civil Disobedience
Henry David Thoreau

QTY

Thoreau wrote his famous essay, On the Duty of Civil Disobedience, as a protest against an unjust but popular war and the immoral but popular institution of slave-owning. He did more than write—he declined to pay his taxes, and was hauled off to gaol in consequence. Who can say how much this refusal of his hastened the end of the war and of slavery?

Law   ISBN: *1-59462-747-9*   Pages:48 MSRP *$7.45*

Dream Psychology Psychoanalysis for Beginners
Sigmund Freud

QTY

Sigmund Freud, born Sigismund Schlomo Freud (May 6, 1856 - September 23, 1939), was a Jewish-Austrian neurologist and psychiatrist who co-founded the psychoanalytic school of psychology. Freud is best known for his theories of the unconscious mind, especially involving the mechanism of repression; his redefinition of sexual desire as mobile and directed towards a wide variety of objects; and his therapeutic techniques, especially his understanding of transference in the therapeutic relationship and the presumed value of dreams as sources of insight into unconscious desires.

Psychology   ISBN: *1-59462-905-6*   Pages:196 MSRP *$15.45*

The Miracle of Right Thought
Orison Swett Marden

QTY

Believe with all of your heart that you will do what you were made to do. When the mind has once formed the habit of holding cheerful, happy, prosperous pictures, it will not be easy to form the opposite habit. It does not matter how improbable or how far away this realization may see, or how dark the prospects may be, if we visualize them as best we can, as vividly as possible, hold tenaciously to them and vigorously struggle to attain them, they will gradually become actualized, realized in the life. But a desire, a longing without endeavor, a yearning abandoned or held indifferently will vanish without realization.

Self Help   ISBN: *1-59462-644-8*   Pages:360 MSRP *$25.45*

www.bookjungle.com email: sales@bookjungle.com fax: 630-214-0564 mail: Book Jungle PO Box 2226 Champaign, IL 61825

QTY

	Title	ISBN	Price
☐	**The Rosicrucian Cosmo-Conception Mystic Christianity** by *Max Heindel* — The Rosicrucian Cosmo-conception is not dogmatic, neither does it appeal to any other authority than the reason of the student. It is not controversial, but is sent forth in the hope that it may help to clear... *New Age/Religion Pages 646*	1-59462-188-8	$38.95
☐	**Abandonment To Divine Providence** by *Jean-Pierre de Caussade* — "The Rev. Jean Pierre de Caussade was one of the most remarkable spiritual writers of the Society of Jesus in France in the 18th Century. His death took place at Toulouse in 1751. His works have gone through many editions and have been republished... *Inspirational/Religion Pages 400*	1-59462-228-0	$25.95
☐	**Mental Chemistry** by *Charles Haanel* — Mental Chemistry allows the change of material conditions by combining and appropriately utilizing the power of the mind. Much like applied chemistry creates something new and unique out of careful combinations of chemicals the mastery of mental chemistry... *New Age Pages 354*	1-59462-192-6	$23.95
☐	**The Letters of Robert Browning and Elizabeth Barret Barrett 1845-1846 vol II** by *Robert Browning and Elizabeth Barrett* *Biographies Pages 596*	1-59462-193-4	$35.95
☐	**Gleanings In Genesis (volume I)** by *Arthur W. Pink* — Appropriately has Genesis been termed "the seed plot of the Bible" for in it we have, in germ form, almost all of the great doctrines which are afterwards fully developed in the books of Scripture which follow... *Religion/Inspirational Pages 420*	1-59462-130-6	$27.45
☐	**The Master Key** by *L. W. de Laurence* — In no branch of human knowledge has there been a more lively increase of the spirit of research during the past few years than in the study of Psychology, Concentration and Mental Discipline. The requests for authentic lessons in Thought Control, Mental Discipline and... *New Age/Business Pages 422*	1-59462-001-6	$30.95
☐	**The Lesser Key Of Solomon Goetia** by *L. W. de Laurence* — This translation of the first book of the "Lemegton" which is now for the first time made accessible to students of Talismanic Magic was done, after careful collation and edition, from numerous Ancient Manuscripts in Hebrew, Latin, and French... *New Age/Occult Pages 92*	1-59462-092-X	$9.95
☐	**Rubaiyat Of Omar Khayyam** by *Edward Fitzgerald* — Edward Fitzgerald, whom the world has already learned, in spite of his own efforts to remain within the shadow of anonymity, to look upon as one of the rarest poets of the century, was born at Bredfield, in Suffolk, on the 31st of March, 1809. He was the third son of John Purcell... *Music Pages 172*	1-59462-332-5	$13.95
☐	**Ancient Law** by *Henry Maine* — The chief object of the following pages is to indicate some of the earliest ideas of mankind, as they are reflected in Ancient Law, and to point out the relation of those ideas to modern thought. *Religion/History Pages 452*	1-59462-128-4	$29.95
☐	**Far-Away Stories** by *William J. Locke* — "Good wine needs no bush, but a collection of mixed vintages does. And this book is just such a collection. Some of the stories I do not want to remain buried for ever in the museum files of dead magazine-numbers an author's not unpardonable vanity..." *Fiction Pages 272*	1-59462-129-2	$19.45
☐	**Life of David Crockett** by *David Crockett* — "Colonel David Crockett was one of the most remarkable men of the times in which he lived. Born in humble life, but gifted with a strong will, an indomitable courage, and unremitting perseverance... *Biographies/New Age Pages 424*	1-59462-250-7	$27.45
☐	**Lip-Reading** by *Edward Nitchie* — Edward B. Nitchie, founder of the New York School for the Hard of Hearing, now the Nitchie School of Lip-Reading, Inc, wrote "LIP-READING Principles and Practice". The development and perfecting of this meritorious work on lip-reading was an undertaking... *How-to Pages 400*	1-59462-206-X	$25.95
☐	**A Handbook of Suggestive Therapeutics, Applied Hypnotism, Psychic Science** by *Henry Munro* *Health/New Age/Health/Self-help Pages 376*	1-59462-214-0	$24.95
☐	**A Doll's House: and Two Other Plays** by *Henrik Ibsen* — Henrik Ibsen created this classic when in revolutionary 1848 Rome. Introducing some striking concepts in playwriting for the realist genre, this play has been studied the world over. *Fiction/Classics/Plays 308*	1-59462-112-8	$19.95
☐	**The Light of Asia** by *sir Edwin Arnold* — In this poetic masterpiece, Edwin Arnold describes the life and teachings of Buddha. The man who was to become known as Buddha to the world was born as Prince Gautama of India but he rejected the worldly riches and abandoned the reigns of power when... *Religion/History/Biographies Pages 170*	1-59462-204-3	$13.95
☐	**The Complete Works of Guy de Maupassant** by *Guy de Maupassant* — "For days and days, nights and nights, I had dreamed of that first kiss which was to consecrate our engagement, and I knew not on what spot I should put my lips..." *Fiction/Classics Pages 240*	1-59462-157-8	$16.95
☐	**The Art of Cross-Examination** by *Francis L. Wellman* — Written by a renowned trial lawyer, Wellman imparts his experience and uses case studies to explain how to use psychology to extract desired information through questioning. *How-to/Science/Reference Pages 408*	1-59462-309-0	$26.95
☐	**Answered or Unanswered?** by *Louisa Vaughan* — Miracles of Faith in China *Religion Pages 112*	1-59462-248-5	$10.95
☐	**The Edinburgh Lectures on Mental Science (1909)** by *Thomas* — This book contains the substance of a course of lectures recently given by the writer in the Queen Street Hall, Edinburgh. Its purpose is to indicate the Natural Principles governing the relation between Mental Action and Material Conditions... *New Age/Psychology Pages 148*	1-59462-008-3	$11.95
☐	**Ayesha** by *H. Rider Haggard* — Verily and indeed it is the unexpected that happens! Probably if there was one person upon the earth from whom the Editor of this, and of a certain previous history, did not expect to hear again... *Classics Pages 380*	1-59462-301-5	$24.95
☐	**Ayala's Angel** by *Anthony Trollope* — The two girls were both pretty, but Lucy who was twenty-one who supposed to be simple and comparatively unattractive, whereas Ayala was credited, as her Bombwhat romantic name might show, with poetic charm and a taste for romance. Ayala when her father died was nineteen... *Fiction Pages 484*	1-59462-352-X	$29.95
☐	**The American Commonwealth** by *James Bryce* — An interpretation of American democratic political theory. It examines political mechanics and society from the perspective of Scotsman James Bryce *Politics Pages 572*	1-59462-286-8	$34.45
☐	**Stories of the Pilgrims** by *Margaret P. Pumphrey* — This book explores pilgrims religious oppression in England as well as their escape to Holland and eventual crossing to America on the Mayflower, and their early days in New England... *History Pages 268*	1-59462-116-0	$17.95

www.bookjungle.com email: sales@bookjungle.com fax: 630-214-0564 mail: Book Jungle PO Box 2226 Champaign, IL 61825

	QTY
The Fasting Cure by *Sinclair Upton* ISBN: *1-59462-222-1* **$13.95** In the Cosmopolitan Magazine for May, 1910, and in the Contemporary Review (London) for April, 1910, I published an article dealing with my experiences in fasting. I have written a great many magazine articles, but never one which attracted so much attention... New Age/Self Help/Health Pages 164	☐
Hebrew Astrology by *Sepharial* ISBN: *1-59462-308-2* **$13.45** In these days of advanced thinking it is a matter of common observation that we have left many of the old landmarks behind and that we are now pressing forward to greater heights and to a wider horizon than that which represented the mind-content of our progenitors... Astrology Pages 144	☐
Thought Vibration or The Law of Attraction in the Thought World ISBN: *1-59462-127-6* **$12.95** by *William Walker Atkinson* Psychology/Religion Pages 144	☐
Optimism by *Helen Keller* ISBN: *1-59462-108-X* **$15.95** Helen Keller was blind, deaf, and mute since 19 months old, yet famously learned how to overcome these handicaps, communicate with the world, and spread her lectures promoting optimism. An inspiring read for everyone... Biographies/Inspirational Pages 84	☐
Sara Crewe by *Frances Burnett* ISBN: *1-59462-360-0* **$9.45** In the first place, Miss Minchin lived in London. Her home was a large, dull, tall one, in a large, dull square, where all the houses were alike, and all the sparrows were alike, and where all the door-knockers made the same heavy sound... Childrens/Classic Pages 88	☐
The Autobiography of Benjamin Franklin by *Benjamin Franklin* ISBN: *1-59462-135-7* **$24.95** The Autobiography of Benjamin Franklin has probably been more extensively read than any other American historical work, and no other book of its kind has had such ups and downs of fortune. Franklin lived for many years in England, where he was agent... Biographies/History Pages 332	☐

Name	
Email	
Telephone	
Address	
City, State ZIP	

☐ Credit Card   ☐ Check / Money Order

Credit Card Number	
Expiration Date	
Signature	

Please Mail to: Book Jungle
PO Box 2226
Champaign, IL 61825
or Fax to: 630-214-0564

ORDERING INFORMATION
web: www.bookjungle.com
email: sales@bookjungle.com
fax: 630-214-0564
mail: Book Jungle PO Box 2226 Champaign, IL 61825
or PayPal to sales@bookjungle.com

Please contact us for bulk discounts

DIRECT-ORDER TERMS

**20% Discount if You Order
Two or More Books**
Free Domestic Shipping!
Accepted: Master Card, Visa,
Discover, American Express

www.ingramcontent.com/pod-product-compliance
Lightning Source LLC
Chambersburg PA
CBHW081915170426
43200CB00014B/2733